IN SPAIN'S
SECRET
WILDERNESS

IN SPAIN'S
SECRET
WILDERNESS

Mike Tomkies

JONATHAN CAPE
THIRTY-TWO BEDFORD SQUARE LONDON

First published 1989
Text and photographs © Mike Tomkies 1989
Jonathan Cape Ltd, 32 Bedford Square, London WC1B 3SG

A CIP catalogue record for this book
is available from the British Library

ISBN 0–224–02716–6

Phototypeset by Selectmove Limited
Printed in Great Britain by
Butler & Tanner Ltd, Frome and London

Contents

For the sake of readers who might wish to follow the journeys described in this book, I have employed the metric system, as used on maps and in Spain itself, for describing distances and heights. For the measurements of creatures and objects, however, I have kept to the more commonly understood system of imperial feet and inches, and pounds and ounces.

M.T.
April 1989

For

Jesus 'Suso' Garzon

1 · *Wildest Spain*

It was bitterly cold in the flimsy wooden hide on top of the 40-foot metal tower. While the late February sun beamed down strongly on the marshes and scrubby bushland in the secret heart of the Coto Doñana wildlife reserve in Spain, an icy wind was blowing from the north east. In two hours I had taken fine pictures of nesting night herons and rare spoonbills courting as they re-established their tree breeding colonies and of red kites sailing into their nest. I had begun to shiver. It was now or never, I decided. I desperately wanted to see in the wild, and perhaps to photograph, the rare and endangered Spanish lynx. In a few hours my visitor's permit would run out.

I climbed down the swaying tower, glad of the warming sun and, keeping well downwind, trekked some distance to a small *camino,* or track, where trapper Rafael Laffitte had shown me that two lynx families came to deposit their scats, so marking their territorial boundaries. I lay in a sand slake gouged out by recent heavy rains, thirty metres downwind of the track, camera poised on the brittle sandy edge. After two hours I felt sure I was wasting my time.

Suddenly there was a movement in the bushes to the right of the *camino,* some 80 metres ahead, different from those being caused by the wind. Out came a blunt nose and muzzle with a little white beard below it. My heart began to pound. The feline face turned towards me, and I was aware through the lens of lustrous greeny-grey eyes and sharp pointed ears adorned by tufts of dark hair. I did not press

1

the button for I wanted the whole lynx to emerge. It soon did so, but too swiftly, taking quick steps towards the *camino* as my camera clicked. While I frantically wound to the next frame, the lynx reached the grassy centre of the track and bent down to sniff at something. It then whirled away, bounded up the track, its short uplifted tail bobbing comically, and vanished back into the bushes. I waited a little longer but it did not show itself again.

Excited by this extraordinary sighting, I walked to meet the biologist who would drive me out to the locked and guarded gate of the reserve twelve kilometres away. I recalled my first real thrill in the Spanish wilds which had occurred five years earlier when I was making only sporadic visits from Scotland to see if I could get on close terms with the wildlife in this vast, spectacular landscape. Before me, only 40 metres away on a wild mountain slope in Extremadura, had stretched an extraordinary tableau. Around a dead goat 61 griffon vultures (a species now declining in Europe) squabbled with each other for the right to feed. Beyond them, like massive prehistoric effigies, stood no less than eight of Europe's scarce and largest raptors – black vultures. Each weighing some 20lbs, they stood quietly, as if awaiting their turn at the goat, with aristocratic dignity. Overhead a lone imperial eagle, one from Spain's 75 pairs – all that is left of the race in western Europe – soared majestically. It disdained to come down and contest for carrion with the vultures.

A late-arriving griffon swooped in. Clearly very hungry, it kept its great wings wide open and bounced up to the others with an intimidating threat display. They quickly made room for it. Soon the senior griffons had eaten their fill and the younger birds converged, covering the carcass with a seething sea of writhing backs and orange-brown wings.

As I crouched in the flimsy canvas hide amid the gum cistus bushes, the corporate power of the huge birds and the noise seemed overwhelming. Loud chattering '*kik kik kik*' calls, and hissings that sounded like steam escaping from a locomotive as the birds fought each other briefly, were accompanied by noisy thumps, grunts and the snapping of bones. Scores of ravens, which earlier had had the carcass to themselves, were now relegated to the edge of the circle, yet a few still angrily tweaked the great vultures' tail feathers.

Suddenly one of the black vultures which felt it had waited long enough ran along ponderously like a taxiing plane, opened its 9-foot span of wings and sailed into the griffons. Lashing out with those wings and making open beak threats, it soon won a place, tore off a chunk of goat flesh and flew back to its own kind. It had only time for a few pecks before another black vulture tried to filch the morsel. Instantly, both leaped into the air like giant fighting cocks, their wings cracking as yacht sails do when jibing in a storm, the meat-owner fighting off the other with downward slashes of its big claws.

There was a loud woofing of wings – all the ravens had flown away. The vultures looked up in alarm, then also left, beating away in slow motion like monstrous dark machines. Presently, back came the ravens to have the carcass to themselves again for half an hour before the vultures, now specks in the sky, saw there was no danger, tumbled the ravens' clever ruse and also began to return.

That early encounter persuaded me of the truth of the Spanish claim to the most spectacular wildlife in all western Europe. Yet it was to take years, and many strange adventures, before I was ready to give a firsthand account of it in this book.

Wild brown bears still roam the remote mountain fastnesses of the Asturias, the Picos de Europa and the Pyrenees. Although fully protected, there are fewer than 100 animals left, and they are seriously endangered. Over 1,200 wild wolves still slip like silver ghosts through the high forests of the north and west central areas. Wild boar root for acorns and mast in many of the high wooded hangars and the lower marshes. The lithe tuft-eared Spanish lynx, though down to some 400 animals, finds strongholds in Extremadura, in Toledo Province, and in the Coto Doñana scrublands and marshes where the mighty Guadalquivir river sweeps down to the sea.

Fourteen-pointer 'imperial' red deer stags, quite common, roar their rutting challenges across many mountain landscapes like those of the Sierra de Gredos, the Sierra de Cazorla and the hills of Extremadura. Besides an estimated 10,000 roe deer and about 1,000 fallow deer, populations of the spectacular *cabra montés*, or Spanish ibex, are to be found on the higher ranges. Smaller numbers of the nimble black and white *musmón,* or moufflon, inhabit some of the highest mountains, while chamois live in the Asturias and Pyrenees. Thirty Barbary sheep from North Africa, imported in 1970, have increased to a vigorous herd of 700 animals in a little hunting reserve in Murcia province. Wildcats and otters enjoy their finest European strongholds in Spain. Foxes, badgers, stoats and weasels abound – as do the stone marten, the genet and the mongoose in lesser numbers.

3

Spain boasts no fewer than six kinds of eagle, including two of the *Aquila* genus, the endangered imperial and the golden eagle. The latter maintains some 600 pairs. The short-toed eagle is abundant, and there are good populations of booted and Bonelli's eagles too. The sea eagle and spotted eagle are rarely seen. The osprey is called the 'fish eagle', but it is rare (about 20 pairs) and is confined to the south. There are four species of vulture — the griffon (3,500 pairs), Egyptian (2,000 pairs), black (250 pairs) and, rarest of all, the lammergeier or bearded vulture, with under 100 pairs left, its last strongholds now in Cazorla and the Spanish Pyrenees. The lammergeier's single wing length of 33 to 34 inches eclipses the 2-foot wing of the golden eagle, and it is marvellous to see this mighty bird wheel in wild courtship display around the massive limestone faces near Jaca.

I was delighted, when driving near Burgos in the early days, to spot a red kite as it flapped ponderously over a farmer's fields. I braked hard, leaped out of my van and took many photos of the great fork-tailed bird, knowing it to be limited in Britain to just 40 pairs in Wales. I was even more excited when I saw my first black kite in Extremadura, for the bird has long been extinct as a breeder in Britain. I did not know then that there are some 6,000 pairs of red kites in Spain, yet they are outnumbered by black kites of which there are some 20,000 pairs.

As for harriers, falcons, hawks and owls, Spain offers a bewildering array for the raptor-starved bird-watcher. The same is true of the myriad assortment of freshwater birds and sea birds, for nowhere in western Europe can offer more of these species, especially in venues like the Ebro Delta and the Coto Doñana. I will deal with these species and their populations later, just as I will try to explain how this splendid variety of wildlife survived in Spain and what conservation measures have been taken.

I first visited Spain in 1952, one semi-lunatic among seven others who had bought an ancient gaff-rigged ketch and set off from Bursledon harbour to sail round the world. We lunged through the Bay of Biscay in winter and landed at La Coruña, looking for cheap repairs to the boat in dry dock, but were ordered to leave by the port police. We sailed up to El Ferrol, where the captain and owner were arrested, and three local guitarists from Coruña, who had come along for the ride, had their heads shaved for leaving the country illegally. When a storm half-wrecked the yacht on our way to the Canaries and a Swedish tanker towed the stricken boat to Lisbon, the party broke up. One other crew member walked with me the 800 km from Lisbon to Madrid, for we had only enough money to take the train home from Madrid. I will never forget that long, hot dusty walk, eating vegetable soup and sleeping in the furrows of ploughed fields at night. I swore then that I would never go to Spain again!

Twelve years later my father and stepmother built a villa at the foot of arid mountains on the Mediterranean coast near Puerto de Mazarron in Murcia Province, and I visited them there from time to time in the late '60s and early '70s. I did not care for their life-style among a group of British, German, Danish, French, American, Norwegian and Swedish expatriates. Apart from the time it took to understand each other, and maintaining the fabric of their villas, all these people had one thing in common: little to do and far too much free time in which to do it. House visits, parties, boozy convivial lunches were the order of the week – a far cry from my lonely spartan life on a remote Scottish lochside.

Then, late in 1978, I received a telegram saying my stepmother had died and that my father had become incapable of looking after himself. Eventually I brought my father back to a nursing home in Sussex and sold his villa to pay for his upkeep.

It was at this time that I formed a close friendship with my father's Spanish lawyer, Gregorio Parra, a big man, as tall as my own six feet, but heavier and two years younger than I was. He spoke fluent English, had written two short works of philosophy and had had a play staged in Madrid. He lived in a large house, full of rare ikons and antiques, near the country town of Totana, some 40 km inland from my father's villa.

While I finished winding up my father's affairs in Spain, Gregorio would urge me constantly to return for a longer period and get to know more of the country, which I had always found too hot and dry for my liking once May turned to June, and where my digestion never seemed quite settled. He wanted to show me a small hunting reserve in the mountains above the town which I assumed was spelt phonetically, as I heard him pronounce it – 'Spoonya' – where lived a goat-like creature known locally as '*muflón*'. It was the mention of wildcats, foxes and even a pair of eagles, however, that made me express some mild interest. My great passion at home in Scotland had been for wildcats (of which I reared three litters and released them into the wild) and the golden eagles that inhabited my corner of South Inverness-shire — and it was to them that I longed to return.

As I headed finally for the French border on May 20, my Volkswagon camping van full of my father's belongings, something happened that urged me to take seriously Gregorio's promise. Having heard that the Ordesa National Park high in the Pyrenees was a paradise of dramatic landscape and wildlife, I decided to make a small diversion and visit the area. None of the roads in Ordesa itself crossed the border, and the next road to the west looked so precipitous on my map that it seemed unwise to tackle it in my overloaded vehicle. Instead, after Zaragoza, I took the small but better road through Huesca and Jaca, with the intention of crossing into France at Candanchu, passing on the way through what seemed like similar terrain. Beyond Huesca I found myself in a wilderness dream. Rushing rivers fed into emerald lakes coloured by the run-off from melting snow. Huge conifer trees appeared magically from wraiths of mist which cooled the heat of the midday sun. And the great crags of the central Pyrenees dominated the distant skyline.

I turned a wooded bend in the road near the village of Riglos and was suddenly confronted by a fantastic panorama. There ahead rose three massive cliff faces of red and grey rock, one to the west and two to the east, vast towering buttresses springing sheer for more than 600 metres from the tops of steep rounded hills. Below them lay green fields fed by small streams, along the grassy banks of which I saw rabbits hopping. I described the scene in my book *Golden Eagle Years,* but I am ashamed to say I wrongly identified nearly all the huge birds which swept into view.

I was just thinking 'There could be eagles here' when one came beating along beside the truck, merely eight yards away! I stopped, leaped out with the camera and took some shots of the golden eagle as it obligingly circled in the sunlight. Then I saw a buzzard, then another eagle. And as I looked up into the sky I saw more huge birds high up, difting towards the western massif. To my astonishment, I counted seventeen huge raptors in the air, eleven of which I identified as golden eagles, and some others where even larger with bigger wings and longer outspread 'fingers' — lammergeiers, otherwise known as European vultures . . .

In fact, apart from the buzzard and one golden eagle, all the birds were griffon vultures. How little I knew then about the wildlife of Spain! Although I discovered my mistake before the book came out, it was too late to have the text altered and it remains a testimony to the naturalist's nightmare — too hasty identification.

All the same, it was that supreme moment which brought me back again and again to explore this vast and beautiful country.

2 · Sorting Sheep from Goats

For the next three years I was completely immersed in my Scottish wildlife studies and did not return to Spain. Then two things happened to change everything. My beloved Alsatian, Moobli, developed severe spinal paralysis and it became clear that he would not survive another harsh Highland winter. At the same time, my father became progressively more miserable in the Worthing nursing home and, as he approached 80, he begged me to take him back to Spain, where his wife was buried.

I left Moobli with a friend who had a large warm house and a sheltered walled garden in Surrey, and rented a villa on the Mediterranean not far from where my father had once lived near Mazarron. For two months he was happier in that small villa, with me looking after him, than he had been for years. Many of his old friends came by, and we visited them. I kept my wildlife column going for a Scottish newspaper, but it was not long before I began to feel trapped. Wildlife expeditions were out of the question for I could not leave my father alone for more than two hours, but his face would darken whenever I asked if he would like to return to Worthing. Eventually I found a former nurse, a woman he liked who had been recently widowed, and she agreed to take care of my father in her apartment. I took off into inland wooded mountains for three weeks while they settled down together.

With Gregorio Parra as my guide, I made for the hills of Sierra

Espuña (still lodged in my mind as 'Spoonya') where, he told me, he had heard there were three pairs of golden eagles, as well as the herd of wild moufflon. We took the mountain road from Totana through walled orchards of orange and almond trees, already blossoming in February with pink and white flowers. Far ahead reared the great white domed peak of Espuña, soaring 1,585 metres high into the drifting clouds. We passed over a bridge above a wide concrete water canal, which Greg explained had been built like that all the way from the mountains 100 km north of Madrid to Lorca, a distance of 500 kilometres altogether. It was a great feat of engineering and one of the longest man-made waterways in Europe. The water, supplemented from natural springs in the Espuña mountains, was distributed through hundreds of small stone and concrete channels to irrigate the orange, lemon and almond tree plantations of the entire area.

Higher up, we drove through deep canyons of sandstone where the slopes were covered with various kinds of pine trees, mostly small rounded ones, with black cones, which Greg said were carrasco pines, capable of surviving in drought. Among them were tall thin trees like pokers – these were winter pines. We passed a beautiful monastery called the Santuario de Santa Eulalia, a long graceful dark-red stone building where white doves fluttered among the towers. It was no longer used as a monastery but was visited for thanksgiving and picnics on saints' days. Up to the left, a steep narrow road led to a huge marble statue of Christ, spreading his arms out to protect the town of Totana far below. As we rounded a bend the whole mediaeval village and castle of Aledo was revealed. Dating back to the tenth century, it is one of the oldest Moorish *pueblos* in Spain and seems to spring from the very rock on which it stands.

After Aledo the road swung right, winding steeply between small farms, and just before we turned up the narrow road that led to the peak itself Greg pointed to a magnificent old red sandstone mansion. It was the last house before the start of the Reserve, and it stood back from the road, beyond a deep gorge, in its own 250 acres of almond trees. It was, Greg explained, *his* Espuña '*finca*' (estate).

The house had 21 rooms! If ever I wanted to live in Espuña, he went on, I could buy it, if I liked, for a mere £50,000! Or a lot less if I did not want all the land.

I gasped. What a bargain – but I did not have that much money, and in any case, what would I, one man, do with 21 rooms?

We stopped at a carved wooden sign that denoted the start of the

14,000 hectare Reserve. (There are 2.47 acres to a hectare). It said: '*Prohibida Toda Clase de Caza*' (Prohibited All Classes of Hunting).

'You would be in trouble if you were caught killing so much as a butterfly here,' Greg said.

It sounded like my kind of place.

He explained that, although it was classed as a 'hunting reserve', the only regular hunting allowed was of the red-legged partridge. Sometimes, when the animals were increasing beyond the capacity of the land to support them, a few hunting licences were issued to cull the wild boar and moufflon herds. Even then, hunters had to pay very high prices, and were led by the two guardas who patrolled the Reserve and knew it well.

As we climbed higher and higher, the road became a series of sharp switchback bends over alarming drops, some of them over 300 metres and sheer. Everywhere there were pine trees, and on the sides of the canyons I could see caves, rock faces, ledges and cliffs which looked ideal for eagle eyries.

It was one of the most unnerving drives I had ever known, yet I had just remarked what a beautiful and extraordinary place it was when we ran into thick mist. We tried to go on, but after a few hundred metres it grew so thick that we could not see for more than three or four metres ahead. There was no choice but to turn back. Greg said that mist was quite rare; usually the mountain enjoyed marvellous light by day, and it remained cool up there in summer while people below in Totana, and even more so in the Mazarron area, sweltered in the heat. I had seen enough and felt my blood stirring. I was a mountain man, not a beach man after all, and I knew I would come back here.

After leaving Gregorio, I ran into a couple of my father's friends (whom I liked) in a bar. Sally and Axel Olhaberry-Compton ran a successful restaurant and camping park outside Totana, and when I said I had just been up to Espuña and wanted to go again, they told me that I was in luck. Camping in their park at weekends was a keen naturalist and expert on Sierra Espuña, a man called Antonio Eguia — I ought to meet him.

Antonio turned out to be a small, wiry and eager man with three sons. The eldest, Sergio, 17, wanted to become a wildlife cameraman. Antonio marked on my map rough areas where bear, wolf and lynx could be found, but said I would be better off visiting the various large reserves run by ICONA (Spain's National Institute for the

Conservation of Nature), where rare animals and birds were kept in relatively large enclosures. It would be necessary to get separate permission for each, and that did not sound like my idea of wildlife trekking. But it might do for a start. One evening, when Antonio gave a show of some of his slides, I was dismayed to see most of his birds of prey wearing jesses. I was not interested in photographing tame and captive creatures but I had enough tact to keep quiet about it. When I congratulated him on a good shot of a golden eagle flying, he said it was a tame bird, flown by a falconer at a safari park near Madrid. He had also flown a griffon vulture to a meat lure. The man who owned the park had been a friend of Spain's most famous wildlife expert, Rodriguez de la Fuente, who had often used his birds in films.

Rodriguez de la Fuente, I was told, had been killed recently in a helicopter crash in British Columbia while filming wolves and grizzly bears. Dr de la Fuente produced Spain's most popular TV show, a weekly programme of films about the country's rarest wild creatures. About 1½ million people flocked to Madrid airport when his body was flown back for burial. In fact his whole crew perished in the accident and there was no-one left to carry on. Spanish television was showing David Attenborough's BBC series 'Life on Earth' to fill the gap. Perhaps I should, after all, heed the advice of my friend Roy Ensor, who owned the local garage, for he had often urged me to buy a movie camera.

It was not until later, when I saw one of the Fuente films, that I realised I had met the man briefly three years earlier while dining with a friend who introduced me to the dynamic doctor in a cafe in Madrid. We had fallen into conversation about the time I had spent tracking grizzlies and cougar from the log cabin I had built with my own hands on the west coast of Canada, and he told me then of his plans to film the great bears, expressing interest in my book, *Alone in the Wilderness*. I advised him to go to Canada and Alaska.

I felt a stab of remorse – despite the fact that, beyond giving him the names of a few useful contacts, I had done nothing to contribute to his tragic and untimely end.

Sally, Axel, Antonio and his family had agreed to meet me on the morning of February 20 to try stalking the wary moufflon goats with our cameras.

On the appointed day we drove up the military road past the sign saying — '*Militar. Prohibido el Paso*'. Antonio's sons had explained that there was a military barracks and radar scanning station at the top, to which soldiers from the area were sent to toughen up, especially in winter, when the temperature could drop to 20°c below zero! People were not prevented from using the first part of the road, and we parked above a vast valley, the far rocky tree-lined slopes of which reared over 1,000 metres into the sky.

'We will probably find moufflons up there,' Sergio said.

As we all piled out with our cameras, I saw two guardas on the far horizon, with the wind blowing from behind them. I said if the moufflons were as wary as they had stated, they would get the guardas' scent and clear the area before we got there. Then Antonio spotted a moufflon herd on a broad steep shoulder lower down. We went there and started stalking across the rocky hill. After 800 metres at an easy amble, despite the steep ground, I realised I was not with professional stalkers for the two younger boys kept talking and we had the wind behind our backs! Naturally we saw no moufflon.

Antonio thought our best chance now was to drive down to where a forestry track went right round the mountain below the peak, and then to trek down to an ancient *finca* called Carrasca where alfalfa was left by the guardas to help feed the animals. We reached the track, to find our way barred by a thick padlocked chain. Again we piled out with our cameras, ready for the 3 km trek down to the *finca*, when we heard the sound of powerful motor-cycles drawing closer.

In a cloud of dust, up rode the two guardas. They were short but stockily built, and tough-looking. They wore green uniforms and both had pistols in holsters strapped to their right hips. They were polite, and said '*Bonna días*' (good day). They had a few words with Antonio, then one pointed to my 2ft 6ins camouflaged lens and said that I was clearly a professional. I could not take photos inside the Reserve without a written permit from the Director, whose office was 35 km away in Murcia! I did not argue, for if I was to work the wildlife in Sierra Espuña in the future I could not afford to get on the wrong side of these two men. We could still walk about, they explained, as long as we did not take pictures. I thought this absurd, for it is the walking about that disturbs wildlife, not the fact that you have a camera in your hands. They shrugged, said it was the law and that they were employed to enforce the law. Just as one needed a permit to '*cazar*' (hunt), so one had to obtain a permit, a '*caza fotográfica*', to take photos. The Eguia family were as surprised as I was, for they had been visiting the Reserve as tourists for five years with their ordinary cameras but had never had permits or been stopped.

I was to discover all too soon that the same situation exists all over Spain. The best wildlife exists in some kind of reserve, of which there are many kinds — national parks, natural parks, hunting reserves, wildlife refuges — and all are protected by guardas who carry guns. While I often found it irksome to have to drive miles out of my way to one big city or another to get a permit before starting work, I soon realised it was a better system than we had in Britain. In this way the authorities know which professionals are in their reserves and what they are up to.

We put our cameras back into our vehicles. The guardas smiled and bid us '*adiós*', and we all set off to trek down to the old *finca* area. Ironically, the next few hours were the best I had spent so far in Spain. I suggested to Sergio that we two should speed ahead of the main group, so we could start stalking properly. We went down the sandy track at a good lick, then cut through the trees. It was rocky between the pines, but it was an easy slope and we kept cutting the corners of the winding track that led down to the *finca*. It was impossible to walk along the stony track without our boots making some noise, whereas the cushion of pine needles on the forest floor made our approach quieter.

Carrasca was basically a ruin which stood near a beautiful natural spring, the lower reaches of which had been dammed up to form a large pool of deep water. Through the trees, we saw there was a small herd of moufflon there, some sipping the spilled water, others tucking into the alfalfa provided by the guardas. I had never seen animals like these before. They were tawny gold in colour, large goat-like creatures, and the few males had huge corrugated horns which swept up and backwards in a graceful curve. The females had horns too, though far smaller. The males had thick tufts of long yellow gold hairs dangling from their chests and front legs. The largest two must have weighed more than 300lbs apiece. And I had no camera!

They heard rather than saw us, and the herd ran a few steps, then stood milling about, looking around nervously, only 200 metres away.

'No *disturbar*?' I whispered to Sergio, and he nodded.

We shrank back until out of sight, then turned to the right and hiked down to an open area, well away from Carrasca. The magnificence of the full spectacular view was now spread out before us. Rocky tree-lined slopes stretched away for more than a kilometre, then rose to a ridge beyond which we could see the sea 50 km away. On the left of the ridge a rounded orange rock cliff face was all that could be seen of a long series of jagged escarpments towering above a vast gorge some 700 metres deep. The broad bosom of land below us fell into another gulch on our right, the far sides of which rose up to meet the end of the primitive forestry track. Above this, more steep rounded slopes, covered with tangles of huge boulders amid the trees, led up to a long white and orange cliff face which was almost as high as the peak of Espuña itself, now above and behind us. I glassed the cliff with my binoculars and saw several dark tufts on a ledge, one of which looked very much like a golden eagle eyrie. If I was right, these eagles would be nesting at the height of Ben Nevis!

I had just said to Sergio that this would be a good place to see eagles when we saw it together.

'*Mire* − Look!' said Sergio, who had a smattering of English. 'There is − águila!'

The eagle was soaring south of the peak but high up. I said that if it was a male, and I thought it was, any moment now it might go into its territorial and courtship dives. Sergio said he did not know what these were.

Right on cue, the eagle soared upwards, closed its wings like a trussed turkey and zoomed earthwards in a fantastic long dive. Then it opened its wings, soared up and dived again − three more times. It sailed along for half a minute, then treated us to five more of these great yo-yo-ing dives before turning and landing on a lower peak. Sergio said he had never seen anything like that in all his life. We looked round and saw that the herd of moufflon were watching us watching the eagle! The great bird stayed where it was for twenty minutes, and we could see it clearly through our binoculars preening its wing feathers. Just then a female moufflon emerged on the peak to the left of the eagle, silhouetted against the blue sky. I could have photographed them both in one picture.

As we walked back, Sergio said he thought I knew more about eagles than anyone he knew, including his father. I had seldom been paid a nicer compliment. Halfway up the hills through the woods we met Antonio and his other two sons, who had been looking for moufflon above the track and had found none. When Sergio told him excitedly all we had seen, he looked quite peeved.

Two days later I was on my way to Murcia for a 10-day '*caza fotográfica*' from the ICONA office. To help with my poor Spanish Axel drove me there in his sports car. Half Chilean, he was related on his English side to Denis Compton, the cricketer. He was a huge man of 6ft 4ins, gruff, sardonic, and looked and behaved like a larger version of Robert Mitchum, whom I had once known quite well in my days as a journalist in Hollywood. He did not tolerate fools gladly, but I got on well with him, perhaps because, when he thumped me during minor arguments, I took the liberty of thumping him back! He could certainly shift his car. I cringed as bends zoomed up at speeds of 70mph, but Axel explained laconically that he had once been an amateur racing driver.

At the ICONA office I was surprised to find he was tact itself. The Director, Carlos Bourcarolas, was a tall solemn man who said that I should have applied in writing first; that was the correct procedure. I sighed and looked despondent. Carlos then turned to me with a look of surprise and said there was no problem. He called in his secretary, who went out and returned with the letter, typed in Spanish, that I should have written. I signed it, and a few minutes later she returned with my typed *permiso* for the full ten days. Of course there was no charge, said Carlos, but if I wanted to learn the best places in Sierra Espuña I could hire either, or both, of the two guardas for £7.50 a day. But I did not have to, he added. Feeling I could thus show good intent, and also make a small contribution to reserve funds, I agreed to hire each of them for one day.

Carlos also told me how the Reserve had begun. At the turn of the century most of the area was owned by a man called Ricardo Codorniu, who loved trees. Few mountains in this hot dry arid region supported any trees and so he had made it his life's work, with a few helpers, to stop soil erosion by planting trees throughout much of the Espuña range. He planted mainly carasco pines, black pines and white pines, and these were complemented by acacias with lombardy and Canadian poplars along the edges of the five river beds. While these 'rivers' were dry most of the year, only running with water when it rained heavily, the soil in them was damper than elsewhere. Other seeds also took root in time so that there were now more than 30 species of tree, including the beautiful flowering madronas, juniper, oak, ash, willow, hawthorn, to be found there. Under their shelter various grasses and bushes thrived because the trees reduced the power of the winds. Planting was basically complete by 1929, and the Reserve was now run by the forestry engineers of ICONA.

The amazing result of all this was the return of a flourishing wild life. Small mammals like mice and voles prospered. Insects burgeoned and lizards and the small birds that fed on them also increased. Hundreds of nest boxes were hung in the trees. Rabbits, fed on the new grasses, multiplied rapidly. Now that they had a larger food source, the few foxes, wildcats and genets in the area also thrived. Young golden eagles, drifting for miles as they looked for new territories, found the rabbits, lizards, mice and voles and the excellent nesting sites, and so now there were the three nesting pairs. There were also two or three pairs of short-toed eagles. Wild boar returned to the area. It sounded a wonderful story, and I resolved to get to grips with Espuña immediately.

When I asked about the moufflon, Carlos laughed and said that the local populace made the same mistake: they were not moufflon at all but *'arrui'* − Barbary sheep. Their scientific name was *'Ammotragus lervia'* and their natural habitat was in North Africa, where they ranged from the peaks of the Atlas mountains to the Red Sea. Because it was found they did not browse young trees, were hardy enough to withstand great differences of climate, and had an extraordinary ability to go without water, ICONA decided to start a small herd.

The first animals, five rams and four sheep, were imported from Ain Sebab in Morocco in 1970. They survived the winter well, and in February 1971 eight more rams and twelve sheep were railed down from Frankfurt Zoo, where they had been breeding too prolifically for their enclosure. From this nucleus the herds in Espuña had grown to 775 animals, and now they had to be culled for their own good. Despite the high fees, hunters came from as far away as North America to bag their trophies − and the fees more than paid for the 250,000 pesetas (£1,250) it cost per year to give the animals supplementary feeding of fresh green and dry alfalfa!

Carlos told me proudly that the lessons in Espuña were now being applied to other dry wildlife areas of Spain, as more private lands came into ICONA's hands.

3 · Where Eagles Fly

Two days later Axel guided me through a maze of stony tracks to the Casa Forestal where I had to present my permit to the head forester, a beaming dark-haired man called José Miniano, and left me with him. José took me in his Land Rover to a place called Collado Bermejo, 1,207 metres high, where the main road ends and many forestry tracks fan out over the Espuña hills. He drew me a rough map, so that I would be less likely to get lost, and told me a good place from which to watch eagles lay round the high peaks beyond Carrasca — the very white cliffs where I had seen the male eagle with Sergio Eguia.

On the way back we saw a small herd of Barbary sheep ahead. He pulled up and after a brief stalk I took three pictures of the great goats through the pine trees. Back at his house, a golden eagle came soaring overhead and I took my first photos of one in Espuña.

Next morning I found I had been assigned as my guide for the day the senior of the two guardas. Casimiro Esteban was a stocky, even plump, man ten years my junior but I soon discovered he could move well over the steep rocky terrain, his short legs looking like tree trunks. He led the way on his motor bike to a crumbling old *finca* high in the hills from which we could see the Casa Forestal, glittering like a jewel 3 km away down in the valley. I would have to camp here for the first few days, he explained, so that they could keep an eye on me. They were afraid of foreign visitors, unused to

17

the terrain, getting lost or falling 300 metres down one of the many precipices. Nor was I to start any fires. If I had not returned to this camp site by dusk they would send out a search party.

We left van and motor bike by the *finca* and he led me up through the pines to stalk Barbary sheep. It was a cold grey day, and he set a cracking pace. Had the sun been out, I would have become extremely hot. The trouble was we went slightly with the wind, and the higher we climbed, the higher went the sheep until they were lost in the trees. We gave up and drove to within 800 metres of Carrasca. A small group of the sheep came towards us, and I took some fine shots of three rams on a rock in a clearing before they galloped away. They had been scared by the other guarda forking alfalfa from a trailer into the feed holders.

I pointed to the great white and orange cliff faces towering away to the west and said I thought there might be a golden eagle eyrie in them. Casimiro looked surprised. There was indeed a *'nido'* up there and he would show it to me right now. He climbed into my van and made me drive round the stony white forestry track for more than 3 km until we reached a pass where the lower shoulders of the range dropped almost to the road. He told me that on one winter's day three years ago he had found two eagles feeding from the carcass of a dead Barbary sheep in those steep hills. A third eagle was perched in a tree and a fourth on a small ridge, with two more in the air. That was the first and only time he had seen six eagles together, and known that there definitely were three pairs in Espuña.

We parked the van and then zig-zagged a long way up the shale and gravel-covered slopes, finding rabbit droppings, the scats of stone martens and also those of foxes which had been left on herb tufts. A red-legged partridge shot up with *'chuckaw'* alarm calls and whirred noisily away on its short wings. We were crossing some jagged white boulders when my foot slipped and I fell backwards, hitting my pack on a rock. I went more carefully after that, especially when we began to inch our way along narrow ledges above sheer crevasses for 30 metres until we came to a natural but thin path which passed dangerously above several steep drops. After a further 500 metres or so it widened out beneath the white and pinky-orange limestone faces.

Casimiro pointed upwards to the clumps of brown vegetation on the long narrow cleft I had seen from so far below with Sergio, indicating the biggest one to the right of the others.

'*Nido!*' he said.

Sure enough, it was an unmistakeable eagle eyrie. A small dead but stout and spiky tree held the great nest of twigs to the rockface. I glassed it but could not see any fresh vegetation to indicate that it would be used this year. I took my camera from the pack and found that, in my fall, I had broken the ring that held the long 640mm lens in place. I cursed and tried to take photos by holding the lens tight on to the camera. I felt sure some light would get in to ruin the pictures. What rotten luck! Just then we were hit by flurries of sleety snow. The wind was bitter, and Casimiro shivered.

'*Muy malo día!*' he said. (Very bad day!)

I forbore saying that this kind of weather was normal at this time of year when trekking after eagles in the Highlands. I was happy to have found Eyrie I in Spain and did not waste the hard climb when the standard lens still fitted. I took several dramatic scenic views from the bottom of the cliff. We went past the faces and climbed down a steeper but safer route. As Casimiro's motor bike was now far closer than the van, he gave me a hairy pillion ride up to the barracks and radar compound on the summit where some 70 soldiers lived. It was even colder up there, and they were camping in large brown tents! Apart from a few ravens nesting on the sheer edges, below the radar scanners, no other wildlife could be seen up there, and I would not need to go there again. Back at the camping *finca,* I paid Casimiro his small fee – he refused a tip. What a superb view of the mountains and valleys I would have from my van! Suddenly I saw an eagle flying straight ahead. I grabbed the camera as Casimiro said the larger female was heading in to join her mate. Again I tried holding the lot together by force and took photos of the male chasing the female and diving all round her. After the guarda left, I spent what daylight was left tying the long lens on to the camera with cord, reinforcing the broken join with black camera tape until it was as rigid as I could possibly make it.

I woke with the van suffused by the light of a red-gold dawn. I made tea and two thick slogs of toast on a Spanish corrugated iron frying pan device. When the sun was high enough to give me good light, I trekked down the wooden valley to the west where Casimiro said I should see Barbary sheep. The yaffling laughter of green wood-peckers rang through the trees, coal tits were flocking and great tits were calling '*Me too, Me too*'. Just like home! Overtaken by an urge of nature, I shifted thick bark debris aside with my foot and crouched down. Just then an odd-looking squirrel came down a nearby tree.

19

I had never seen one like it before. It was grey with a thick creamy elongated patch along its flanks. I reached for the camera. A large grey soft-looking hawk with a barred chest wafted silently over my head and landed in a pine next to the squirrel, which immediately shot away. I tried to take a photo of the goshawk but, unsteady with pants round my ankles, I missed it.

Climbing out of the valley, I hit a dirt track and was hiking back to the van when I saw an eagle sail across the gulch and land with slow sweeps of its wings in some white cliffs high above the tree line. I noted the position − about 400 metres west of the wide red cut of a firebreak. There could be an eyrie up there. I drove right round the wide valley on the rough track until I reached the firebreak.

It was a hard steep climb, as high as yesterday's, and even worse when I left the firebreak and headed over large serrated rocks towards the cliffs. I was now carrying both my cameras, the second for scenic shots with standard and wide angle lenses, for I dare not tamper with the tapes on the first, which I had to nurse in both hands like a rifle. There was nothing on the north-east faces but I took two photos of an eagle's lookout rock which was striped with white splashes. Encouraged, I clambered on, negotiated a nasty drop, then went low again into the tree-line to get round a long sheer bluff to check the middle faces.

I had just rounded the bluff when an eagle launched itself from what looked like a crevice near the highest peak in those faces. It flew fast, and because I was low and among the trees, I could not get a picture. I climbed up to take a closer look at the crevice, but such was the formation of bulging buttresses the higher I went the less I could see. Back down I went again and glassed the face of the peak. It was quite a small crevice but I could see the thick grey twigs of a short nest under a perfect overhang of reddish rock. Here was Eyrie 2, found in record time. It was, however, an impossible place to work for there was nowhere to put a hide to overlook the nest. There was nothing in the west faces of the cliffs. As I turned to leave, I saw the eagle doing golden ball dives far across the valley. A flock of 21 ravens and jackdaws launched themselves from the great white Espuña peak, loving the high wind, zooming round each other and calling. Some of the ravens were performing courtship flights, pairs gliding along close together and enjoying aerial chases. I took some good photos.

After a knee-cracking descent, I drove to the *finca* camp site for lunch, so that the foresters in their *casa* two miles away could see I was still alive. I then drove to the chained road, hiked the 3 km down to Carrasca and spent the afternoon taking pictures of Barbary sheep after brief stalks through the dappled sunny woods. Now there were no rams among them so I had to be content with just the smaller females and yearlings. Once a sparrowhawk zoomed by, twisting and turning through the pines, giving me no time for a photo. As ever with this dashing cavalier of the woods, a brief glimpse is all you get. A small flock of magpies were at the feeding area, chasing insects among the alfalfa.

Tired now, my feet sore, I traipsed back up to the van. As I drove back to my camp site I saw a red-legged partridge at the side of the road, pecking away. It was turning over stones with its beak. I took two photos through the windscreen, then stepped out and tried to get nearer. I was only four metres away when it saw me, squeaked and took off.

The next day was a Sunday. I had been told that tourists would come to various public picnic sites and walk about on the mountain. I decided to give my aching feet a rest and go to Sally and Axel's camping park for a shower and to stock up with food and water supplies. I met Antonio's family again. They were amazed at the speed with which I had operated for they had never found an eyrie in five years. They had hired Casimiro yesterday, to show *them* the nest. Now they intended to put a rabbit 100 metres from the cliff and from a hide made out of canvas and curtain rails try to get pictures of an eagle taking it. I had worked with bald eagles in Canada and golden eagles in Scotland with my own type of 'invisible' hides for many years, and I offered to show them how to make one. None of them seemed interested, not even Sergio.

Later I met Gregorio Parra, who invited me down to the Puerto for a sea trip in his new cabin cruiser. Unfortunately, his heavy duty battery, which he had had on charge all week, would not turn the engine over; nor would one we borrowed from the port manager. I managed to persuade the disgusted Greg not to dump his duff battery into the sea, and took him out for an early supper to compensate. When I told him of my adventures in Espūna, he said he would love to come with me but could not do so during the coming week as he had to defend a burglar in the Murcia courts.

It was a cold night, up there in the ruined *finca* at 1,300 metres, but I woke to clear skies. Though the sun was hot, a cool north breeze was blowing, making it an ideal day for trekking. I hiked down to Carrasca, still 1,146 metres high, intending to try for some Barbary sheep, and would then head down the long valley and up on to the ridge where I thought there might be an eagle eyrie in the rounded orange cliff I had first seen with Sergio.

I moved slowly and as quietly as I could, trying to avoid the frequent beds of dead pine branches and twigs which crackled under-foot. Before reaching the dammed-up spring above the old *finca* I saw a huge herd of the sheep in the woods to my left. The trouble was the sun was behind them, lighting up all their outer hairs into bands of gold. I could not see their eyes. I paused, wondering how to tackle the stalk when I saw a pine or stone marten with a white throat patch go down a conifer trunk and become hidden by the foliage of smaller trees. A blackbird sang nearby, a woodpecker called its yaffling song, and the blackbird immediately imitated it. Suddenly there was a whirring scratching noise and up the bark of a carasco pine shot a squirrel which stretched, flattened itself along a branch. I managed one photo before it disappeared into the thick upper foliage.

Shrinking back, I stalked down in a semi-circle to my right and took a few better-lit photos of some Barbary rams in a clearing, then my film ran out. To put in a new one I had to undo the tapes and cord truss and put them back again afterwards. It seemed to take ages, though it was probably only a few minutes. By that time the sheep had moved higher and were lost in the trees. This meant the sun would now be on them fully, so I went after them again. I had only travelled fifty metres through the forest when I heard a scuttering sound and saw a small brown and cream squirrel shoot up a dwarf oak. It stayed briefly with its head behind the trunk, then leaped to a bigger black pine and climbed up it. I stole round the thick trunk and saw it holding a cone in its pinky buff hands, its thick brown tail held up tight behind its head. It was watching me, staying perfectly still.

Slowly I raised the long lens. I was too close to bring it in focus! The only way of getting far enough away without actually walking, which would have scared it off, was to sink slowly down on to a bed of rushes, lie on my back and start taking pictures. Unfortunately, in the act of lying down, the tapes gave way and the lens parted from the camera. I forced it back together, only to find the end of the tape was now in vision. Then a second squirrel came down from the high foliage, posed for a perfect shot I could not take, and disappeared into another tree. Luckily the first stayed where it was as I worked the tape clear and squeezed the lens back on to the camera.

I lay still, and after a while it decided I was harmless and began to eat the cone. As I clicked away it turned the cone round in its mouth with its hands as we would eat a sweetcorn. Little bits of wafer thin husk kept floating down in the breeze. A beautiful fat-faced creature with huge eyes, it had a reddish nose, creamy cheeks, huge ear tufts and thick creamy patches on its chest and flanks. This was no ordinary Spanish squirrel.

Suddenly there was a thundering noise in the woods above, and a cracking of twigs. Something had scared the herd of Barbary sheep and they were stampeding. Some of these huge-horned rams weighed over 300lbs, and I did not want them stampeding over me. I stood up, ready to run for the shelter of the black pine's trunk as they headed my way. But as soon as they saw me they split into two bands and disappeared into the trees in opposite directions. I decided to carry on and check the rounded cliff that stared over the great crevasse 1,500 metres away.

Reaching an open area beyond Carrasca, I glanced up at the towering white and orange cliffs that contained Eyrie 1. There was a small dark lump on the second peak to the left. Through the binoculars I saw it was a large golden eagle, and perched only two metres from her was the smaller male. Hoping I might actually see them mating, I hid behind a dead tree, rested the camera on it and took a photo. Just then the female flew off, circled and vanished over the far side of the peak.

No sooner had I set off again than seven ravens came over from the Espūna peak, but when they got near the perched male eagle they veered off. There must have been something frightening about the way he turned quickly towards them. Suddenly he launched himself into a jet glide, travelling south east on the north wind, soon catching them up, flapping hard though they were. Squawking with fear, like crows, they turned to head back to the peak but the eagle quickly gained on them. I pressed the button for a shot of him zooming along, wings back like a huge swallow. One raven cut out from the group and swerved south and the eagle went for it. With apparent contempt he dived down on it with a great rush that made the raven swerve wildly and shoot upwards and head off fast to join its cronies.

The eagle then sailed airily back, performed one golden ball dive, and landed in a niche to the right of Eyrie 1. It certainly looked as if they were going to use that nest this year.

I trekked on down the gorge on the right, took a gentler traverse up its far side and then had to work on a compass bearing as the orange face was now out of sight because of the forest. I toiled on until I reached the lip of the great chasm to the left. Holding on to a pine on the serrated white crags above it, I steeled myself to peer over. I had never been more terrified on a mountain. The cliff was not sheer, it sloped *inwards* above a drop of more than 650 metres. I felt the solid rock on which I stood might at any moment break away and precipitate me with it down into the gorge. I walked thirty metres back into the pines and ate a sandwich lunch to calm my frayed nerves. Then, keeping the edge of the crevasse in sight as much as possible, I climbed over bluffs and down into gullies, until I came to the rounded sandstone face. By now the sun had gone behind a dark cloud as well as behind the face, and it was cast in gloom. I scanned the great cliff with the binoculars and there, I was almost sure, was Eyrie 3. It looked like a nest, an old one, of sticks and small branches resting on a ledge. If it was a nest, it had not been used for several years, but it would be easy to work from a hide, for the rounded escarpment on which I stood was level with the nest and there was plenty of pine tree cover. I took a few photos, hoping the camera could better catch the detail I could not see with binoculars in the dark light. I realised as I made the long hike back to my van that it was more like 3 km, distances being so hard to judge when unused to such vast terrain. It was 6.45 p.m. when I reached my camp site.

Next day, realising it was foolish to keep messing about with cord and tapes and risking useless photos, I went to buy a new adjuster ring for my best camera. I called at Greg's house early, as he was about to set off for Murcia. I saved him the drive, for he came in my van. After his morning's work at the Courts, he came with me to the store, where the manager sold me the ring and threw in a new camera battery for free. Later I gave Greg a show of my best wildlife slides at his home. He too said I should switch to making movies. One day, if one of my books made more money than usual, I might. By dusk I was back at the camp site.

The following day was the last under my permit, and I went out with the second guarda, Pedro. He was even shorter than Casimiro, slimmer, but also strongly built. He had thick folds of flesh over a

The huge rams of the Barbary sheep weighed up to 300lbs and were hard to stalk. They can be located in hilly woodlands by the clicking of their hoofs on the rocks.

The 'rosy eagle' turned out to be Europe's rarest raptor.

The lammergeier pursued the mobbing raven, displaying its 9ft wing span.

This rare sub-species of the Spanish squirrel is found only in Sierra Espuña.

The griffon vulture zoomed into her cliff nest, so close she sounded like a plane about to crash.

Near Una village a vast rampart of orange cliffs reared into the sky, home for a griffon colony.

There are still wild brown bears in northern Spain but they are endangered. This 500lb female and her two-year-old cubs lived in an enclosed valley.

Ravens courting, the males bowing and swelling out their throats while their mates gently preen them.

rough handsome face into which his eyes sank when he smiled, which was not often. He looked dour when I said I wanted to concentrate on eagles and to go up to Eyrie I again. He chose a shorter, steeper route than Casimiro had done, and went at a faster pace. When he saw that I could keep up, carrying my big pack of camera gear while he took nothing, his manner changed. I took photos of a few Barbary sheep on the way, then of the eyrie again, in better light than before. Although we waited for almost an hour, the eagles did not appear for the closer flight shots I wanted. Pedro said he knew of two other *nidos* within 5 km and flashed down the steeps at a great pace, his short legs twinkling like a goat's over the rocky boulder-strewn terrain. I fell over twice trying to keep up. We drove almost to the pass and as we alighted from the van saw three ravens chasing a large falcon which gave as good as it got, twisting on its side to slash at the ravens when they came too close. My photos later showed it was a peregrine!

Pedro trekked down through the woods to the east. I had the feeling he was making for the rounded orange face where I thought I had found Eyrie 3 two days ago. I did not stop him, for I wanted to double check it myself; in any case, he might know of a different nest. Sure enough, we came out at the orange face, the sun now blazing on it. There indeed was Eyrie 3, but it looked old, unused for years, the sticks blown away, and rock was showing through its centre.

I told Pedro that if the eagles were old birds they would prefer a lower site so that they would not have to flap and work hard to carry rabbits and other prey up to great heights, as at Eyrie I. This would also be true in a harsher than usual spring. He laughed and said he had not thought of that. He would now show me another *nido*, and also a high place where I could photograph flying eagles, often when *above* them. We hiked up to the van, drove over the pass for 3 km until near an abandoned village called El Pinillo, then went up a high rough track. It was only 12.30 p.m.

This long climb was mostly over hard basalt rock, with many sharp projections that twisted my ankles and hurt my feet even through the boots, the soles of which seemed to be rapidly thinning after the onslaught of the past week. He took me to the edge of another great cliff, and when I looked over I again recoiled with instinctive fear. Here the sheer drop was a full 800 metres (that is as much as 2,500 feet). He pointed to a spur on a bulging buttress almost halfway down and said the nest, Eyrie 4, was just behind it. He leaned over at an alarming angle and said that if I did the same I would be able to see the outer sticks of the nest.

'Fuck that!' was all I said, glad he couldn't understand my crass choice of English words.

It was an impossible nest to work but Pedro said it could be seen easily from the valley floor, though it was '*muy lejos*' (very far away). We waited half an hour, but no eagles flew by.

After lunch we tried to drive up a steep shaley forest track to overlook Eyrie 2 from a distance, but without 4-wheel drive my van could not get far enough. We spent the rest of the afternoon near Carrasca. On the way Pedro showed me another spring where he and Casimiro had made a concrete pool, complete with an easy walkway so the sheep could get to water. Beside it they had put slabs of mineral licks too. I told him how I had been scared when the big animals had stampeded in the woods, but he laughed and said they never attacked man. I was glad to hear it!

As we walked down to Carrasca there was a loud thump among the pines nearby, then the sound of crashing twigs as some animal ran away. Pedro smiled and said it was a '*jabalí*' (wild boar). I did not really believe him for I had never seen one, or signs of one. It could just as easily have been a Barbary sheep.

I slept like a hibernating dormouse that night and was surprised, while typing my notes next morning, when Pedro and Casimiro came to the camp site to wish me '*Buen viaje*', and to tell me to come back. I knew I would return to Espũna, and get those eagles at a nest if it half killed me.

I now had to head back to Britain, pick up my poor semi-paralysed Alsatian Moobli and return to Scotland for what I was sure would be both his and my last wild season there. I packed up my rented villa in the Puerto, then went to visit my father again, to see if he was still happy with his new nurse and companion. I asked if he wanted to go back to Worthing. He almost snapped at me.

'No! I do NOT want to go back to Worthing, Michael. I want to stay here!'

So, that was that. Mission accomplished. I made sure the financial arrangements were still working smoothly and said goodbye.

That night, as I camped by the sea, I heard on the radio news that the ferries at Santander in northern Spain would be on strike for at least a week. I decided to use the time to visit a place Antonio had told me about – the Sierra de Cazorla, where he said there were large red deer stags, wildcats, wild boar, eagles and even a few pairs of the rare lammageier or bearded vulture. I took the road through Lorca, Velez Rubio, with its twin-spired cathedral, and Baza, then turned up the country road through Pozo Alcon. The landscape was spectacular – high wooded mountains and rugged cliffs, and the lovely village of Tiscar perched on rocks above a rushing river. From Cazorla I took the steeply winding road down to where the Guadalquivir river was just a stream near its source and camped at dusk in a pinewood. I found deep trotter marks in the red mud there, but they disappeared in the pine needles on higher ground. I did not see the wild boar I was sure had made them.

Next morning, March 6, I kept seeing odd flashing lights, like mirrors, in the river and stopped to find that they were being made by grayling-like fish turning on their sides as they flicked up stones in search of food. Further on the river opened out into a beautiful lakeland vista which reminded me of the view from the log cabin I had built years ago on the Pacific coast of Canada. Rocky pine-covered spurs sloped down to the etiolated shore of Embalse del Tranco, in which a large wooded island rose from ruffled deep blue waters under a cobalt sky. Yet I saw no water fowl through the binoculars, nor any other sign of wildlife, except for one eagle, far off. Maybe this place would be better in the nesting season.

With the ferry strike still unsettled, I decided to drive all the way to the French Channel coast for a short sea crossing. I wanted to have another crack at the eagles and vultures on those massive cliffs near Riglos, so I headed for Zaragosa and arrived at the Mallos de Riglos in mid-afternoon after a bitterly cold night camped by a lonely haystack. Immediately I saw griffon vultures soaring into holes in the great sandstone cliff where they obviously had nests, but so high that even a 2,000mm lens would not have secured good photos. According to the map, this was the Sierra de la Pena, and my dictionary told me that 'pena' meant pain, mental sorrow, but also 'to be worthwhile'. How apt!

I camped in an open spot below the twin peaks and decided over supper there was only one way to obtain good pictures of those great birds, and that was to get up there with them! Next morning I drove as close as I could to the foot of the lefthand mountain, found a small gap in the rock and swung the van into it. I set off fast, hoping I would not be seen, for I had no permit, though I was fairly sure this place was not a reserve.

27

It was the hardest climb I had ever made. I scrambled across deep holes covered with dry grass between great rocks, the slope so steep that longer rushes poked their tips into my eyes. Festoons of brambles, alive and dead, tore at my clothes. I forced my way up, sweating like a horse, negotiating gorges, scrub pines and thorn bushes that ripped my legs. I kept the last of the trees at 700 metres between me and the grey and red cliff. An eagled circled, and then the sky was empty. I prayed for twenty minutes clear before the vultures returned and went as fast as I could up steep slippery shales above the tree-line. As I reached the shadow of the great rock wall seven griffons appeared from the south west and began to circle, reminding me of old-time aircraft displays I had seen as a boy at Tangmere in Sussex. I scrambled up to a large rock surrounded by bushes – a perfect natural hide – and tried to conceal myself.

Suddenly what I thought was a male eagle came over, close. Then I saw that its tail was too long, and it had a reddish orangey breast. Its wings were long and slim, like those of a giant peregrine. What on earth was it? It clearly saw me, but did not seem to care, for it did not swerve or alter its flight pattern. Then the 'rosy' eagle began wheeling between two griffons that flew in from the west, none taking any notice of the others. The larger griffon landed at a dark cleft in the rock face just as a slightly smaller vulture left it. Griffons lay only one egg, and here the female was taking over incubating duties from its mate. Her large downy white head turned towards me and she yawned before contemplating the roof of her nesting chamber. She was not one whit scared. More vultures soared above me as I heard the sound of powerful engines approaching. Two jet aircraft roared past less than 100 metres from the circling birds, yet they did not alter their course.

When the 'rosy' eagle came sailing back, I saw that its long tail was wedge-shaped, like a magpie's. It landed on a rocky spur half-way up the face, its head gleaming brassy white in the sunlight, the long wings dark. It crouched down and appeared to rub its orange-red chest and belly on the rock, like an animal getting rid of an itch. The griffon stayed on her nest as two ravens arrived making noisy 'krock' calls, but the 'rosy' eagle gave chase when one of them flew close. The raven dodged all over the sky, flying up and down the cliffs, over the top and back, while I clicked away. The raven is a large bird, but seeing the two together, I now appreciated the immense wing span of the pursuer, which I put at almost 9 feet. The raven's squawk sounded more like a cackle than a cry of terror. Once, turning faster than the big bird which flapped its wings slowly, the raven dived on the eagle. It seemed a kind of game, and before long 'rosy' flew off. I took my final picture of it perched on the peak, its chest blazing in the sun like a flame.

I wondered what these huge birds fed on. While I filled up with petrol, the garage attendant, who turned out to be an amateur ornithologist, told me about the artillery camp at Jaca nearly 25 km away where horses, mules and donkeys were kept. When an animal died, the soldiers took the carcass up into the hills for the vultures to dispose of it. So these vultures depended on the Spanish army! He said that they could travel four times the distance in search of food.

I said goodbye to the great cliffs with regret, but it was time to take Moobli back to Scotland. His last wild summer there was not an unhappy one, his abiding joy now that paralysis kept him close to the cottage was to swim in the loch. For me it turned out to be the finest season ever with nesting eagles and the black-throated divers, and I described it in my book *On Wing and Wild Water*.

In late May my father died, ending his days where he was happy, and was buried next to his wife. The end came for Moobli in the early autumn, and it was a crushing experience after all we had been through together. I tried to banish grief with hard treks into the hills until, in late November, ferocious storms almost completely wrecked my boat and came close to costing me my life. I could not endure another lonely winter below Moobli's hillside grave, and left for Spain.

4 · Fit for the Hard Life

In mid-December I took the overnight ferry from Plymouth to Santander and drove to Madrid to have lunch with a leading conservationist, Imre de Boroviczény. It had dawned on me that I could spend a lifetime tramping the mountains and amazing range of habitats in this vast country without ever getting to close quarters with the rarest species. I needed guidance from someone who really knew. Imre, a Hungarian with Austrian nationality, was chairman of the Spanish section of the International Council for Bird Preservation, founder and vice president of CODA (Co-ordinating Federation of the Protection of Birds), and a consultant to the International Union for the Conservation of Nature's Species Survival Commission. He was also an excellent field naturalist who also wrote nature articles, one of which I had tucked in my wallet. Written for *International Wildlife* magazine it was called 'Man On A White Horse', and was about an amazing man called Jesus 'Suso' Garzon fighting a lone battle to have the Spanish government declare an area of the mountainous Extremadura region a national park in order to prevent the paper industry from destroying the natural trees and planting eucalyptus in their place. The region was a stronghold of the rare black vulture, imperial eagle, black stork, eagle owl and lynx, as well as many other uncommon species. I very much wanted to meet Señor Garzon, even work with him if I could. Imre was a good friend of Garzon and promised that I would meet him. He also told me of a unique reserve in the high mountains above Cuenca where a family of wild brown bears lived in a valley surrounded by high cliffs.

When I showed him my pictures of the 'rosy' eagle, Imre gasped and wanted me to mark on his map where I had found this bird.

'That, my friend, is the rarest raptor in Europe!' he exclaimed. 'It is the lammergeier, or bearded vulture. There are fewer than a hundred pairs in the whole of Europe! These pictures of it chasing the raven are unique. I wish I had taken them!'

The lammergeier is also known as the 'bone breaker', for it carries the large bones of dead animals high into the air, drops them on to rocks so that they break, then flies down to eat the marrows and smaller fragments. It will even smash open poor live tortoises in this way.

When I told him how it had crouched down and appeared to rub its belly on the red rocky spur, Imre said few people had observed that. For some unknown reason, the bird rubs its chest and underparts on walls, damp ledges and rocks to get the stain of oxides on to its feathers. I said maybe it had a cosmetic purpose, to make itself more attractive to its mate in courtship. Imre thought that was certainly possible. I began to feel quite proud of myself. We agreed to meet again in the spring, and perhaps tackle some rare species together.

I could not attempt any new wildlife treks yet, however, for I had to finish *A Last Wild Place*, the book on which I had been working for four years. Knowing there were a few villas available on winter lets, I headed for the area where my father had lived. There was a range of arid rocky hills behind his old home which were dominated by a conical mountain, on the 1,000 metres high peak of which I had once found a green coot's leg. Since only an eagle could have carried it there, I had dubbed this hill Eagle Mountain. I arrived in the dark and was cooking supper in the van up a lonely road when I saw a movement under the light of a single street lamp forty metres away.

A large fox climbed up the steep rocky slope on the far side of the road and started sniffing round a single dustbin. Moments later a smaller fox, a cub, followed the first. The big fox reared up, put its front paws on the top of the bin, took steps back with its rear feet and hauled the bin over. Both foxes ripped at one of the plastic rubbish bags, ate something from it and padded away, as softly as cats, with their brushes balancing airily behind them. They vanished round the side of an empty house. The sighting seemed a good omen, for when

I was not working on my book I could at least resume my wildlife studies.

Next day I rented an isolated villa overlooking the Mediterranean, not far from the mountain. In the marvellous light, with electricity and hot water laid on for the first time in sixteen years of wilderness living, I could finish the book in a third of the time it would have taken me in the winter gloom of a Scottish lochside. I would not have to spend nearly half the day chopping wood just keep warm. Each night I set out scraps of food on a rock below a window which I could overlook with my camera. At first they were not taken.

By December 28 my book was going so well I took a morning off to explore the gorge of a deep *rambla* on the east side of Eagle Mountain. I felt reasonably sure that, if there were any fox dens, they would be high up on the left side of the gorge where the stunted palms and other bushes grew more thickly. First, knowing foxes like to keep low in daylight, so as not to be seen, I climbed down to check the sandy bed of the dry river. Within minutes I found adult fox tracks, along with those of a cub, smaller I thought than the cub I had seen. Near by were the rounded four-toe prints of what must have been a feral cat.

Working my way up to the bushy ridges, I located several holes in the rocks with scuff marks in them, which seemed to be foxes' day time resting places. Lower down I spotted what looked like a certain den, with much scratched-out earth and many tracks going in and out. When I got there the hole proved to be too small, so it was just a play area. In the sand were the heads of two large lizards, four times the size of British lizards. Clearly, these animals were taken as prey. I also found some deep and wide-apart dog fox tracks that must have been made by a sprinting animal. The right hand tracks were less deep than those on the left, so it was likely the fox had an injured foot.

I slogged upwards again towards the bushy ridges, perspiring in the heat, until I was climbing over large rocks between the dwarf palms. There was a small red cliff face about 5 metres from the top of the gorge and as I climbed towards it I found another lizard's head, almost 1½ inches wide, and then a large fresh fox scat, still damp. It seemed I was getting nearer. I climbed on up to the cliff face, and there was the breeding den.

Below the face was a triangular hole between the slabs, from which branched two narrow tunnels. There were fox prints everywhere, including very small ones of cubs. A cuttlefish bone lay in one tunnel, and in the other a crabshell and an empty sardine tin. Outside the hole were pieces of newspaper to which were stuck remnants of a chicken carcass. The foxes had obviously carried much of this alien food up from the dustbins a kilometre below! I felt happy at finding the breeding den so quickly on my first time out.

To leave as little of my scent as possible, I backed away, climbed down to the *rambla* and up the steep far side until I found a clump of bushes in which I could sit and overlook the den. From there I could see right down the valley as well.

Before dawn on December 31 I threw meat from gloved hands ten metres below the den, then hid myself in the bushes, camera on tripod. Although the wind was in the right direction to blow the meat scent to the den, a cold three-hour wait produced no foxes. Suddenly I heard a '*yak*' bark high in the hills to the north. Then another. It could have been the vixen returning from night hunting and warning the cubs to stay inside, or a dog fox that had spotted me and was warning vixen and cubs in the den. I decided to investigate, climbing up and peering over each herbaged ridge with great care before moving on. Another bark helped me locate the fox.

It was a large sandy, almost white, dog fox and it was sneaking along a ledge far higher up. I took a distant photo. It drifted along the narrow ledge, turned into the mountain, then came out on to a flat rock for another picture. The creature glowed white in the rays of the rising sun, the first albino fox I had ever seen. It vanished for a while before my eyes picked it up again a good two hundred yards to the south east and I got another photo of it, slinking along with its mouth open, as if panting. It was limping slightly. I climbed up to where it had disappeared over a far ridge but did not see it again. He would not come back until sure I had gone. Neither would the vixen stir from the den, if she was in it.

Although I was wearing only light trainer shoes (so I could move more silently) and the sharp rocky terrain had made my feet sore, I took a wide traverse above the gorge and found eight more day time fox dens, all with prints outside them. I came out on to the highest stony road of the little empty urbanisation and found that a tap on the open water pipe which led to the villas from a reservoir was leaking. In the damp sandy earth all round it were many fox prints. They clearly came here to drink. I now realised why they had chosen the tunnels beneath the little cliff face for their breeding den. They liked to be near the human dustbins for food, the leaking tap for drinking, and the high arid bushy hills for escape.

Anxious for closer shots of the albino fox, I trekked the mountain again two days later. The food scraps had been taken from below the den, so I put down some more. Sometimes the food I left below my window had gone by morning, but although I put in several short vigils I never once saw a fox take it.

Apart from the sand martins which nested in the sandstone cliffs below the villa, and flew past my window with '*zit*' calls, the only other obvious wildlife round me were the black wheatears, which enjoy the Latin name of *Oenanthe leucura*. They were soft and dumpy, like little blackbirds, with snowy white rumps and tails, and are found only in Spain, Portugal, the extreme south of France and South Africa. Several pairs were re-establishing their nest sites near the tops of rocky gullies. The cocks flew straight up into the air emitting shrill little songs, then floated down again with quivering wings and fanned tails to land beside the females they were courting. Sometimes they chased off a rival male, flitting fast between the rocks like black and white bees. They would not, however, come to the food I set out on the parapet of my verandah, where I was hoping to get close photos of them.

On January 16 two local lads, Alex, 17, and Diego, 18, called at my villa to ask me to take them up Eagle Mountain to see the foxes for themselves. Alex carried a cheap little 8mm battery-run movie camera as I led them up some 800 metres of gently rising scree-covered rock. We were approaching the steep stuff when Alex asked impatiently how long it would take us to see a fox?

'It took me five years in daylight!' I said. 'But we might be lucky.'

I was heading for a big pink cliff, to check for nests, when I heard two '*kaow*' barks high up on the hill. They did not hear it. Just then there came a louder yapping bark.

'I think it is a dog,' said Alex.

'Could be,' I said, 'but it's more likely to be a vixen telling her cubs to lie low.'

I scanned the ridges and with the naked eye saw the fox running, barking as it went. I pointed it out. Alex saw it but Diego did not. Then it vanished. I said our only chance to photograph it was to run up to the ridge. I took my camera from the pack and set off. We got over the ridge and saw the vixen with a white tip to her tail. She bounded along, running upwards, and I took five pictures as I heard

Alex's little movie camera whirring. Finally the fox disappeared over the far shoulder. Both lads were amazed for it was the first wild fox they had ever seen. We did not find a den anywhere but saw where the vixen had regurgitated chicken guts and feathers, as if leaving them for her cubs.

We set off for the peak after finding three more day dens. It was hard steep going, up and down, up and down, over the shale-covered rock, and after half a mile the lads were asking when we were going to eat. I said it would be better to get to the top first for it was no good climbing on a full stomach. After another two hundred yards they yelled they were going to stop and eat now; I need not worry for they would soon catch up with me. I slogged on at my own pace over the terrible ground, the summit always beyond the peak ahead. There was a new eagle pellet on the ground when finally I reached the top. It contained the remains of a seagull. I had seen no eagles at all since arriving, and thought it must have been left by a migrating bird. I ate my sandwiches and waited a further forty minutes before the lads puffed up, surprise on their faces.

'How is it you are fifty-five years old and can beat us?' asked Deigo.

I said it had nothing to do with youth, strength or fitness, but was due to years of experience. It was most important that you placed each footstep carefully, on tufts of vegetation where possible, on the flattest part of any rock, and never on shale or scree, or even one loose stone. After years of practise this became instinctive, so one could get into a rhythm even on the hardest terrain.

'Never mind,' said Alex. 'We will beat you home!'

For a time I was sure they would but I thought I would give them a good run for their money. They took the shortest route, running and leaping dangerously over the rocks. Then they came to a sheer face and spent some time working around it. I was now well ahead. As I went up the ridges I let them catch up a little so that they felt sure of overtaking me. As soon as I was on the far side, out of their sight, I went as fast as I could, so when they reached the tops they would see I was as far away as ever. This was what I called 'the heartbreak treatment'. I was at the villa for six minutes before they arrived.

I put in another dawn watch overlooking the foxes' breeding den on January 19. I lay between the bushes, camera resting on a rock, for three hours without a fox emerging. The sun climbed high and it was hot. I had just decided to get back to my book when I discerned a slight movement two metres to my right. A large black-patterned

35

snake, about six feet in length, with thick powerful jaws, slid by. It saw my head turn but it showed no fear. Its thick jaws indicated they held venom sacs, and its air of quiet confidence was quite unnerving. Moving very slowly, I took its picture, then got out of there as fast as I could.

On February 3 I went for my weekly keep-fit run along the sandy coastal tracks and back through the deep valley below Eagle Mountain. I was plodding rather than jogging up a steep gully with high banked sides when I heard harsh squawly cries, '*rowl rowl*', like those of a fighting cat. I felt sure it was a fox. I stopped and saw it just forty metres ahead. It ran up the bank to the right, trotted about, walked to the edge to look at me, barked again, then ran away to the right. It was the albino fox. His injured foot must have healed for he was no longer limping.

Gregorio Parra took me out to sea in his cabin cruiser at the weekend. A fair wind was blowing when we reached the harbour and the boat's stern was bucking up and down a good metre from the quayside. Without hesitation Greg, who was quite plump, leaped safely on to it while I waited a second or two before timing my leap. Greg held the wheel proudly, and looked at me through his spectacles like a boy with a new toy.

'We are the wolves of the sea!' he beamed.

'Pirates of the Barbary coast!' I rejoined.

We had a marvellous day out on the frothy blue ocean trolling for tuna, which Greg said could be caught in the Mediterranean between October and March before they headed out into the Atlantic, but we caught none. We were slapping along some four kilometres out, my villa just a white dot on the sand-coloured coastline, when we saw something bobbing and dipping ahead. It looked like a small whale fluke, or the top of the tail of a big fish. We got too near for it to be a healthy fish just basking at the surface. Sure enough, as we came close it waved more frantically, but still feebly, and took a few seconds before getting under way and going down. It looked like a dying fish to me, perhaps one that had been injured by a boat.

We cruised in gentle circles, then saw it again on the surface. It was about two metres long and looked like a giant dogfish. Greg said it was a *tintorera,* a type of shark which predate on other fish. These *tintoreras,* which can grow to 10 feet long and weigh as much as 450lbs, were more abundant in the Mediterranean than they are today, though they are still fairly common in the sea round Mallorca.

They rarely attack humans. In the past guards of island prisons used to encourage them by feeding scraps and offal to them. The idea was to make prisoners think twice before trying to escape and swimming to freedom! Once again the fish struggled, then swam weakly down into the dark depths.

Later two big black fins showed ahead. They rose and fell in perfect unison three times, then leaped almost clear of the water, revealing the blunt snouts of porpoises. We were soon among a school of them and I took a few photos. The battery in the camera went dead and the shutter stuck as one pair came close to investigate the boat.

I threw bits of bread into the sea to attract black-headed gulls but none bothered to dive for it until I dispensed half a slice from a sandwich. A large skua appeared in the haze and chased a gull with fractured wingbeats, forcing it to regurgitate bread, which the skua caught in mid-air, while the gull flew off with protesting shrieks.

After going out in the boat again next morning, Greg produced two bicycles after lunch, a little fold-up model and a real racer. I had not ridden since I was a cub reporter in Chichester more than thirty years earlier, when I had lived for amateur cycle racing and had won a few cups and medals on the sprint track. I had given it all up when I made it to Fleet Street – and I did not believe that plump old Greg could ride at all. But off he went, sailing along like a professional racer, his hands off the bars, as I laboured and wobbled behind on the silly little fold-up. When I had a go on his machine, the wind whistling past my ears, some of the old power returned, and from that day to this I have preferred cycling to running in my attempts to keep fit for trekking up mountains. While you use the same muscles for both, it is impossible to strain your legs on a racing bike (which I hastily acquired) for your strapped-in feet are limited to the smooth movement of the pedals, whereas every step in running is a jolt to tendons, ankles, knees and hips. All the trouble I had experienced with osteo-arthritis disappeared when I took up cycling again.

A week later Roy Ensor, who had once been chief mechanic with the Lotus racing team, accompanied me to Murcia for minor repairs to my van. His fluent Spanish also helped smooth the way for another week's permit for wildlife photography in Espuña. I gave Director Carlos Bourcarolas copies of some of my pictures and he gasped with surprise when he saw that, unknowingly, I had photographed a unique sub-species of the Spanish squirrel which is found only in Espuña – and as far as he knew, it was the first time ever. He was delighted, and two prints from my slides now hang on the wall of his office.

Afterwards Roy took me to El Corte Inglés to show me a new lightweight video camera. As the obliging manager put the camera through its paces I thought hard. I had heard that Rodriguez de la Fuente used 24 video cameras to make his marvellous television films at the rate of one a week. He would focus one hidden camera on an eagle's nest, one on that of a buzzard, one on a peregrine's, and so forth, each with tapes lasting 3½ hours. Tapes would be played back and the camera shifted elsewhere once good shots were obtained. He seldom endured hours in uncomfortable hides, as people often thought. I had spent hundreds of hours in my type of invisible hide in which you could only lie down, and I was no longer sure they were a good idea in Spain after my experience with the poisonous snake. I resolved to buy one of these cameras when I found a publisher for a new book.

While I was making my bed back at the villa that evening, I saw a movement outside the window. A tawny fox with black tips to its guard hairs was sneaking past a eucalyptus tree, sniffing the air in an excited way. It sidled down to my food scraps, seized a lamb bone in its teeth, then ran over the rocky ground and vanished into a deep gully. I put out more food, but it did not return. The next evening I heard foxes making a racket near the breeding den. I went there and kept watch from some bushes but saw nothing. All the food I had put out as bait had gone when I returned to the villa. It was almost as if the foxes had made the noise to get me out of the house.

By mid-February Imre de Boroviczeny had smoothed the way for me to visit a bear reserve near Cuenca, where there was also a lynx, and Jesus Garzon far away in Extremadura, but he left me to make final arrangements for which, he warned, I would need to brush up my Spanish, for neither the bear warden Francisco Rojo nor Garzon spoke any English. I asked Greg for help and he offered to make the calls with me from his home in Totana. The town was then under deep snow, and the temperature on Espuña peak was 12 degrees below zero. If the weather did not improve it would be worse than winter trekking in the Highlands.

When I drove to Totana on the appointed day, all the snow had gone and Espuña peak was basking in bright sunshine, like a white beacon in the sky. Greg phoned warden Rojo first, only to be told that the bears were asleep in their dens in winter hibernation! Until then I had believed that in sunny Spain bears would forage all the year round, but the temperature in the Cuenca mountains was an unusual 7° below zero. I would have to take a chance on the bears being out when I met Rojo on March 5. Jesus Garzon said he would be glad to see me at his house on March 9, when he would show me rare black vultures if I paid for an old goat for bait. I quickly agreed.

I now had a tremendous schedule ahead, for I was booked on the Santander ferry on March 15. After a week's work in Espuña, the driving to Rojo, Garzon and then the ferry would amount to nearly 1,700 km. I left Greg, presented my permit to the head forester, and camped in a glorious sunset. I decided to get the worst over first and make the long slogging climb up to Eyrie 1.

As I set out in hazy sun next morning a chain of fourteen pine processionary moth caterpillars crossed the track, each with its jaws clamped on to the rear of the one in front as they followed their leader to find a new pine in which to build the webs where they would live and feed. I did not touch them for their hairs are poisonous, causing acute irritation of the skin and breathing passages. On the way up I located small herds of Barbary sheep, not by sight at first, for they were among trees, but by the clicking sound of their hooves on the steep rock over which they moved like the true mountain goats they are. Now and again, a youngster would slip, and one even fell for about three metres. It must have hurt its leg for afterwards it limped. It was easy to envisage a young or very old animal falling to its doom in this way, so providing easy food for eagles and foxes. I found several stone marten droppings filled with the elytra from large beetle wings, and a few fox scats which contained red-brown berries from a juniper-like plant. Reaching the high path, I worked my way over ledges above the awful chasms and was soon beneath the eyrie.

The nest had been built up, and I could see fronds of pine and juniper laid across it. No eagle had flown from the nest, and I had seen none in the sky, so it seemed that even in this climate, it was still too early for eggs to have been laid. I tried to climb up to a spur on almost the same level as the nest but it was very steep and covered with a thick layer of small rocks which shifted unnervingly underfoot. A hellish place to try and put a hide without a companion and a rope. Going back down I had to use hands as much as legs to avoid sliding.

Fortunately, I made it back to the road safely and then hiked for nearly 2 km until I reached its tightest bend to the right. I turned back and glassed the northern face of the white peak — and there was Eyrie 5. It was an old unused nest just above a bush but on a fine ledge with a perfect overhang of pink rock above it. It would be an easy place to work for there was a broad shoulder overlooking it only 30 metres away.

Because he was interested in my techniques and hoped to see eagles close, I later took Greg with me. I now had the key to unlock the chain on the forestry road and by driving almost to the pass we cut out two miles of wasteful foot-slogging. As soon as we alighted from the van I heard the faint clicking of hooves up in the trees of the slopes to Eyrie 1. Greg would not believe that I knew there were Barbary sheep up there. After a short stalk upwind we found them in a conveniently open area of young pines and took our first photos. As we came down again, guarda Casimiro bumbled up on his motor-bike to tell us that these slopes were out of bounds after 3 p.m. because of partridge hunting. I said we had no need to go there again as I had already checked the nest. He thought it was the one that would be used this year. After he left, Greg told me that in English the name Casimiro meant 'Quietly I look', and he laughed louder than I had ever heard him before when I said —

'No wonder he had to get a job in the woods!'

We drove back along the stony track for some 850 metres, then trekked down through the woods and gullies. The lie of the land looked different from here and I was working by instinct. I was as surprised as Greg when, after about a kilometre we came to the great chasm and the exact viewing spot opposite Eyrie 3. This nest too had been a little built up, the rock in its centre now overlaid with sprays of pine. If this had meant the eyrie would definitely be used, I would have cancelled the ferry and stayed to work it, but eagles usually decorate several nests before making a final choice. I climbed to a high rock to look up at Eyrie 1 — and saw both eagles circling above it. It seemed Casimiro was right. As we stood above the yawning drop where I would have had to put a hide, Greg said he did not care for such heights. Suddenly a large hawk-like bird with silvery underside and dark wings soared out from the rocky ridge above the nest and winged away from us. I took a distant photo and through the lens identified it as a peregrine falcon. As we hiked out again, Greg moving well despite his bulk, I took a picture of a buzzard flying overhead with nesting foliage in its claws.

After a lunch of bread, cheese, ham and onion, we drove to below Eyrie 1 and hiked up to a rocky pinnacle to keep watch. Immediately an eagle sailed over from the east, made two dives, and I saw it was an immature bird, with a white band in its tail. It landed in a bush just two metres above the ground and stayed there, a dark blob. Within minutes we saw the male eagle displaying before it landed on the peak above the eyrie. He was followed by the larger female, which soared round the northern shoulder with a clump of vegetation in her talons and landed on the nest. There was little doubt about it now. Greg put down his binoculars, amazed delight on his face, and said it had been one of the golden days of his life. He had never seen an eagle nest before, or the great birds so close.

Again he urged me to buy one of his *fincas*. Later we drove round the area and looked at three I had not seen. One was an orange farm called La Isla, perched on a knoll above two dry rivers, but he said his workers were often there tending the fruit trees. There was a small cottage, right by a road, and he had sold a plot not far away to a Dutch couple who were building a home there. The third was a huge isolated fortress of a building with over 100 windowless rooms amid 1,000 hectares of land, but there was a spring near the house to which all the sheep and goats in the area came to drink every day. I liked the red sandstone villa in Espuña best, but to buy it and put it into shape was beyond my means. Greg said he had three other *fincas* less isolated than these. I looked at him in surprise. I had not realised my good quiet friend Greg — barrister, writer and philosopher — was also a multi-millionaire!

On March 3 I closed up my rented villa, loaded my gear into the van for the eventual return to Scotland, and drove back up to Espuña. I had niggling doubts about Eyrie 5, so I parked at the tight bend and made the steep climb up to the broad shoulder. I had just time to see it was not a nest, but an unusual flat dense bush growing from the ledge, when a thick grey mist came down from nowhere, obscuring the peaks and the land two hundred metres below me. Everything was blotted out and I could see no further than a few metres. I managed to climb down safely, drove to where I had parked with Greg and hiked down to Eyrie 3, hoping the eagles would be driven down to it by the upper mist.

The woods were as dry as tinder, the twigs and dead branches cracking like bones beneath my feet. One carelessly discarded match here and the whole area would become a raging inferno in minutes. There would be no escape. I moved carefully, stalking round wide of the rounded eyrie face so that trees hid me, and sat down behind a bush. To my horror, more mist crept up the chasm to my left and blotted out that nest too. It thickened rapidly and I just managed to take a compass bearing on a knoll above my parked van before, once again, I could see nothing ahead. Without the compass I would undoubtedly have got lost in that woodland of deep gulches and high rockfaces. With the nights still below freezing at this height, I would then have been in real trouble. I emerged thirty metres from my van, drove off and hiked down to Carrasca, which was oddly free of mist, and took even better photos of Barbary sheep.

It was dusk when I arrived at the high camp site by the old *finca*. Up here I could get the BBC on my radio. I switched on to hear that one of the modern writers I most admired, Arthur Koestler, had committed suicide at the age of 77 after a long illness. Shortly afterwards his wife had followed suit. It had been a pact between them. As tributes poured in, some said his act had been wrong. I did not agree, and felt as I had when hearing of Ernest Hemingway's suicide. When an intelligent creative person becomes old and trapped in physical or mental illness and knows that only deterioration lies ahead; when he or she knows that creative work is impossible and does not want to become a burden to others, then to end one's own life seemed to me an act of immense and rational courage. Somehow the news made me feel more lonely than ever. I too, if a mountain did not get me first, might have to face such a decision.

Next day I made the long drive to near Hosquillo, the bear reserve in the high mountains 100 km beyond Cuenca. I turned left before Murcia on to the N301 to Albacete, passed through the ugly town of Molina de Segura, and then it was orange groves and almond plantations all the way to Calcarix. After that came a pine tree area and a comely village called El Pinar; then I was in Jumilla wine country, where men were pruning off last year's shoots in the vineyards. The by-pass round Albacete was easy to follow, but I missed the N320 turn-off beyond La Gineta and had to take the smaller C312 road from La Roda. It was a pretty route, with poorer homes along it, still running small vineyards. After the lovely old town of Tarazona de la Mancha I went through Motilla and then some pine-covered mountains to reach Cuenca, where houses looked as if they had been thrown around by giants but miraculously had all landed on top of a hill the right way up. I was making for Majadas, the last village before Hosquillo, and someone had told me to go through Villalba de la Sierra and look for the signpost.

Beyond Cuenca a series of great high cliffs towered over the beautiful Jucar river, which was lined with plane trees, poplars and willows. After Villalba the road became very twisting as I climbed higher and higher. I was running short of petrol and stopped to ask some giggling children the way, but they took one look at my bearded face and ran off! I must have missed the little turning that I had been told was signposted for I saw no sign of Majadas until it was indicated 24 km away, and Hosquillo was some distance beyond that. The road turned downhill at a very steep gradient, and suddenly my brakes failed. The intense heat from constant friction was causing the brake fluid to boil. It was also growing dark. I pulled off into a small wood and came to a halt by bumping into a tree — and there I camped for the night.

In the morning I found the ancient village of Majadas deserted. A passing lorry-driver stopped at my frantic wave and said there was no petrol to be had in the village; I would have to go all the way back to Villalba for it. I hoped that warden Francisco Rojo would have a little to spare and drove on. There were no more signposts, but my instinct took me aside up the correct sandy track for suddenly huge 30ft-high wooden gates appeared ahead, with a rotund grey-haired fellow in green cap and uniform standing before them.

5 · *Naked in the Wild*

Francisco Rojo greeted me with a cordial '*Hola!*' and I understand enough Spanish to know he was saying that I was in luck. The bears had come out of hibernation two days ago. He shut the giant gates as if expecting something akin to the siege of Troy and locked them with a key so large that he had to use both hands to turn it. He said I could go with him on his feeding rounds of the various animals, the rarer ones of which were kept in huge wild enclosures. Although visitors were admitted on Sundays and holidays in summer, they had to travel in special buses. No-one was allowed to walk around alone. There were 15 bears in captivity and another 16 roaming wild.

A four-year-old mother bear with a pair of two-year-old cubs were kept in a unique enclosure at the end of the Reserve.

The Hosquillo Park, founded by ICONA in 1964, was an extraordinary place for it consisted of 970 hectares in a natural valley surrounded by mountains and high cliffs. It was fenced in along the tops but only the *cabra montés* (mountain goats) were capable of climbing up there. The Escabas river flowed through the valley and provided uncontaminated water for all the animals. We climbed into a jeep and roared off. While Rojo and his assistant off-loaded foodstuffs, I took pictures of fallow deer in a 10 hectare enclosure, and then of moufflons in a 25 hectare enclave. These huge dark-brown and white goats were wary, and I had to stalk them up to a rocky plateau to photograph them among the pines. We drove across the stony bed of the river to a blind end where Rojo said there was a 30 hectare enclosure containing *cabra montés* surrounded by cliffs 70 metres high. But when I climbed out of the jeep I could not see a single animal. Rojo explained that, when they heard his engine, they always ran up into the cliffs and hid among the trees. We drove on to the bear compound, 8 hectares of rocky wooded hills on each side of the start of the river, hemmed in on three sides by huge high cliffs on which three pairs of griffon vultures were nesting. To keep the bears in, a strong high metal fence had been erected across the bottom. In the centre of the fence was a tall wooden tower, made of logs, and I helped Rojo to lug a sackful of bread loaves smeared with margarine up to the platform at the top of it.

We spotted the bears at the far end of the compound at the same time as they saw us, and they began to wander through the trees towards us. The mother bear weighed about 500lbs and she sauntered heavily along on the rounded pads of her feet, her great claws scuffing at the rocks. The two cubs, more than half-grown, followed her. They were in no hurry, and now and again the two cubs biffed each other round the ears with their heavy front paws while the mother turned on them with brief growls, as if telling them to behave. It was marvellous to see them, for although they were not truly in the wild they looked very natural here, and I took many fine pictures.

They reached the ground below us and the mother reared up easily on to her haunches, despite her great weight. Her big flat muzzle twitched, like a huge dog begging. Rojo tipped out the sack of loaves and the bears pounced on them. He explained that while they obtained some wild food from the land, their diet was supplemented by the bread, vegetables like potatoes, greens and maize, and also some meat.

When we climbed down again, the larger male cub looked at me in an odd way, sauntered placidly up to the fencing and shoved his big right paw through in the region of my ankle. He held it there, seemingly in a friendly and expectant way. I had never shaken hands with a bear before. I put my right hand down and gently clasped his paw. Instantly he tightened his big claws, hauled my hand towards the fence with enormous strength and made a gnashing bite. I pulled my hand away just in time. Rojo told me off for my foolishness. He said the bears were still very wild and if you went into the enclosure, or fell off the walkway, they would kill you without hesitation. With two cubs, the mother would certainly attack. He said I had been lucky to get any pictures at all at this time of year. The bears had hibernated in their rocky den in the forest from mid-November, and due only to the lower altitude than where one would expect to find completely wild Spanish bears had they come out so early — the day before yesterday. He was not sure how many wild bears were left in Spain, fewer than a hundred he thought, and they were mainly in the mountains of the Asturias and the Picos de Europa. I resolved to get to grips with the truly wild species.

Rojo then drove up a long dusty track to another enclosure. In it stood what looked to me like a small grey Alsatian. It was a placid she-wolf which had been owned by Dr Rodriguez de la Fuente and was used in some of his films. He said they were trying to trap a male wolf as a mate for her.

On the way back Rojo stopped by another large compound in which I could see nothing but thick bushes.

'*Lince,*' he said almost in a whisper.

But the lynx did not show itself. Rojo said they seldom saw it. I asked him to wait, put my mouth to the back of my hand and blew the kind of squeaks a Sussex gamekeeper had taught me, which sound like a rabbit in distress. Suddenly, from the bushes, out popped the lynx's head! I took a couple of pictures, but the jeep's engine was vibrating the camera, so I asked Rojo to switch it off. As I climbed out, the lynx stayed looking up at me for a few seconds while I clicked off two more photos, then withdrew as silently as it had appeared. Rojo said they were trying to trap a female for it, and if they bred, some of the progeny would be released into the wild.

The ICONA biologists' headquarters here were built entirely of logs, as skilfully made as any log cabin I had seen in Canada. Two plots of flowers and vegetables were fenced round with red deer antlers. Most of them had been found in the nearby mountains, and the tines had been cleverly interwoven to form an impenetrable barrier to grazing animals. Hosquillo had won the national award for the best heads of roe buck and moufflon in Spain. The moufflon had not been shot by a hunter but was a legendary wild animal which some photographers had tried to get in their sights. One season it failed to appear at all and after a long search the guardas had found the old monarch dead in the hills.

Rojo gave me some late lunch before handing me a 4-litre can of petrol siphoned from his own jeep. When I asked what I owed him for this and all his time and help, he laughed and said '*Nada!*' All I could do was promise him some pictures for the Park's museum.

On the way back to Villalba de la Sierra I took pictures of the vast canyons above the Jucar river. Near a village called Una a vast rampart of dramatic orange cliffs reared into the sky above a high steep rocky wooded hill. Griffon vultures were sailing overhead, pairs gliding close together to maintain their bonds in the breeding season. There must be nests up there, I thought. I'll come back here! The petrol ran out just before I reached the garage but I had just enough impetus to free wheel to the pumps. I had driven more than 70 km from Hosquillo through these steep mountains and this was the first petrol station. I filled my tank with what was liquid gold in this area, then drove back to the vulture cliffs.

Feeling good after the easy morning, I stormed up the gabbro-covered rock, which was treacherous in places, until I reached the end of the tree line 350 metres higher up. At first I thought I had been spotted for no vultures appeared, but after half an hour one great bird came sailing round the cliff. I took photos until it came so close I could not get it all into the frame. More griffons came and gave me a wonderful display. Choughs were also nesting in small holes in the cliffs. As they made their twisting, rolling aerial courtship dives, calling loud '*chiaw*'s, I could clearly see their red legs and down-curved crimson beaks. Choughs are now rare in Britain, confined to western seacliffs in Wales, Ireland and in smaller numbers in Scotland. I was glad to see them, though they are very common in Spain. There were ravens and jackdaws up there too, the sharp '*chack*' calls of the jackdaws shorter than the more drawn out cries of the choughs. It seemed only moments before dusk began to fall, ending a wonderful day, and I had to climb down to make a lone supper in the van before turning in.

I was cleaning the inside of the van next morning when a red kite flapped past a field on the other side of the road. I dived out for a picture and glanced up at the towering ramparts, but I did not see a griffon until 11 a.m. Maybe they waited until the thermals of warm air were rising from the sun-heated land to make it easier for soaring. Once I saw a juvenile golden eagle with a white bar in its tail and creamy underwing patches sailing along the peaks from the north. A pair of peregrines appeared, dashing about the sky at great speed as I clicked away. Then one of the falcons dived on the eagle, mobbing it, dashing and diving round it like a silvery light.

At 2 p.m. I made the laborious climb again, with all the camera gear and a tape recorder, but when I reached the tree line I found all the ravens and choughs were gone. They flew and dived about and made a lot of noise in the mornings and evenings, but clearly by day they went away to feed. This time I went the whole distance until I was right under the vast orange cliff. I looked up. It was not sheer but bulging out over me, and I felt a sudden awful claustrophia. I told myself it had stayed up there for hundreds of years and would be there for many years more. The top, 200 metres above, leaned out at such an angle it seemed impossible for it to remain there. If one chunk fell off I would be buried under a thousand tons of rock. It also hurt and strained my neck to look up at it from where I stood. I quickly shifted lower down.

I found two mammoth rocks projecting from the ground like rotten molars and sat in their shade, not only to escape the intense heat of the sun but because the shadow would better hide me from the vultures. For an hour nothing happened, then I saw three griffons high up. They circled, dropping lower and lower, their claws out, and vanished behind one of the great rocks under which I was sitting. I could not bear the suspense. Had they landed by a carcass on the other side? I crept out and saw that they had landed on a low ledge. They took off again, and I moved higher so that the rocks would not block my view.

For the next two hours, as I sat in the open, they kept coming over my head. The largest of them sailed in with its claws extended, as if to land on the cliff, but it turned behind the rocks and swooped close over me, turning its head to one side to give me an intense scrutiny. It repeated this manoeuvre, turned as I saw it had vegetation in its claws, and finally zoomed past so near that the rush of the air through its great feathers sounded like a plane about to crash. It landed on its nest ledge just above me, dropped the vegetation, then hopped like a gawky parrot on to a dead branch that projected from the ledge and gazed down at me. It did not seem to be afraid, wondering perhaps what in hell brought a human being so far up the mountain. I decided to let the others get back to their nests in peace and went back down.

Another marvellous day was only slightly marred when I reached the van. My second pair of trekking trews, which I had washed that morning and left spread out on the van to dry, had been purloined!

After a bitterly cold night I woke to find the van windows iced up inside and over the ground a thick hoar frost which soon melted away in the rising sun. I set off for the 500 km drive to Extremadura and my last wildlife venture this trip.

I was passing through wheat country by the time I reached Carrascosa del Campo, and there was a big flour mill in the town. On seeing a '*supermercado*' sign I parked and went to stock up my provisions. As in most villages and small Spanish towns, the shop had no windows or even lights. No doubt the grocer wanted to sell his goods but for a couple of minutes, before my eyes got used to the gloom, I could not see what was on display. I walked round with a jerrican looking for '*kerosina*', which I had been told was the Spanish word for paraffin, as I had run out of it. I used paraffin to light two hurricane lamps which supplemented electric lights running off the van's battery. I tried two garages without success and could find no-one who had even heard of '*kerosina*'. I had to settle for a box of candles instead.

The N400 became a smaller road after passing through small hills of stunted pines around Tarancon, traversing country as flat as Saskatchewan in Canada. Vineyards appeared again at Santa Cruz de la Zarza, and as I drove over the beautiful old bridge high above the broad Tagus river at Toledo I saw a few white egrets and a white stork in the marshy area round the ancient, empty and windowless water mills. Beyond Talavera de la Reina, famous for ceramics, I took the mountain road towards Arenas de San Pedro, hoping to camp beside water or interesting cliffs. For a long way the land was fenced close to the road, but eventually I saw an opening over a cattle grid, crossed it and drove for 200 metres to camp under a cork tree.

I was relieving myself in some bushes after supper when I heard heavy crunching footsteps and saw a large black animal form swishing past me. Probably just a cow, I decided. At 4 a.m. I was woken by a noisy diesel engine, the slamming of doors, loud voices and a torch being shone through my windows. Two Guardia Civil policemen, with the customary pistols in their belts, wanted to know who I was, what I was doing there, and why I was carrying so much gear. I climbed out naked, hastily pulling on my trousers, and showed them my passport. I explained that I was a wildlife photographer and was writing a book about the wild creatures of Spain. The two men showed great interest in my book, and one said in Spanish:

'Ah! You are the Rodriguez de la Fuente of England!'

Knowing the respect in which the Doctor was held in Spain, I hastily agreed. They were extremely polite after that, and told me I could stay as long as I liked. They even said I should have a señorita with me. When I looked sad and agreed it was my biggest problem, they roared with laughter. As I was handed my sweater and urged to put it on before I grew cold, they told me they had stopped because I was camped in the middle of a fighting bull ranch and might have been up to no good. The black animal I had seen when *déshabillé* the night before had been not a cow but a fighting bull! I was lucky not to have had some extra cleavage added to my rear region.

Bowling along the main road ten kilometres before Navalmoral de la Mata, I saw some large black and white birds circling which I took to be white storks. Further on three more stood in a field by the side of the road. With their big white bodies and black edged wings, they looked like elder statesmen as they stalked over the ground on their long red legs among a small flock of magpies and jackdaws, picking up food with their huge red bills. I took my first close photos of white storks from the van.

Nearing Almaraz, where Spain's first nuclear power station glistened in the distance, scores of beautiful birds kept me company, flitting from tree to tree in the orchards. They were almost the size of crows, with what looked like black stormtrooper helmets on their heads. Their bodies were pink, with creamy throats, and their wings and diamond-shaped tails were a brilliant blue. I was seeing my first azure-winged magpies. They flaunted their gorgeous colours, made loud '*cheese*' calls, and flirted their startling tails as they landed on branches.

I crossed an arm of the Tagus river after Almaraz and found myself in the typical terrain of Extremadura. Great rolling mountains stretched ahead as far as I could see, real bosquy wooded land with many bushes and holm oaks, holly oaks and cork trees. The whole region of Extremadura is pierced by the life-giving waters of great rivers like the Alagon, the Alberche, the Guardiana, the Tiétar, the mighty Tajo (Tagus), and further south the Guadalquivir. All of them, like Spain's other large rivers, often open out into broad stretches of water, called *embalses*, which fill valleys. Some of them are so vast that when standing on their shores you can believe you are looking out to sea. All this water not only helps arable farming but sustains an extraordinary variety of wildlife.

At Jaraicejo I turned right up a little farm road which would take me up to Torrejon el Rubio and then to Salto de Torrejon, the small village where conservationist Jesus Garzon lived. My passage was temporarily blocked by a herd of sheep and goats with clanking bells which emerged from the bushes and took several minutes to cross the road. The shepherd invited me to drive through them. I gave him a cheery wave, told him I was in no hurry, and waited until the last goat had filed across. There were now olive groves and patches of vegetables between the cork trees and holm oaks, and I saw several red kites dangling like fork-tailed anchors above the fields.

After Torrejon, a steep winding road, with many tight bends, descended to the broad lake-like waters of the Tajo river. I crossed the long bridge, drove another kilometre and rounded a tree-lined bend. The towering peak of Penafalcon suddenly hit my vision. I had never seen anything like this great pointed fang which soared up from the river for over 500 metres, its rugged grey and white limestone surface covered in yellow and green lichens. I passed a pillar of rock on my left, which overhung a 200-metre sheer drop from the road, pulled into a tiny open space on the right, and got out. I felt I had been transported to another world, one long lost to man.

From the summit of Penafalcon, like squadrons of First World War planes, soared scores of vultures. I counted 73, most of them griffons, but here and there glided the more graceful forms of cream-winged Egyptian vultures, with distinctive white magpie-shaped tails, looking like small lammergeiers. Dwarfing them all, massive as condors, their outer pinions spread wide, floated a few black vultures, like relics from a prehistoric age. As I stood entranced, taking photos, I had a sudden fright.

A huge griffon emerged from behind the rock pillar and came winging towards me at the level of my head. I was too stupefied to raise the camera, and it sailed past 15 metres away. I could see its eyes, the way its head was tucked back on its neck. Far below a smaller bird with blackish wings fringed with brown was circling above the river. When I saw its tail, forked but less so than that of its red cousin, I realized I was seeing my first black kite. This was the best place yet.

Before dusk, I drove until I came to a sign that indicated Salto de Torrejon to the right, and pulled into an open area to camp. The ground was covered with odd little piles. I climbed out to find that they were scores of groups of pine processionary moth caterpillars, all holding on to each other, but as it was cold the leaders were not moving. They would clearly wait for the morning sun to warm them up before continuing their journeys. I avoided them as best I could.

Next day I drove across the huge hydro-electric dam which had been built at the confluence of the Tajo and Tiétar rivers, ignoring a sign that said '*Se Prohibe Pasar*', and eventually located Jesus 'Suso' Garzon's humble terraced home. I rang the bell and waited. I wondered what sort of reception I would have, and how we could communicate, for Imre had warned me that he spoke no English. The door was opened by a little four-year-old girl who said her '*padre*' was on the phone. She invited me inside. I entered and went down two small steps into the gloom. The man at the desk said '*adiós*' and put down the phone.

6 · *Fight for Monfragüe*

Jesus 'Suso' Garzon did not so much stand up from his chair as unfold. To my surprise, the legendary 36-year-old conservationist was a giant of more than 6ft 4ins. Slim but powerfully built, he had the good looks of a movie star, and his greeting handshake was like a vice. My second surprise was that he spoke quite good English so that with a little of my fractured Spanish we found we could understand each other well. We had two hours to spare before Imre de Boroviczény was due to arrive from Madrid. Suso Garzon ushered me into his red Spanish Ebro jeep and drove me round while he told me of his battle to establish nearly 18,000 hectares as the Monfragüe Natural Park. He was a professional surveyor of fauna and flora, and had been preparing a report on Spain's endangered raptors when he first visited the area in the late 1960s. What he found had astonished him.

'I soon realised this was not only one of the finest wildlife areas in Spain but in all Europe,' he told me. 'There was an even greater diversity of fauna here than in the Coto Doñana, which was then becoming famous for its wildlife. The black vulture is extinct in western Europe, except in Spain, yet it is the world's third largest raptor; only the torgus of Africa and the South American condor are bigger. In Monfragüe live 70 out of the 100 pairs surviving in Extremadura. The rare black stork has declined all over western Europe, with just a few pairs left in West Germany, Austria and Greece. Here is the main population.'

53

The table below sets out the extraordinary facts which Suso Garzon gave me about the rare birds in this area:

Species	Monfragüe	Extremadura	Spain
Black vulture	70 pairs	100 pairs	250 pairs
Egyptian vulture	15 "	200 "	2,000 "
Griffon vulture	150 "	400 "	3,500 "
Imperial eagle	8 "	25 "	75–85 "
Eagle owl	30 "	200 "	2,000 "
Black stork	11 "	80 "	140 "

Almost ten years later, as this book was going to press, he gave me the population figures for 1989, which reflect the success of some of Spain's new conservation measures, though the Egyptian vulture has lost ground.

Species	Monfragüe	Extremadura	Spain
Black vulture	120 pairs	200 pairs	500 pairs
Egyptian vulture	15 "	200 "	1,500 "
Griffon vulture	250 "	500 "	4,000 "
Imperial eagle	8 "	30 "	120 "
Eagle owl	50 "	1,000 "	3,000 "
Black stork	12 "	150 "	200 "

'Here too is one of the last strongholds of the Spanish lynx,' he continued, as the jeep rattled along. 'We also have wildcat, mongoose, red deer, otter, stone marten, genet, and booted, short-toed, golden and Bonelli's eagles, as well as red and black kites, falcons, hawks and all the owls. In winter many species migrate through here, and we have seen white-tailed eagles, ospreys, and common cranes by the hundreds.'

As we drove past the two great hydro-electric dams I asked him what effect their building in 1962 had had on the area's wildlife.

'Mainly the effect was very bad because they flooded the valleys of the Tajo and Tiétar rivers behind,' he replied. 'They also flooded areas where formerly small fish, frogs and other amphibians flourished. With the water higher than normal it is now much worse for the fishing of the black stork.'

He pulled up on the high bank above the Tajo, pointed to some low cliffs on the far side and said there was a griffon vulture and an Egyptian vulture incubating eggs on their nests there, with two griffons perched on a rock near by. I could see nothing. Huge birds like that, yet I could not see them. I would not have given such low cliffs a second glance. Only through my binoculars, and with his instructions, could I locate the birds. Big though they were, they were perfectly camouflaged against the rocky faces.

Suso then drove me past Penafalcon and up a steep winding track to the ruin of the ancient Castillo de Monfragüe, perched high on the opposite cliffs. This castle holds the key to the area's history. Before it was built in the 12th century the early human inhabitants lived largely in harmony with nature, finding enough fish in the rivers and game in the forests for their needs. The conquering Romans hunted wild boar, deer and now-extinct bears, and called the area Monsfragorum, meaning impenetrable craggy mountains. Around 713 AD, the Moors who had driven the Romans from the Toledo and Merida areas renamed the hills Al-Mofrag, meaning chasm or abyss, and built the castle. After the Spanish army reconquered the area, the two names merged and eventually became Monfragüe. Apart from the small village of Villa Real, now the public headquarters of the Park, no other permanent settlements were made because of the poor soil and the inaccessibility of the mountains. The wildlife was largely left alone.

Inside the castle was dark and damp, like a vault, the steps of the spiral staircase both steep and deep. One slip going down here and one would suffer severe injury, if not death. As we reached the short ruined battlements I recoiled in fright when I saw the drop. It seemed to be sheer for all of a kilometre. Suso saw my fear.

'Here,' he said. 'I stand in front of you. Look over my shoulder.'

I was amazed at his trust of a total stranger as he shielded me from the drop. But he had to stoop before I could see over him. On the far hills across the deep valley he pointed out trees used by nesting imperial eagles and black vultures. They would be easy to find when tramping that terrain, and easy to work from a hide, but Suso explained it was one of the Park's reserved zones where visitors could not go without special permission.

As we drove away again, I heard more of this man's lone fight to save the area from development. He explained that before and since the Spanish Civil War most of the land had been held by large estate (*finca*) owners, who came only to hunt wild boar and deer, or at weekends and on holidays.

'The few people who still live here all the time remain in harmony with nature. There are a thousand goats roaming the hills with their shepherds. Ten per cent die each year, which means a hundred dead goats to feed the rare vultures.'

In 1974 came the threat of disaster. Plans were announced to build a nuclear power station and a large paper mill on the shores of the Tajo river. The paper industry persuaded landowners to bulldoze all the natural vegetation – the three evergreen oaks (holm, cork and holly) and the dense covering of bushes like lentiscus and gum cistus – and replace them with fast-growing eucalyptus for the mill. The Ministry of Agriculture's Institute for the Conversation of Nature, at that time still run largely by the old type of forestry engineer who held the view that there would be enough remaining land for the rare species to survive, agreed to fund the entire enterprise, including the paper mill. They would supply heavy equipment, the labour, the know-how and the young trees to be planted. In all, 70,000 hectares of Extremadura (15,000 of them in the Monfragüe area) were to be blanketed with eucalyptus.

Alarmed, knowing it would destroy a superb eco-system which had taken thousands of years to develop, Garzon wrote a 36-page report on the unique biological importance of the area, listed all the species in it, and sent it to the government and every influential body he could think of.

'The government thanked me, but as the months passed it was clear they would not stop the development,' Suso told me. 'You see those evergreen oaks? They are ecologically important trees. Their root clusters are large and prevent soil erosion, and they retain the watershed, which is important, for we have had three years of drought here. Rare birds like imperial eagle, black vulture and black kite nest in them, so do short-toed eagles. The branches are used to heat homes, or for cooking, and give excellent charcoal. The leaves are good food for cattle and goats, so are the acorns which grow from October to January. Pigeons, doves, wild pigs, cranes and other species also eat the acorns. The leaves are thick, retain water and are wonderful for producing organic materials for the soil.'

He waved to the arid terraces on the bulldozed ground. 'You see those eucalyptus? They grow fast, they pump water *from* the soil and release it into the air. Their thin leaves are acid, have almost

I had a bigger shock than the ravens when a huge rare black vulture landed beside the goat carcass.

The ravens took revenge by tweaking the vultures' tails. The black vulture tried to retain its dignity . . . then it was a griffon's turn.

A hungry griffon vulture bounced up to the goat carcass with his wings open in an intimidating threat display. In this way he won his place at the feast.

Usually black vultures await their turn with aristocratic dignity, but this young bird had waited long enough.

Two black vultures battle like giant fighting cocks over a morsel of meat.

Jesus 'Suso' Garzon, who fought a brilliant one-man battle to save Monfragüe's rare wildlife, helps to disguise the hide.

The wild flowers in Spain begin to bloom in mid-January.

no nutrients, and contain toxic bacteria which kill useful micro-organisms in the earth. No birds nest in them. No vegetation grows under them, and soil erosion is increased.

'It was once a superb area for lynxes here, with the dense cover of vegetation between the oaks, with many clearings for rabbits on which the lynxes depend for food. But when they cleared it over large areas, the lynxes began to die out. Imperial eagles also take rabbits, so they were affected. The goat herds were to be removed too, the main food source for the vultures.'

It was early in 1977, when he found government bulldozers actually knocking down oaks containing black vulture nests, destroying trees round an imperial eagle's nest, that Garzon pulled out all the stops. He mounted an extraordinary one-man campaign. He reported it all to the World Wildlife Fund, which had already approved his report on Spain's endangered raptors. They gave him a modest annual grant, on which he was still living, and he hiked the hills photographing the bulldozers at their destruction. He even took photographs of a black vulture chick watching another nest tree being destroyed. He wrote articles, went to Madrid and besieged ecological journalists on every major paper and magazine, which began to print his superbly researched facts and photos. He went on radio and television, wrote countless letters to the government, universities, nature protection bodies and leading conservationists like Imre de Boroviczény. All of them threw in their support.

With money of his own, Suso leased an important estate of 4,330 hectares which he could personally protect, touted for donations, and built a small observatory opposite Penafalcon from which to show naturalists and government officials the rare wildlife and the dangers to it. Slowly his indomitable persistence paid off. Plans for the paper mill were shelved. The bulldozers were removed, but not before some 5,000 hectares had been planted with eucalyptus.

In 1978 ICONA acquired a new Director who was for and not against Monfragüe's protection. In April 1979 the Council of Ministers declared 17,852 hectares as the Monfragüe Natural Park. Today no landowner can develop without permission, the eucalyptus planting has ended, and the Park is run by new and more nature-minded officials and biologists.

At first Suso, the fighter and pioneer, was left out in the cold and not appointed to the Governing Board. Was he bitter about that?

'Not at all,' he smiled cheerfully. 'My job is basically done, but I'm keeping a very alert eye on what happens here now! As a matter of fact, I have ideas for 60 more areas of Spain which should also be protected Parks.'

He pulled up on the road opposite Penafalcon and took me down to the little observatory he had built among the trees. Through a powerful telescope I could see the nesting vultures on the massive cliff. Just then a black stork flew by, its long red legs trailing and its crimson bill stretched out like the tip of a lance. Suso moved the telescope and showed me one of its nests, on a bowl-like ledge, just a few metres above the river. It would have been impossible to make it out with the naked eye.

As we climbed back up the hill to the jeep, a car pulled up near by, two men and a girl got out and one of the men began throwing rocks into the river. Suso said something. The tourist, also a big man, argued with him and kept on throwing the rocks. Suso went over to him. He was clearly furious, but he spoke rapidly and quietly. I do not know what he said but the man's face changed, he apologised, and the three of them got back into their car and drove off. I made a mental note that Jesus 'Suso' Garzon was not a man to cross. I had had a glimpse of the forceful personality that lay behind the gentle exterior, the steely mind that had overcome the opposition of big business to have his Park established.

If I was amazed at Suso's single-handed achievement, beside which my attempts to campaign for better protection for species like the golden eagle, the otter, the wildcat and the pine marten in Scotland seemed rather feeble, I was even more astonished by his sheer kindness and patience with me. He drove me a long way to various *fincas*, making enquiries, until we met a shepherd who had a big old goat with a huge festering growth, almost the size of a football, on its front leg. It was clearly done for, limping along far behind the herd, and was due for slaughter. I paid the 3,000 pesetas (£15) the owner wanted. We put the goat in the back of the jeep and drove back to Suso's home. His attractive dark-haired wife Isabel, who had spent some time in America and spoke faultless English, was waiting for us. With her was Imre, who had driven from Madrid in three hours, wearing a neat Tyrolean hat and puffing away at his eternally-lit pipe. Although it was nearly 2 p.m., we all felt it would be cruel to leave the goat in the hot jeep while we ate. We would take it to the vulture feeding site right now. I felt sorry for the poor old goat, but Suso said it was better to feed the rare vultures with it than to let it go for pet meat.

We drove a few miles along the Tiétar river, then up a bumpy sand track to the ICONA biological station at Las Cansinas, the one *finca* the government had been able to buy. Carlos, the new young biologist who got his job through Suso's work, complained that I should have a written permit from the Park's Director, but Suso soon talked to him and then drove us another 2 km into really untamed terrain.

There, among the gum cistus bushes on a wild broad slope overlooking a breathtaking view of wooded mountains and the Tajo river, was his hide. It was a canvas affair but twice the size of any I had seen. Suso gave a slight smile and nodded with approval as I rearranged the camouflage netting and stuck fresh vegetation into it. Then I heard a loud 'Bang!' He had shot the goat in the back of the head. I set up my camera to check the distance, then dragged the dead goat further away as it was too close for my long lens. Suso pegged it down with cord and a stake, explaining that the vultures would drag it about, maybe behind bushes where I could not take photos. On the way back, as I tried to memorise the wild route, Suso indicated a spot by a small stream under the cork oaks where I should camp for the night. From there I would have to walk the 2 km to the hide before dawn.

7 · A Feast of Vultures

A heavy dew lay on the cold ground as I set off in the pre-dawn gloom. The long wet leaves of the tall gum cistus bushes hung limply. I could not see for more than a few yards, so I tried to keep to the tracks made by Suso's jeep. I was moving quietly over an open area near a small pond when I heard a splash. A loud snorting grunt made my heart leap. Then I saw a large dark animal form swerve from the pond and wheel away into the thickets with a scratchy pounding of its feet. I felt scared, unsure whether to go on. It had been larger than a dog but smaller than a cow, and heavy for its size. Maybe it was a wild boar; Suso had told me there were some in the area, but not wanting to appear cowardly, I had avoided asking him whether they attacked man. Obviously the creature had been afraid or it would not have run off so fast. Then I saw a huge bird winging towards me, obviously disturbed by the 'boar' dashing through the bushes. I could just make out its piercing orange eyes as it passed by and shot away on wings as large as those of a buzzard. It was an eagle owl.

The distance to the hide seemed longer than I had remembered, and I was alarmed at the speed with which the light was improving. I reached the white quartz rock I had left as a marker and turned in through the bushes to reach the start of the open slope where the goat was staked down. I heard ravens croaking, and then saw a crowd of vultures on the ground 40 metres below. A raven flew overhead giving a loud '*Krok*' call. The vultures looked up, leaped into the air and beat away on monstrous wings. Hell! I had blown it already, a bloody amateur in Spain. I located the carcass and then the dark mass of the vegetation-covered hide in the bushes. There was only one thing to do. I walked round it in a large semi-circle, as if leaving the area. When I was sure there were no birds in the sky, and the bushes were thick enough to screen me from the cliffs across the river where they might have landed, I crawled swiftly on all fours into the hide. I set up the camera on its tripod and found that, with only a mat to sit on, I had to kneel up to see through the viewfinder. It appeared that I had a long, uncomfortable wait ahead.

Only moments later I heard ravens croaking all around me and some landed near the hide. I kept still, and in twenty minutes there were 26 ravens quarrelling over the half-eaten carcass. A comic pantomime now took place, and the variety of vocal sounds the birds made was surprising — '*Wug*', '*Grok*', '*Gibb*', '*Ger ger*', '*Kwark*', and odd burping noises too. Sometimes a raven turned and fed a snippet to its mate; others took to fencing with their stout black bills before attacking the meat again. One raven waddled over to another which had removed a long thin piece of the entrails, weaving to and fro as if courting, and grabbed the other end of the entrail. The two then had a tug of war.

By 8.40 a.m. there were only eight ravens left at the carcass, suggesting that the others had eaten their fill. One pair walked off together and stood close to each other, the smaller lowering her beak while the larger male preened the back of her neck. Two had a fight, sitting back on their tails and grappling with their claws. An hour later five more ravens had flown in, and I saw two pairs which had eaten enough, walk off to the side. I took fine photos of the two males courting their ladies, swelling out their neck feathers, fanning their tails and giving graceful bows. One pair played 'footsie', each moving out one foot to grapple fondly with that of the other.

At 10.40 a.m. sure I had spooked the vultures for the day, I looked through the viewfinder to see a beautiful black vulture standing by the goat. These birds weigh up to 22lbs, and it looked massive, dwarfing even the big ravens. Then I saw that three griffons had landed 30 metres to the right, and heard the loud swish of great wings as more landed. They stood apart for a while before three hop-jumped gawkily over to the goat, one holding its wings out like the open doors of an aircraft hangar. A raven seemed to take exception to the black vulture, which was still just standing by peacefully, and waddled towards it. The vulture looked down, cocking its head sideways, and gave it a look as if to say, 'Now then small fry, watch your step.' With great dignity, the vulture turned and started to walk away, whereupon the cheeky raven stepped forward and, with its beak, tweaked the great bird's tail!

Before long there were six griffons pulling at the carcass, and the social interaction was fascinating. Sometimes they momentarily threatened each other with half open beaks, giving out a noise like steam escaping through a vent, like a mute swan hissing but much louder. Others, when approaching the carcass, had brief fights, jumping awkwardly at each other with chittering noises and making downward slashes with their claws. These short brawls, never lasting more than a few seconds, seemed more symbolic than serious. The more vultures that went to the goat, the more squabbles occurred. They made lightning beak stabs at the heads and necks of those beside them, though it was clear they were really intent on feeding. Sometimes, one bird looked at its neighbour and lifted its huge foot high, as if to say, 'This is what I would like to give you, but our rules don't allow it!'

I now saw that eight black vultures had landed and stood aloof, quietly, as if waiting their turn with aristocratic dignity. Two preened themselves while another courted its mate, twisting its head on one side and looking tenderly into the other's face. A new griffon swept in, landed near the goat with a clumsy bumping run. It kept its great wings open and bounced up to the feeding birds with an intimidating threat display. They quickly made room for it. The strange thing was that all the younger griffons, smaller, thinner and darker-looking, were kept to the sidelines, and when one approached the goat it was driven off by an adult with wing flaps and beak threats.

As soon as the seniors had eaten their fill, the youngsters moved in and all hell broke loose. The goat could not be seen under a seething mass of backs, wings and orange and brown feathers. The noise was tremendous — chittering squeaks, steam-like hisses, wing snaps, accompanied by grunts, thumps and the snapping of bones. None of the vultures attacked the ravens which were relegated to the edges of the fray, sneaking in now and then to tweak the vultures' tail feathers, sometimes pulling hard as if hoping to haul the big birds off the goat!

One of the black vultures evidently decided it had waited long enough. It ran ponderously like a plane taking off, opened its 3-metre span of wings and sailed into the griffons. It lashed out with its wings, made open beak threats and soon won its place at the feast. This was the signal for three more of the blacks to fly into the mêlée, and as they easily battled their way to the carcass, their greater size was obvious. There were now eight black vultures and 61 griffons around the goat, which had been reduced almost to a skeleton.

The first of the blacks was evidently in luck for it broke away from the imbroglio with a large chunk of meat in its beak and flew back to where the other four of its kind were still waiting. It had time for only a few pecks before one of the others tried to steal a piece. Both birds immediately leaped into the air, wings cracking, battling like giant fighting cocks, the meat owner forcing its opponent off with powerful downward slashes with its claws. It hopped ponderously back to the morsel. Up came another black vulture, looked into its face with a gentle solicitous twisting of the head, and was allowed to share the food. They were clearly a mated pair.

Suddenly there was a loud woofing of wings, and I saw that all the ravens had flown away. The vultures looked up with alarm, then also left, beating away in slow motion like monstrous machines. Immediately, the ravens returned, and had the feast to themselves for half an hour — until the flying vultures tumbled to the ravens' clever ruse. As soon as they saw that there was no real danger the vultures began to return. Then suddenly a male griffon jumped on to a female's back and mated with her.

It was 1.35 p.m. when I heard Suso's jeep approaching. I had been in the hide for seven hours and my knees were aching. As I dismantled the camera my legs trembled with excitement and the strain of having to keep kneeling up to see through the viewfinder. I had everything packed away by the time Suso opened the hide's rear flap and greeted me with —

'How are you, sir?'

Sir? From *him*?

It seems he had been looking through four of my wildlife books and thought highly of them. He told me I could return to Monfragüe any time. After such a wonderful morning, I thought I would sell the remaining lease of my Scottish Highland home and settle here for good. That night, I managed to persuade Suso and Isabel to let me take them to dinner while a neighbour looked after their children. That was all he would accept for his help, and he refused to let me make a donation to Park funds. Before we parted he invited me to lunch next day.

I spent the morning typing up my notes. When I arrived at Suso's home, I found not just lunch but an intimate gathering of his parents from Madrid and his closest friends. It was his 37th birthday party. I was accepted as one of the family and felt overwhelmed by their kindness. We drank wine, ate huge prawns, canneloni, fillet of pork roasted in orange sauce, topped by coconut flan and the finest schnapps made in the Picos de Europa, which Suso said was his favourite hunting ground for wildlife.

'You want to see imperial eagles displaying?' Suso asked later. He led me up to the roof and we had only half an hour to wait before a pair flew over from their nesting hills across the river. The male started diving on the female above our heads. She rolled over and presented her talons to his several times. We could hear their short harsh '*Gak gak*' calls clearly as I clicked away.

I discovered that Suso had written important papers on species like imperial eagle, wolf, bear and lynx, and said I would like to see them. He immediately took me to the office of the dam company and had them photocopied. As he handed them to me he said with mock severity –

'I hope no more wild men come from Scotland wanting me to copy everything!'

Again he would take no fee, but I managed to force upon him a new tape recorder which I had in the van, as his had broken down. When it was time to say goodbye, I felt what for me was the rare emotion of gratitude.

'Why did you help me?' I asked. 'And give me so much of your time?'

'It is important to help,' he said simply. I have never forgotten those words, nor the incredible goodness of this man.

Next morning, after tape-recording partridge and raven calls, I left Monfragüe and began the 500 km drive to catch the Santander ferry in two days' time. Though I had little time, I intended, on the way, to take a look at the Picos de Europa, where Suso said there were still wild bears, and at Covadonga National Park, where I ought to find capercaillie. Before Plasencia I took pictures of a flying black kite and a red kite perched on a pylon. I saw several more along the N630 road to Montemayor, where the high mountains are of granite. Descending into rolling arable plains, I took some good shots of nine red kites flapping over a rubbish dump, the most I had seen of these birds together. Palencia seemed an interesting little town, with lighted bars, attractive shops, and pretty women walking about, but I did not stop. After taking the small C615 road towards Riano, which Suso had said was his favourite mountain town, I camped in an open field just before Villoldo.

Up early, I drove through flat lands to Guardo, with its huge cement works, and then climbed into high mountains to cross the 1,433-metre high pass of Puerto de Monteviejo. I could see the first peaks of the Picos de Europa all shrouded in clouds. The road was rough and windy, but by 1.30 p.m. I reached the beautiful village of Riano, set in the middle of vast mountains that dwarfed it. Beyond reared the great domed peak of Mampodre, 2,190 metres high and covered with snow, and near Puerto del Ponton the winding road passed through deep gorges with the mountains pressed tight up on each other, making the region seem claustrophobic. I also ran into pouring rain and mist before reaching the villages of Corriglos and Tournin, where the mountains open out and the road travels alongside a fine river with beech hangars, sallow, willow and poplar growing along its banks.

In Covadonga I passed a noble old monastery perched on a crag, and some children were singing hymns in a cave by the side of the road. A steep little road took me to 850 metres and the heart of the Picos. One peak, snowcapped like all the others but not named on my map, reared to 2,648 metres. High though that is, it does not compare with Spain's highest mountain, the 3,482 metres Mulhacen in the Sierra Nevada, nor the Pico de Aneto, which soars to 3,408 metres in the Pyrenees. The hills around me now were rounded, with many granite outcrops, covered with heather and short grass where sheep had cropped it. I saw a wood up to my left and parked so that I could take a look through my binoculars.

I could hear strange clicking and popping sounds followed by a scissoring noise. It sounded like someone grinding a knife on a primitive, creaking foot-driven wheel. I glassed the bottom of the wood, expecting to see a human but instead saw that the tuneless cadence was being made by a large bird, a cock capercaillie. It was strutting about, keeping to an area roughly one metre square, with its dark tail fanned up and round like a turkey, its head up in the air.

In my part of the west Highlands there are no capercaillies, and this was the first I had seen giving its posturing courtship display. The trouble was that I could not see any hens. The light was bad, with mist drifting about. I tried to get nearer for a photo, but there was no cover between me and the bird, and it vanished into the forest gloom. As I walked back to the van a huge female golden eagle came sailing down from the north, keeping below the thicker mist now advancing from the peaks, and I took a shot knowing the light was really too poor for photographs.

Not wanting to be trapped in mist, I drove back down and, after a long search, because all the land was fenced close to the roads for sheep, cattle and goats, I found a camping spot in an old timber yard. Next day I caught the ferry home from Santander. The wild bears would have to wait until a later visit. I was resolved now to sell up in Scotland, buy that video camera and return to Spain.

This plan went wrong from the start. On the drive back to Scotland I visited Tony Soper of the BBC Natural History Unit in Bristol, who had given my book *Golden Eagle Years* a wonderful boost on their regular radio programme. Over lunch I received a shock when members of the television team told me that ordinary video tape was not good enough for transmission. I would have to buy equipment costing £50,000 to gain the quality they needed. Even the films made by Rodriguez de la Fuente did not meet their standards. If I wanted to make movies, I would need a good Arriflex camera with tripod and an assortment of lenses, and at the time that sort of outlay was beyond my purse.

My attempts to sell the remaining lease on 'Wildernesse' also floundered. Freak storms blew up on each occasion when I boated across the loch the two families which had answered my advertisement. Their faces paled at the idea of such a hazardous access, and I never heard from either family again.

But by the end of the summer, when I had found a publisher for my book *A Last Wild Place*, I blew the first part of the advance on an old Arriflex ST 16mm movie camera and some lenses. When I returned to Spain in late December, I took the outfit with me, filming first some flying red kites at El Espinar. With a new book to crack, I rented once more the clifftop villa overlooking the Mediterranean near Mazarron which I had come to call 'Sunny Alcatraz', and moved in on Christmas Day. On my first trek round Eagle Mountain I found that a family of feral dogs had taken over a small cave in the *rambla*. They would certainly keep the foxes away. They were noisy, ranged the hills at night, and I saw them taking the food I set out for foxes.

By New Year's Eve I was suffering from a form of writer's block and had written no more than 2,000 words. I was struggling with a chapter on Scottish foxes oddly enough, and just before midnight I climbed up to the high ridge overlooking Eagle Mountain's broadest valley in order to renew my wilderness vows. It was a clear cold night, the stars bestowing a soft glow to the landscape, and I could see Orion up there, just as I had from my woods in Scotland. Suddenly a dog fox ran past me, making '*rowl rowl*' barks.

'Rowl, rowl!' I barked in just the same way.

To my surprise, the fox stopped and looked back at me, just a few yards away, its nose quivering. For a few seconds our eyes held, then it turned and slipped away into the gloom. It seemed a good omen with which to end the year.

8 · *Hide and Seek*

I climbed halfway up the white-peaked mountain in Sierra Espuña and found what seemed an ideal position. I had seen from the valley floor a young golden eagle flying near Eyrie I. There were bushes behind me, a thick pine tree screened me from the sight of any eagles flying over the valley to my right. I looked up to the nest at a slight angle and tied the monopod of the heavy movie camera and lens to the pine for stability. After a three hour wait I checked once more round the side of the tree with binoculars.

There were three eagles in the sky — the youngster with white markings in its plumage, a smaller male and a huge dark female. The juvenile was as large as she, and must have been their eaglet from the previous year. Although it was the breeding season once again, they made no effort to drive it away.

As the movie camera whirred, the male dived twice on the female and she turned half over, but their talons did not touch. The pair circled above the eyrie without the youngster then flew back to it and all three sailed round each other. Once again the male dived down, more purposefully this time, and the female turned right over. She appeared to take a small stick from his talons. Perhaps she would take it to the nest.

Quickly I shifted the camera to the lefthand side of the tree and focussed on to her again as she made a small aerial circle. Then she zoomed along the faces, made a few slow pulling-up flaps and landed right on the eyrie. She probed about with her beak, putting the stick in three different places, then looked out into the void. I kept the camera trained on her and filmed her flying off, sweeping along the rock faces before rocketing out into the blue. She circled again, and I saw the male diving past her just before the spool of film ended. I threaded in a new film and was just shooting a pan sequence of the eyrie cliffs when a chough appeared in the lens making its madly flapping courtship flight. Then the chough dived with a harsh '*keerk*' call, its red legs stretched out.

Filming wildlife in such mountains was a far more difficult proposition than merely photographing it. I was now carrying 48lbs of gear rather than 15, and while Scottish hills contained slushy peat, tussocks and heather, the terrain here was composed of steep hard rock, with gabbro and shale on that rock. One slip on sliding shale and one could be away to a gouging painful death. Twice, as I weaved my way up the sheerer parts, I felt convulsive griping pains in the centre of my chest – my heart protesting at the extra burden. It is true that I would sooner go while working on a mountain than in a hospital ward, but I did not *want* to die, so I made a point of slowing down. That morning I had taken the far easier path down to Carrasca, but had found only a solitary Barbary ram feeding from the alfalfa the guardas had spread out. I had stalked into the shadow of some pines and filmed it, with the sun shining in its eyes and climbing up a little cliff, before walking away. It was while eating lunch that I had seen the young eagle fly past the eyrie.

Next day there were no Barbary sheep near Carrasca and I saw no eagles, choughs or even crows or ravens. A great mist began creeping in high from the south. I climbed 130 metres towards Eyrie 1, hoping to get the eagles before the mist arrived, and was just focussing on the nest when the young eagle swept off it, too fast for me to film! I had just caught up with it when it dived and vanished behind the trees as the mist obliterated all the peaks. There seemed little else to do but hike down to overlook Eyrie 3 and hope the birds might appear there.

Although some new moss had been added to the nest, they had not shown up after a two-hour wait, so I searched around for a future hide site. I was sure this eyrie would be used sooner or later. I found the ideal place, between two stunted pines right on the lip of the great chasm. From there the nest loomed large in the lens and I would be able to film the eagles leaving, flying along the sandy coloured rock faces and soaring out into the blue. It was in fact the best situation I had ever found.

Between the edge of the forest and the two little pines was an open area of convoluted rock that sloped downwards. It would be impossible even to belly-crawl over this rock without being seen from the nest. I spent the next three hours building a long screen of rocks, on top of which I piled dead branches so that one day I could crawl behind it unseen. (It was three more years before the eagles used this eyrie but how glad I was then that I had taken this trouble.) By now the mist had cleared completely from the tops. I drove almost to the pass and found a new camp site from which I could overlook all the white peaks surrounding Eyrie 1, and much of the valley besides, albeit at a fair distance. After a short climb, I filmed sequences of the female flying, and once being mobbed by choughs, before landing again on the nest.

Next morning I drove to Mazarron for petrol and to order two new tyres from Roy Ensor. He laughed when I told him what the BBC had said about video cameras, but was pleased to see all my movie gear. On the way back I found a traffic-killed little owl, and was surprised to find its wings spanned 21 inches.

I climbed twice as high as the day before and found a rocky fissure six feet deep, but such was the formation of the rocks that I could not get them to hold the monopod steady. I negotiated a 100-foot drop by crawling along a ledge, hauling the big pack of movie gear behind me, and found a small flat arbour of trees which gave me a panoramic view of the valley and the cliffs. I cut a hole in the little owl's chest and pushed into it half a handful of red mince, then placed the bait on a flat boulder 50 metres away before returning to set up the camera against a madrona tree.

At 5.28 p.m. I heard '*kewp kewp*' calls and saw the young eagle flying below me. It passed over the owl without appearing to notice it, then suddenly began beating away to the east. As I looked up, there were the two adults. I filmed the female gliding along, the male performing shallower dives than usual with his wings half open instead of shut, and at last of the female flying into the nest. They both ignored the owl. Then, as I saw her tugging sticks about, I heard a flapping noise from inside the camera – the film had run out. I knew for sure now that this eyrie would be used again this year. Hell!

For most of the next month I locked myself away in 'Sunny Alcatraz' and worked on the new book. I could not take time off to study local foxes, for two more feral dogs had set up home in a ruined farmhouse on the south slopes of Eagle Mountain, while a bulldozer was busy with foundations for a new urbanisation on the high eastern slopes. The foxes had gone elsewhere.

The only wildlife experiences at this time were provided by the dumpy little black wheatears. Apart from courting, they were at last coming for the scraps of food I set out. I saved bits of chicken, rice, mussels and prawns which I put in a pile on the wide parapet surrounding the terrace, to thwart the feral cats. I was at my desk one morning when a swift shadow crossed the window, and I was delighted to see a wheatear land by the food, bob up and down like a robin, seize a piece of chicken in its beak and make off with it.

After a few days of these 'grab-and-run' raids, he brought his mate, and it was soon clear they preferred the chicken; prawn heads came second and rice third. I set camera on tripod and with a remote control cable could press the button near my typewriter as I sat at my desk working. Once I got a picture of the male suspended in mid-air as he jumped off the parapet before opening his wings.

During this sedentary month I tried to keep fit by taking the occasional run and averaging 60 km a week on my bike, including a few hard sprints.

On March 7 I spent a hot sunny day back in Espuña. After carrying the movie gear down to Carrasca I saw a huge Barbary ram out in the pasture. No sooner had I set up than it saw me and broke into an uncharacteristic sprint, its hooves scrabbling on the loose soil, its belly almost touching the ground, and vanished into the trees. There were no others in sight. As I climbed back through the woods I heard a loud humming or buzzing noise. There seemed to be a large swarm of bees flying round a water conduit below some bushes. When I drew closer, I realised they were much bigger than bees and must be some kind of hornet. The pipe was cracked and leaking water, and the hornets were landing on it to drink. They were large, dark in colour, and looked both socially intelligent and very aggressive. I filmed them with a 300mm lens but dared not go too near. A swarm of angry hornets was dangerous, and could kill me with poisonous stings.

Later, as I was driving round a tight bend on the forestry track leading to the high white eagle crags, a small herd of Barbary rams burst out of the trees on my left, dashed in front of the van, making clouds of dust, and vanished up the wooded slopes. I parked and stalked them, carrying the movie gear in my hands so as to be instantly ready. It was hard steep going, but after a short distance I saw them again. They now behaved cleverly; they did not run but hid. Moving slowly, each one shrank behind a bush and kept dead still. If I had not known they were there I would not have been able to see them.

I too slipped behind a bush and we had a game of hide-and-seek. When they could not see me, each ram put its huge horned head out from behind its bush and peered. As soon as I moved my head out, they would shrink back again. This happened several times. I was still too far away for filming and so I tried to stalk nearer, but there were now so many dry twigs underfoot that it was impossible to move quietly. Gradually they slipped away like tawny ghosts. I climbed down, drove on and soon saw them again. This time I tried a very slow 'dead' stalk, moving straight ahead but each foot shifting only a few inches each time. They hid the same way as before, but still I got good footage, proving their ability to conceal themselves.

After loading some firewood logs into the van, I climbed a third of the way up the white-peaked mountain, glad of my hard bike training, for I carried both sets of camera gear, weighing over 60lbs. I puffed up to my favourite arbour below the little pines, set up and was ready for the 'eagle show' by 5.20 p.m. They usually came, I had noticed, just before half past five, but now that the sun was higher in the sky and lasting longer, I reckoned they would be a few minutes later today. They arrived at 5.48 p.m!

I was watching some choughs performing their short roll dives, which ended with suddenly opened wings and '*chi-aw*' or '*kiaow*' calls, when a raven came from behind me, croaking and flapping hard in fear. Sailing along behind it, as if enjoying the fact that his easy glide was giving his black tormentor a hard time, came the male eagle. I filmed the choughs dive bombing him until he disappeared round the far ridge. A few minutes later he returned and I filmed him soaring down towards Eyrie 3, until the film came to an end. The light was fading by then, so I packed up in time to see the female flying close past me and land on a bush to the left of the high nest. Not on the nest itself, I noticed. On the way down I found a large area of scuffed earth, as if a giant badger had rooted there, or some big animal had shifted the stones and soil to make itself a cool bed. It could have been done by a wild boar, I thought, but since I had never seen one in all my visits to Espuña, I had begun to think the guardas were pulling my leg.

Four days later I packed up the villa ready for twelve hard days of driving and wild camping. On my way I spent one more day in Espuña, to see whether the ideal Eyrie 3 was being used. While trekking down to it I filmed a fine squirrel dining area, filled with cones stripped of their seeds, and also a big drey in a black pine, but I saw no squirrels. The eyrie was definitely not in use. Just as I climbed out again and reached the forestry track I saw the female eagle fly into Eyrie 1 with a branch about 18 inches long in her talons. I filmed her perched on a branch of the dead tree, looking like a sparrow against the great ball of a nest. She had not laid eggs yet, which surprised me in this warm climate. I was to find out later that golden eagles lay only about a week or ten days earlier than their Scottish counterparts, despite the sunny weather in Spain.

It took me two days to reach Suso's place in Extremadura for I kept stopping to film things — a huge sierra of corrugated red mountains near Jabalcon, the beautiful wooded heights before Cazorla where the blue of the sky and the green of the trees made a superb contrast to the chimneys and buttress shapes of the white and pink rock. Just before Bellerda and Tiscar I saw two long-winged birds with coffee cream breasts sailing along through a gap in the trees. I went round a dangerous bend, saw they had landed on a flat peak above a spectacular gorge, and pulled up. While I filmed them preening, I saw that they had broad heads and almost white tails. A raven landed near by. I did not know it then but I had just filmed my first booted eagles. There were also griffon vultures on the peaks above Bellerda.

Next day, as I drove up the country road from Jaraicejo to Torrejon el Rubio, I saw two huge white storks beside a farmer's slow-moving tractor and plough. The farmer took no notice of them while ploughing every inch he could, ducking his head under the cork tree branches as he passed below. I stopped, shoved the long lens through the open van window and was filming the storks when I heard an odd shout. The farmer threw his hands in the air in fear. He must have thought I had a gun and intended to shoot him. I waved and smiled, and pointed to the big round of the lens before he realised it was just a camera. Then he laughed and waved back.

I camped before Penafalcon, and in the morning took some fine sequences of flying griffon and Egyptian vultures, and also a rare black stork that was soaring round the peaks even more gracefully with them.

Suso was waiting outside his house at the appointed time and shook my hand so hard I could not restrain a grimace. He said he had to go to Santander that day, not on the 17th as Imre had told me. There had been a mix-up, and I felt a keen surge of disappointment.

'Oh well,' I said. 'I wanted to get vultures at a goat again now that I've got this movie camera, but don't worry. I'll go back to the vulture cliffs.'

'Oh no,' he assured me hastily. 'Of course we will get a goat. It is no problem.' He put a huge arm round my shoulders and took me in to Isabel, who was cooking lunch. I felt perplexed.

'If you have to go all the way to Santander today,' I said, 'you have no time to help me to find a goat and take it all the way to the hide . . .'

He raised a hand to stop me.

'There is always time, for everything!'

Over lunch he and Isabel plied me with questions about Britain's conservation systems, the government licences for photographing rare species, how reserves were run, whether hides were built to encourage public interest, and so on. I told them all I could, promised to look out some licence forms and all the written information I had, and give it to Isabel on the morrow.

In his red jeep we drove after lunch over miles of rough tracks, careered through marshes and across dry river beds, until we found an old shepherdess who had a dying nanny goat. I had forgotten to bring my wallet and Suso said I would have to pay her 4,000 pesetas tomorrow. The price had gone up! I cradled the poor goat's head in the jolting jeep all the way to the wild vulture site.

The old hide had disintegrated, and while Suso staked out the dead goat, I reset its poles and macheted gum cistus bushes to obscure it. He returned as I was tying a cord round the middles of each side of the hide and asked why I was doing it. I showed him how such a cord held in place the bottom of greenery hanging from the top and also the tops of the fronds propped up from the ground. A dark eagle flew over, slightly smaller than a golden eagle. Suso said it was an imperial. The movie gear was in the hide but I clicked off two shots with the still camera. I asked him if myxomatosis had ever been a problem in Spain.

'Yes, it began here when a French farmer deliberately introduced it on his estate, and the disease spread through France and down through Spain. It killed rabbits and had a big effect in this area on the imperial eagles which prey on them – and also on the lynx which does not catch pigeons or partridges too well. Myxomatosis is not a big problem now, but we have had three years of drought here, which has been bad for the grasses. This has also kept the rabbits down.'

Before we left I noticed he cut off the tagged ear of the goat. He explained that the shepherdess would send it in and collect 8,000 pesetas compensation from the government. I remarked that the Spanish were more generous to farmers over livestock compensation than was the British government.

'Many of these people have no other living than their goats, sheep and a few cows,' he said. 'If the government did not support them, many herds would die out. Bad for the rare vultures, and many other species!'

Suso drove me back to my van at the camp site by the stream in the cork tree woods and said goodbye. It was nearly 6 p.m. and he was clearly overdue in Santander! I cleaned and checked all the photographic gear and I cooked supper. It began to rain. I hoped it would clear away by the morning, but it did not. I was woken several times during the night by great plops of water splashing down on the van roof from the cork oaks. At dawn it was still pouring with rain, and all I could do was to sit gloomily in the van. By 8 a.m. it seemed to clear slightly, so I put on wellingtons for the first time in Spain and carried the 54lbs of gear, which included lunch and a litre of milk, up the squelchy track to the hide. I could see no vultures, nor even ravens, anywhere. Still I kept the hide between me and the goat as I made my crawling approach. I set the camera up on the tripod Suso had lent me and heard a raven nearby. Then it began to rain heavily again. I saw the raven fly to the goat and hack away with its beak as it tried to puncture the skin, but I was darned if I was going to remove the lens cap and risk the rain flooding the glass just to film one solitary raven.

The roof of the hide had many small holes and water leaked through on to my head, shoulders, and the camera. Soon the ground was awash. A cold wind blew from the north, almost freezing the wet on my neck, face and hands. My jacket and trousers were soaked and water seeped down to half-fill my boots. I felt sure the vultures would not fly in such rain for their huge feathers easily get wet and heavy. It was as cold as any hide I had used in Scotland, and before long I was shivering. I gave it five excruciating hours, then packed up at 1 p.m. I trudged back to the van under dark lowering clouds, my knees aching with the cold and my wet trousers making the insides of my thighs sore. Well, I would at least put the afternoon to good use.

I drove to Torrejon to fill up with petrol and visited Isabel, who had a friend with her. I gave her all the promised information, including a copy of Britain's Wildlife and Countryside Act, 1981. She told me Suso had been too late to make his long drive last night and so had taken the jeep to Madrid that morning to catch the train to Santander. I felt guilty and hurried away to pay the old shepherdess for the goat. She began looking into my van and talking excitedly. She was furious that I had not brought the goat's tagged ear. In his haste, Suso had forgotten to drop it in to her. I said the ear was in his jeep, and he would bring it to her on his return, which of course he did.

The sky had begun clearing, but it still looked dark where the goat lay. It was 6.30 p.m. and Suso had said that if the vultures did not come by four o'clock they would not be seen that day. I decided not to risk another wasted trek.

Next day I woke at dawn to yet more splashing rain. I waited impatiently. Then Carlos, the young ICONA biologist, drove down to tell me that he had seen many vultures in the sky the previous afternoon. Maybe the goat was gone! I hoped not. Still it poured until, at midday, a hoopoe landed near the van. I eased down the window and filmed a fine sequence of it running about, probing in the wet earth with its long down-curved bill, pulling out grubs and worms and swallowing them. It seemed to find food easily. Well, I had something good.

By 1 p.m. the rain had almost stopped, the sky looked lighter to the west, and I buckled on all the gear and hiked back to the hide. I had almost reached it when I saw two black vultures standing near some bushes 200 metres to the right, a spot where I had thought none would go. They caught a glimpse of my head before I bobbed down and away they went. *Damn!* I crawled in, set up the equipment and looked through the lens.

The goat had been entirely consumed! Its bloodied ribs stuck out like a broken zip-fastener. The vultures must have come down yesterday afternoon when the rain had lessened, just as Carlos had thought. What a terrible error of judgement on my part. I should have stuck it out the whole day, though I had never been colder or wetter in a hide in my life. It rained heavily again for almost an hour as I went through my vocabulary of curses – and even invented a few new ones. The sun came out. At 4 p.m. an azure-winged magpie flew to the carcass, soon followed by four more. They flitted all over the remains of the goat, picking off the tiny scraps of meat left, and at least I got some good film of them. By 6 p.m., knowing no more vultures would come, I returned to my camp. I decided to move on, and give myself a day filming at the great vulture ramparts near Una.

I called on Suso next morning feeling guilty that I had let him down. He was also disappointed by my failure. He was sorry that still I had not seen the Egyptian vultures come to a carcass. They used to be the pets of Egyptian kings, he told me, and they were rather like kings themselves. They always approached a carcass delicately, tweaked pieces off and then retired a few yards away to eat them discreetly.

'Never mind,' he said as he came out to see me off. 'It is just bad luck. But, you have fed the vultures, and you have brought the rain. For three years we have drought here, but you are the great rain maker! Come again!'

As I drove away I felt again a sadness at saying goodbye to this man. I stopped at Penafalcon and made up slightly for my earlier blunder by filming Egyptian vultures mating high on the crags, the male whinnowing his great wings slowly as he took almost half a minute to complete the act.

I made a good run almost to Cuenca and decided to camp in a wood at a height of 1,150 metres, just after Puerto de Cabrejas. It had been raining here too and the ground was sticky. The back wheels spun, dug in, and I could not move. Shivering with cold, I tore my fingers throwing in handfuls of frozen rock and gravel to give the tyres more purchase. Only by using a branch like a ski-stick and pushing down on it hard with my right hand through the open door as I drove, could I extricate the van. Finally I camped down a broad side road behind some tall reeds.

Next morning I queued for petrol at Villalba de la Sierra before driving on to the vulture ramparts beyond Una. There were none of the great birds in the sky. Was I wasting my time again? I strapped the pack of movie gear on to my back, seized the support pod and began to climb. It was 500 metres of very hard going under my 50lb load, and as it was almost sheer in places I did a lot of weaving to and fro to reduce the slope. One fortunate effect of all the recent rain was that it had melded the dust into a glue which held the gravel firmer. I could dig my boots in rather than have them sliding off on the loose stones that covered the steep rocks.

At the top I had to search for the right place in which to work. The rocky ground sloped away from the bottom of the cliff. I tried beneath a pine, but its foliage obscured the sky. There was a hump of rock that gave good cover but such was its shape that no part of it would hold the pod steady. Finally I found a rocky crevice I could back into and still have a good view of all the mighty orange cliff faces.

Almost immediately the griffons appeared, winging past in pairs and threes, shimmering like prehistoric ghosts as they filled the lens. I took a sequence of a peregrine falcon flickering along, her hooked beak opening as she gave harsh '*raich raich*' cries. One griffon began circling more purposefully, a fair distance out from the cliff, so I focussed on it. After another half circle, it began to zoom in to its nest, but I could not follow it all the way for it passed right over my head and the camera hit against the pod, unable to take the acute angle. Once the vulture was on the nest, I walked to another high rock. While it watched me, it did not fly off. Then I filmed it preening its outer primary feathers with its beak while perched on a stick projecting from the nest. I was adjusting the camera, making sure that the heavy 500mm Kinoptic lens was well seated, when the vulture's mate came in to take over, and the first one left. The new bird walked over the nest, vanishing into the deep rock crevice where, presumably, it was attending a recently hatched chick. There was no other action before I left shortly at dusk. I had missed the takeover but at least I had made up a little for the awful fiasco at Monfragüe.

I slipped on the way down and had to grab at a bush to arrest my fall under the heavy weight. A thorn went into the palm of my hand and the poison caused swelling and some discomfort for the next few days. You have to be efficient or the wilderness teaches you just how old you are getting. All this driving and finding new places in which to camp, all the cooking, the trekking with heavy gear, the nervous energy needed for filming, the constant loneliness — all this was wearing me out. No wonder wildlife films are usually made by teams. This life would do me in yet.

At dusk there was a knock at the van door. It was the shepherd, and at first I thought he wanted a lift to the village, but no, his wife was coming to collect him in their car. He just wanted to say he knew that I was the man who liked to photograph the vultures on his land, and I was welcome to do so at any time! No Scottish shepherd had ever said anything like that to me.

9 · Bird in the Hand

The marshes and salt lagoons at Santa Pola run alongside the coastal road from Cartagena to Alicante, and as they came into view I felt disappointed that I could see none of the stars of these wetlands – the greater flamingos. Never mind, there were grey herons, a few coots, and two white egrets were skulking in the reeds up one shallow channel. I parked and ambled slowly, casually, towards them, trying to look disinterested, and was rewarded with a fairly close picture before they spread their snow-white wings and flew off. I carried on up the channel until I came to a tall screen of thick reeds behind which I could hear strange muted gaggling sounds. I parted the reeds and there they were – the elusive flamingos. They had not seen me but had clearly heard my approach, or else the flight of the egrets had alerted them.

Some were gracefully stalking along knee-deep in water, occasionally paddling with their feet to stir up aquatic insects and small water-life which they sieved out with their quaint Roman-nose beaks. Others seemed to be watchdogs, or sentries, for they were fully on the alert. They held their bills high and were stalking away from me, looking back over their shoulders with suspicion. It was too good a chance to miss. I tried to slide my long lens quietly through the reeds but the sentries saw the movement and gave odd goose-like gaggling calls as they sprang into the air. That was the signal for the lot to go, about 40 of them, and it was marvellous to see the spreading of their pinky-crimson black-tipped wings as they rose into the sky like a flying sunset, their long necks and grotesque beaks stretched out in front to counter-balance their lanky legs stuck out behind. From the side each one looked like a bag of flying bones.

These greater flamingos puzzle me, for there is a colony of up to 500 of them on these marshes for most of the year, yet on some days you can see none at all, no matter how hard you search. The flamingos have not bred at Santa Pola for some 20 years. Usually there are grey immatures among this flock, and the theory is that the adults are non-breeders, either too young or too old, and all have assembled here between the main west European breeding grounds – in the Camargue in southern France, in Málaga Province, and at the main Spanish site in the Coto Doñana.

The greater flamingo, a very rare bird in Europe, is now an endangered species. Its breeding is erratic, to say the least. If a colony is upset – one group of nests was ravaged recently by wild boar in Doñana – the birds may not breed again for several years. Their breeding places, or *pajarerías*, are hard to find, sited often on remote mud islands deep in the *marismas* (marshes). The nests are round upraised bulwarks on dry mud, and the islet can look like a potter's table with two dozen unfinished pots on it. The birds lay unusually late; one or two long chalky white eggs in May which take a month to hatch. When the chicks are ten days old, they leave their individual nests and join together to form a crèche in the centre of the colony, and are fed communally by all the adults. By the time they can fly at 2½ months old, however, the waters of spring have dried up and the colony is surrounded by thousands of acres of sun-baked cracked dry mud.

The flamingos I had scared did not go far, and I saw them wheel round and go down into the last of the salt water lagoons. There were coots, moorhens, various ducks and a few grey herons not far away. After taking more pictures, I turned to go back and found a dead avocet in the grasses. Both its legs were broken, as if by a shot, and it was very thin, probably having starved to death. This rare wader, which returned to nest on the Suffolk coast after an interval of 120 years, is not common in Spain either. This one measured 15ins long, with a wingspan of 28ins.

These Santa Pola marshes seem to be an important staging post for migrating waterfowl in this dry and arid region. Together with the lagoons of La Mata and Torrevieja, they were designated a protected area by the local authorities a few years ago. If I were running the marshes, my first priority would be to construct as natural an islet as possible for the flamingos to nest on. To have these marvellous and scarce creatures nesting in Alicante Province would be some achievement.

Later, I drove up through Totana, parked by the locked chain below the peak of Sierra Espuña, and waited until guardas Casimiro and Pedro had gone by on their bikes on their way to lunch. Then I scrambled down past Carrasca and took a look at Eyrie 3. The nest was even more blown away than it had been before. I hiked out, up to the track, and then climbed to within 130 metres of the high Eyrie 1. It had been built up yet again, with fresh twigs and greenery draped all over it. Damn. It was impossibly high to work, and the best one could hope for there would be eagle flight pictures. I had more than enough of those from Scotland. But there were compensations − red beaked choughs were squabbling over nest hollows below the peak, ravens were flying, and in the pine woods one could find jays, magpies, mistle thrushes, fieldfares, and great and coal tits. There also I found a wild boar's bed. The animal had scuffed the sandy earth up in a big cool bowl almost one and a half metres long and one metre across, and near it was a stone marten's scat. Would I ever actually *see* one of these animals?

February 28 found me heading for Extremadura again. 'Suso' Garzon had now been appointed Director General of the Environment for the whole of Extremadura Province, which also gave him virtual control of Monfragüe Natural Park, but this elevated position did not prevent him promising to help me again to film vultures at a carcass.

I took a new route, west along the N342 to Guadix, where the high pinnacles strathed with brown rock and snow gave the first panorama of the Sierra Nevada, and then turned right up the winding N324 country road towards Jaen. Around the insular village of Huelma I saw that all the hills right up to their crests were covered with olive trees, and men were knocking the olives on to nets with sticks and cutting leafy branches as fodder for their animals. There were many spectacular cliffs and nesting sites near Jaen but not a single raptor did I see. There would not be much prey in these olive groves, where the earth beneath the trees was tilled free of all growth on which rabbits, voles and mice could feed.

I camped on the soft loam of a grove but was woken at 4 a.m. by rain thumping on the roof; in a few minutes the place would be a quagmire. I groaned and hurriedly dressed, but even after throwing down branches and heaps of stones, the van wheels spun uselessly. Only by putting the engine into first gear, letting out the clutch slowly, and pushing, did I get the vehicle free. Then I had to leap in, let out the clutch, and apply the brake before it took off down the track on its own. The odd thing was that the roof was covered in sand! It had probably been gathered up in a dust storm somewhere and had come down in the rain drops all over my van, which of course had been especially cleaned for the trip.

Next day, near Córdoba, I saw a white stork on a nest perched precariously on an electric pylon in the grounds of a newly built garage that was not yet operational. After the old ramshackle village of Espiel, the road degenerated, and I was lucky not to break a spring, but it improved again before Llerena, where I had time to film a red kite hunting the fertile red fields and vineyards. I dodged below Merida to take the Trujillo road and was surprised to locate six white stork nests on the roofs of two huge empty buildings on the outskirts of Miajadas. I could not see any storks actually in or near them, which seemed odd. Maybe they were just away feeding. I camped again by a bridge over the Burdalo river and filmed jackdaws nesting in holes in the stonework.

Before meeting Suso, I filmed griffons flying at Penafalcon, and also a rare black stork that was winging gracefully over the peaks with them, its red beak and legs showing clearly. A new large wooden public hide was being built at the Mirador de la Tajadilla, opposite the low vulture cliffs beside the dam. From it I located six nests, on four of which griffons were incubating their single eggs. Clearly Suso's plans to build hides and look-out posts for biologists and photographers, and to interest the public in the rare wildlife of the province, were going ahead quickly.

I found him with two biologists from the Balearic Islands, Juan Mayol Serra and Jorge Muntaner, who spoke good English. They had been checking black vulture nests, and the two men were taking back with them two black vulture chicks to rear to maturity in Mallorca before releasing them in the wild. The colony of this rare species on Mallorca had dwindled in recent years; indeed, in the previous year only a single chick had flown. Suso said the black vultures were now doing exceptionally well in Monfragüe and it was safe to allow a few to be taken for restocking former areas where the food supply was adequate. The two biologists assured me this was so in Mallorca, and invited me to visit any time I liked.

Suso talked more about the area's vultures. Monfragüe Park itself was important to them for breeding and nesting cliffs, but they ranged far beyond the Park boundaries for feeding. A griffon could range 30 km from its nest site, but the large black could range up to 50 km afield. Both birds could reach the foothills of the Sierra de Gredos from here! When hunting, they usually formed rough grids over the sky, high up, so that they could see one another over a vast area. One bird on the far side of the grid would spot some carrion and begin to go down to it. That purposeful downward flight would be seen by the next bird in the grid, and down it would wing too. Its rapid descent would be witnessed by the next, and the next — all the way back to birds still perched on the nesting cliffs. They too would fly off and join in the feast, though they might arrive an hour after the first birds had gone down. Vultures always scan the ground for dead animals and carrion but find such food more often by just watching each other.

While there are roughly 1,000 goats living in Monfragüe itself, providing say 100 dead animals a year for the vultures, over the entire area covered by the vultures there were 50,000 sheep, 10,000 cows, 18,000 goats, as well as many horses, pigs, wild red deer, wild boar, and *cabra montés* in the Gredos mountains. Imperial eagles do not range as far as the vultures, not more than 20 km from the nest.

I asked Suso how the lynxes were faring, and he replied not very well. I played what I thought was a trump card.

'Why don't you start a breeding project of rabbits for them? Get a hundred pairs, a hundred hutches and runs, and release the progeny into the wild? Imperial eagles would benefit too. I'd like to run such a scheme!'

Suso smiled. 'We are doing just that! We have got 30 rabbit breeding bunkers already, and round them we have planted 14 hectares of corn so the rabbits will go wild naturally.'

There would not be much I could suggest to this man that he had not thought of already, I reflected. When I told him that I would like to get another dead goat for the vultures, he introduced me to a tall young man with sleepy eyes whom I had not met before. José Antonio lived at Las Cansinas and had just been appointed Warden of the Park. The two men talked, José nodding his head occasionally but not smiling. Suso then turned to me and said that if I met José at midday he would have a dead goat for me, and it would cost 5,500 pesetas. The price had gone up again!

Next day we rattled over the sandy tracks out to the vultures' feeding site with a dead black goat and a new hide. To my surprise, José allowed me to choose where to put the hide. I found a spot between the thickest gum cistus bushes and faced it north, overlooking a flat open area which would be lit up by the sun from behind for most of the day. José spoke no English whatever but I understood him to say he had some German photographers coming in a few weeks and so he was glad to have help with erecting the hide. I used the twiggy debris left from the old *escondite* to bank up the bottom of the new one. These twisted stems also held up sprays of newly cut vegetation to help obscure the canvas walls. The tops of these sprays were held in place by a cord round the centre of the hide, and to this I also tied a wad of vegetation in order to camouflage the sides of the large twin camera holes. The top was also covered with cistus, pampas grass, rosemary and some kind of giant heather. I could see that José Antonio was watching all this very carefully. When I set up the camera and fixed heather sprays over the top of the long lens cap with a green elastic band, he whistled under his breath. As he wired the outer tops of the four poles to rocks, he told me he had never seen anyone camouflage a hide so much before. I said it was possible the birds would accept a plain canvas hide in time, but I had only a day and a half, and I wanted them to accept it immediately. It is always better to take trouble from the start and, if possible, to make a hide that the birds will not even notice. It marks the difference between professional and amateur. By the time we had finished it looked just like a natural dark part of a thicket in the bushes, and a human at 30 paces would not have known it was there. I think it was the way I built that hide that made José Antonio more friendly towards me than he might otherwise have been.

We staked the goat out 50 metres away, feet towards me this time. I rested its head on a flat rock, so that the camera would be able to see one eye and its horns clearly. It then began to rain. Would this be a repeat of the earlier disaster? But by 6 p.m. the sky had cleared again. Unable to turn my van on the soft narrow sandy tracks, I had to back it for a kilometre until I found a suitable camping spot for the night.

I rose in the dark, a quarter moon already rising. I had to hurry. I gulped down some toast and tea, put bread, cheese, two boiled eggs and tomatoes into my pack along with the movie camera gear (because of the rain shower I had left only the tripod and camouflaged lens hood in the hide) and tramped down the track. We had done our job so well I could hardly find the hide, but was set up by 7.16 a.m.

At 7.51 I was startled by harsh croaking calls. A raven had landed in a tree 50 metres away, but it flew off again after six minutes, passing right over the goat without going down to it. Soon a group of red-legged partridges went by the hide, making muted '*chuckar*' calls to each other, but they did not go into the open area where I could film them. Then three azure-winged magpies landed near the goat and began looking for food on the ground. At 11.50 a.m. two black vultures landed and stood 50 metres north west of the goat, half hidden by small cistus bushes. A minute later a third arrived but stood 25 yards east of the first two. They all looked about, scratching their heads or preening feathers. They did not seem to be at all hungry! Six minutes later two more blacks arrived, and one made a brief run over the ground with its head lowered but not towards the goat. Just past midday the first griffon landed behind the other vultures and stood still, occasionally preening.

At last I was able to film something more interesting for now the first pair of black vultures indulged in some courting behaviour. Both huge birds reached their beaks slowly down to their breasts, raised them again and touched the tips of each other's beaks as if offering a plucked feather but, in fact, no feathers had been plucked. They did this several times more, turning their heads from side to side as they nibbled affectionately at the tip of the other's beak. There was no doubt about it — the movements were gentle and loving. They were, in fact, *kissing*!

After some 20 minutes of this, the griffon walked over to the two blacks, as if to take a closer look at what they were up to, stood beside them for a few seconds (they made no attempt to drive it away), and then flew off and did not return. Four minutes later the lone black flew away, soon to be followed by the second pair. This just left the courting couple whose territory I presumed this was. At 12.54 one walked slowly behind the other, and they nibbled each other's beaks many times and also groomed each other's lower neck feathers. I changed lenses, so as to show more of the landscape, but when I looked back these two had also gone. None of the vultures had approached the goat after standing not far from it for more than an hour. Hell! Obviously they just were not hungry.

I was nibbling lunch at 1.25 p.m. when a huge white mastiff dog, one of the giant *mastíns* being bred at Las Cansinas, came out of nowhere and started sniffing at the goat. I took a few feet of film, then gave two loud roars which sent it scampering off through the bushes like a colossal puppy. Maybe it had been close much of the time and had scared the vultures away. Perhaps they would return now. At 3.00 I heard clonking bells, and a goat shepherd came over the ridge a kilometre away to the north west, bringing his herd nearer and nearer. It took them 40 minutes to reach the vultures' clearing. I had to walk out and try to tell him I was filming vultures. I think he said he had grazing rights in the area but would take the herd down to the shore of the Tagus river and back the way he had come on a lower route. As I went back to the hide he shouted at the goats, throwing stones to turn them round. The white *mastín* (which belonged to the shepherd) barked at me before leaving with its master and the goats. Naturally, although I waited until 6.30 p.m., to complete a 12-hour watch, the vultures did not return.

Next morning I was back in the hide by a minute after 7 o'clock. Nothing had touched the goat overnight. Two hours later a raven landed, walked round the goat but showed more interest in some remnants of old dried bone lying near by, for it tweaked off little pieces and swallowed them, as if needing the calcium. Maybe it did, for the eggs it was about to lay. After twenty more minutes there was a rush of air by the hide and a black vulture shot by; it swooped up briefly and landed three metres behind the goat, walking towards it, then stopping and preening its neck feathers. The raven glared at the black giant, waddled up to it, reached down and tweaked its tail feathers with its beak. The vulture did not appear to mind this treatment in the least. It walked to the piece of dry bone and picked it up. I stopped filming briefly, not realising that the raven was really intent on annoying the vulture, for suddenly it leaped into the air, bounced its feet off the placid vulture's head, landed beside it, strutted to the left and flew away. It was so funny I could hardly stifle a guffaw, particularly as once again the vulture made no response whatever. It just blinked, sadly, as if one just had to put up with this sort of treatment in life. A few minutes later the great bird crouched down momentarily and flew away. At 10.21 a.m. I saw that it, or another one, had landed 50 metres to the left of the goat. It stood about for a long time, occasionally preening, then walked straight past the carcass, stood for several minutes four metres to the right of it, then also flew away. And that was that.

I ran into José on the way out and told him I had been unlucky, but as the goat was untouched he should go in himself and get some good pictures, which he did. He seemed genuinely sorry, and said he hoped I would return and stay longer! He was right, of course. I should have had more than a day and a half in hand when trying to attract vultures to a fresh carcass. I had not realised just how lucky I had been that first time. But I had no complaints. Film of black vultures courting was a good deal rarer than of them feeding from a goat.

As I drove north to catch the ferry, fresh wonders of Spain appeared to my traveller's eyes – the beauty of Salamanca cathedral at sunset, new vulture ramparts past Villasquieza de las Torres with the birds wheeling over the lush pastures of the Rio Pisuerga, a quarry of nesting choughs and jackdaws near the 987-metres high Puerto de Pozazal, quaint mediaeval Reinosa with *áticos* jutting out over the narrow streets, all bustling with life . . .

For the first time, I boarded the ferry to return to Britain with reluctance. I knew the time had come for me to leave Scotland. As I watched through my porthole the lights of Spain slipping by and the dark open sea became my only view, I knew that once I had finished my new book and my Scottish wildlife film I would return here and find a new path. I would aim to leave on June 30, when 20 years of living in wild remote places would be completed.

Although I succeeded in filming the nesting divers on my home loch, the rest of that season was the most disastrous I had ever known in Scotland. A fox hunt blew up an eagle eyrie crag, apparently to free hounds trapped in a fissure below it. Eggs disappeared mysteriously from the best eyrie near me, and other nests failed due to cold wet weather. A fish farm moved tanks too close to the nesting divers, putting them off their eggs and allowing a predator to eat them. In order to get the tanks shifted back to a safer distance before next season, I stayed on nearly four months longer than I had intended, but it was worthwhile for it also ended in success. In mid-October I sold the remaining lease of Wildernesse to a lifeboat-man from Wales, who promised to let me visit whenever I wished. After a sad *au revoir* to Moobli's grave I returned to Spain. I did not take the movie equipment with me. After three years work I had been unable to sell my film to a television network and I could no longer afford the cost.

Black clouds filled the sky and rainstorms lashed the van as I drove south from Lerma almost to Honrubia de la Cuesta. Near the turn-off for Maderuelo I saw in the distance a farmer ploughing a field, with flocks of crows and ravens following behind the tractor. Some red kites were homing on to the area, and high in the sky about 20 griffons also headed in. The kites were attracted by the movements of the crows and the ravens, and the griffons saw all this and sailed in to investigate. They did not go down, however, but veered away to the south and vanished into the dull sky, having covered a great distance in mere minutes.

With the M30 Sur motorway running through the city, Madrid must be the fastest European capital to cross, and I was on the far side in 20 minutes without encountering a single red traffic light. The first thing I saw as I turned down the narrow bumpy little road from Totana to Mazarron was that all the trees that once lined it had gone, and with them had gone the nesting and hunting cover for some five pairs of little owls. Bulldozers had removed the lot and were now busy laying a wider road. What a diabolical lack of conservation there seemed to be in the development of this area. I saw only one little owl perched miserably on a low rock by the side of the road, staring at the ground for beetles on which to pounce. It was not much of a perch from which to hunt.

I rented the same villa as before and soon got down to the lonely slog of writing *Moobli,* the book I had vowed to write about my beloved and departed Alsatian. Once again I kept fit while I worked by taking long hard bike rides. More bulldozers had been at work here during my absence and I could find no trace at all of the foxes. Once I ran into, or cycled into, another aspect of the poor nature conservation in the area. I was returning from a long ride at about 20mph on the road from Mazarron to the Puerto when I saw a thick fog lying over the tomato fields and the road ahead. Thinking it was just a sea mist, I sped through it, breathing normally but heavily. I felt nothing untoward at the time, but my lungs hurt by the time I reached home, I could not stop sneezing and my eyes swelled up so much I could hardly see. I had to bathe them with clean water from the sides. It had not been fog or a sea mist at all but a cloud of pesticide, sprayed indiscriminately by a small plane. Here was the main tomato growing area in Spain, and this blanket spraying occurred at least twice in the season. No wonder there was such a dearth of small insectivorous birds in the region.

Just after Christmas, while I was driving through the mountains to Mazarron market, a small browny-blue bird shot out from the foliage and I heard a slight clonk on the bonnet. Looking back through the mirror, I saw it lying in the road. I was sure it was dead until I saw a wing move. I reversed the van and found the bird was still alive. It had grey-blue plumage, in fact, and bright red eyes. Its wings did not appear to be broken. I was sure it would die, however, for it had suffered quite a bang. I had seen a similar bird flitting about the bushes near the villa, and now that I had this one I would be able to identify it from my books. I put it on a woolly cloth in a cardboard box and took it home. It turned out to be a Marmora's warbler. I left it in the dark for a few hours. When I looked at it again at dusk, it kept raising and lowering its tail and fluttering its wings. I shaved tiny morsels of raw chicken, sausage, cockles and strewed them round the bird with breadcrumbs. I put a tiny pot of water in the box, then carried it to the top bedroom. I left the blind half up so that when dawn broke, after another long rest in the dark, it would see the food and eat it, or die.

Next morning the little bird was not only still alive but was out of the box on the tiled floor. It let me pick it up, looked at me without fear, then flew to the window sill. It had a bit of chicken on its beak but more than half the food was still uneaten. I picked it up again and let it go from the outdoor balcony. From its insectivorous beak I could see that it would be as hard to feed and keep alive as a wren. Outside, in the sun, lay its best chance. It fluttered down and landed in a bush. Immediately it started hopping about and climbing through the twigs, looking for food. I looked out again at lunchtime and was astonished to see that the other lone warbler of its kind had found it and the two were foraging for insects together. It was good to know that not only had the accident with my van not killed the little bird but that it might even have helped it find a mate.

10 · Nesting Eagles and the Red Villa

As the weeks passed and the typed pages of my book piled up, I began to miss the wildlife experiences I had enjoyed in Scotland. I needed a break from the routine of work at my desk and long lonely bike rides. On January 19, having obtained a new permit from Murcia, I hurried to Sierra Espuña convinced that, although it was not the nesting season, just to see an eagle would buck me up. I might even find some new eyries.

There were some low cliff faces east of Eyrie 3 and far below and south of Eyrie 1 in the high white and orange walls. I climbed down the gorge below Carrasca, negotiating small but deep *ramblas* on the way, and was surprised to find it was nearly 700 metres deep. I crossed the dry river bed and started the hard climb up the far side, pausing twice as my heart began pounding a bit too hard for comfort. Eventually I got up to a ridge at about 300 metres, which gave me a perfect view of the faces I had come to scan. Within moments I had located Eyrie 5, a deep nest which appeared to have been used during the last four years and was in the shadows at the bottom of the righthand face.

Needing a rest, I decided to stay awhile and keep my binoculars trained on the ridges above Eyrie 1 where I had often in the past seen the eagles. Within two minutes the male came sailing over. He landed on the peak to the left of the nest and right beside a brown lump, which, through the glasses, I realised was the female.

He raised his wings, made two clumsy hops and was on top of his spouse. He flapped his wings more slowly then, with curving whinnowing movements as if to keep his balance, and I realised he was mating with her. It was the first time I had seen eagles mating in Spain, and only the fourth time anywhere. I clapped on the X2 extender and took two pictures, but they were still too far away. After a few seconds the male flew away again, circling in the sun, showing fawny feathers on the underside of his wings. He headed right over the Espuña peak, ignoring the military encampment and the radar scanners, then treated me to four 'golden ball' yo-yo dives towards earth with his wings almost closed before sailing away to the south east. I waited almost an hour, but the female just stayed, preening her neck, chest and wings. Surely she would not use that high impossible eyrie yet again? On the hard return hike up the 700 metre gorge I went as of old, my heart apparently slotting back into the old trekking rhythms.

Early next morning, as I headed along the south side of the long valley of the Rio Espuña below the Morron (at 1,446 metres the second highest peak in the Sierra), I kept a sharp eye on the sky. Suddenly I saw a huge dark female eagle fly over the road ahead, sweep across the valley and vanish behind a tree-lined ridge which had a square rocky hump on it. It was a purposeful flight, not a wheeling, soaring, hunting flight, and she did not reappear. It was just possible there were some cliff faces behind the ridge and that she might have a nest in them. I made a note of the surroundings, especially the square rocky hump, for there was a firebreak in the trees leading almost up to it which would make climbing easier.

On the way back from the Casa Forestal after handing in my permit, I located Eyrie 6. The nest was on the left of a big orange double cliff, 800 metres past the first ruined building across the chasm. Further on I saw that there were indeed some cliffs behind the square hump, and that they contained a blob which could have been an eyrie. I would check there in the morning when the sun would be in the best position.

Next day brought the worst weather I had known in Spain. In the blizzard Espuña was out of the question, so I spent time writing some of the script of my unsold Scottish wildlife movie. With only two days left on my permit, and the weather little improved next morning, I drove back to Espuña. Snow lay about in small drifts and all the peaks were shrouded in mist. I contented myself with a drive round the north side of the mountain range, looking for eyries up small sand tracks. I found none, nor did I see an eagle, although there were many tall gloomy cliffs.

I felt I was wasting my time. As I headed down the east side of the Sierra towards Alhama de Murcia, I saw a large brown bird heading out from a fold in the hills. At first it looked like a large buzzard but its wings were too long. As it neared the van I leaped out to take a photo and saw it was a male golden eagle. It turned and circled over a small wood a few times, then carried on to the north east. It had come from the Barranco de Carboneras (gorge of the charcoal makers), which looked like ideal eagle territory. It was also far harder terrain for me to work than that of the pair on the west side of the Sierra. I drove back to Collado Bermejo, tramped down some wooded tracks, hoping for a glimpse of a wild boar, then camped early for the night.

The mist cleared next morning to reveal a fine sunny day, and I wasted no time. I drove up the gravel road on the north side of the Rio Espuña *rambla* below the looming Morron peak until I located the firebreak in the trees I had seen two days before. From that closer angle I could not see the tree-lined ridge with the square rocky hump on it. With heavy pack, I climbed up about 350 metres and was beginning to feel that I was on the wrong firebreak when suddenly, to my right, loomed up the square hump. It was at least seven metres across at the top. I scrambled round the lefthand side of it, where the terrain immediately began to descend again. Ahead were the cliff faces I had seen. It took only minutes to confirm that the blob I had glimpsed was indeed an eagle's nest. Here was Eyrie 7, built at the end of a long narrow ledge above a small ravine, and roughly at my eye level. It was directly in line with the route the female eagle had taken when she swept up this gully, but I could see no fresh leafy vegetation on the nest.

Maybe she would fly in again. I hiked down to the left until I reached some small pines, then set camera on tripod and focussed it on the eyrie. I was hidden by the trees from all but a direct frontal approach, yet I had the view of a wide panorama of sky. I sat down on a rock, ready for a long wait. After a few minutes I thought I might as well take a photo of the eyrie, stood up and did so, and was about to sit down again when something caught my eye near the top of the ravine to my left.

A huge female eagle was lurching ponderously through the air towards the eyrie no more than 30 metres away. I made the minimum movements back to the viewfinder, and I do not think she spotted me for she did not change her flight. The Spanish golden eagle belongs to the North African race and is said to be slightly smaller than the Scottish breed — an inch or so — but through the lens she was a galleon of a bird, as big as any I had seen in the Highlands. Nearer she came as I clicked off pictures, and while she *looked* cumbersome and even unwieldy, she glided along with majestic ease. She passed the eyrie, went away to my right, appeared to spot something, made two powerful beats of her wings and dived at great speed towards a red circular patch of earth below more high cliffs, then vanished behind a ridge.

A smaller male eagle flew up from where she had dived, then she too returned and flew up to join him. The two sailed and circled round each other several times, mounting higher and higher into the sky until they finally disappeared in the clouds. The day's sightings had been wonderful, but I was just as pleased by the fact that I had now located the territories of all three pairs of eagles in Sierra Espuña. After lunch I laboriously checked the first four eyries again, but none showed any signs of being freshly built up. Well, it was only January 23, still early yet.

This latest visit to the mountains made me more dissatisfied than ever with the boring and disturbed wildlife scene around my rented villa near the sea. Why did I not come and live here? My lawyer friend, Gregorio Parra, had offered to sell me his huge old sandstone mansion that stood in 250 acres of pines and almond trees on the edge of the Reserve five years ago, and the place was still empty. Maybe he would rent it to me for a few months. On the way down the mountain, I drove up the winding track to what I had come to call the Red Villa. Immediately a hoopoe flew up from below the two huge wooden front doors. A pair of jays rasped harshly from the nearby pines, and a swallowtail butterfly was flitting among pink and blue flowers already in bloom. There were no pesticide problems here.

To my surprise, Gerg said he would rent me the place, if we could agree on price. We met in Totana on February 4, so he could show me inside. To open the front doors, which would not have looked amiss on a cathedral, he produced a key nearly a foot long. It took a double wrench with both hands before the bolt crashed back and one door opened with loud groaning creaks. Inside, the Red Villa looked enormous, with a ballroom, and 20 other rooms. To my horror, the back door had been completely smashed in. The place was not secure, but Greg said he could have it all repaired. Upstairs was an attractive complex of three south-facing rooms, linked by delicate French windows with red lace curtains. The white ceilings were beautifully beamed and the floors were of smooth red tiles. I opened the long shutters in the central room, which I saw as my study, and found no glass in the windows. In fact, there was no glass in any of the windows in the entire mansion, except for a few panes in the room I chose for my bedroom. Well, I could use thick plastic sheeting in the few rooms I would use; the rest could just be protected by their shutters.

There were other drawbacks − no telephone and no electricity. The kitchen, which contained only a tiny marble sink and a small table, had a huge open fireplace ventilated by a wide chimney, down which icy gales would blow in winter. The bathroom contained a small shower unit, lavatory and washing basin, none of which worked as there was no water supply to the villa! All the pipes had broken down years ago and would cost a fortune to replace. Well, at least I would not have to battle up stormy lochs to reach the place, even if it would be the first remote home I had lived in without even water.

I took a look around the back and found a huge concrete reservoir filled with rough water from an irrigation channel, which was used some six times a year to flood the terraces of almond trees. This water was not drinkable, but a 120-foot siphon hosepipe would get it from the tank to the mansion, where I could fill three giant pitchers that stood in the kitchen. From them, I could extract jugs of water for washing and for flushing the loo. Water for cooking I could fetch in containers from a pure spring half a mile up the mountain about once a month, and in Spain I always bought my drinking water anyway. I have never cared much what a house is like as long as the roof does not leak. The surroundings in which the house stands have always been far more important to me, and on this Thursday afternoon the Red Villa in its pine tree setting, nestling below the great Espuña peak, seemed like another quiet paradise.

In the discussion that followed, I pointed out the lack of windows, phone, electricity, and water, and the shortage of furniture. Gregorio replied that he would have to repair the back door, that there were 21 rooms which could be used for many purposes, that it was peaceful and ideal for a writer . . . The upshot was that he rented the Red Villa to me for £5.50 a week! That was a fifth of what I was paying for the villa near the sea.

For a month I worked hard on the Moobli book and got up to the last three weeks of his life. I could not face writing about his end just yet, so I used the move to Red Villa to help me escape from painful memory. Twice I drove there with fully loaded van. I soon had the water siphon system working, a two-burner camp gas cooker installed, and thick PVC sheeting covering the missing windows in my upstairs study and bedroom.

It seemed a ghostly place on that first night of gales. The wind sighed through the mansion, the shutters rattled, the doors and beams creaked, and the spiral staircase made odd cracking noises. 21 rooms and air conditioning too! But the gusts died down next morning and I was woken by loud yaffling laughter as a green woodpecker landed on a lone snag near my van and made its maniacal calls. I could hear the songs of chaffinches, blackbirds, the twittering cadences of serins and the clarrion tones of a mistle thrush from further away. Outside I saw two swallowtails and a brimstone type of butterfly, with bright orange spots on its yellow forewings, all flying to the flowers for nectar. I was living in Sierra Espuña at last. It was the nesting season and time to start working with the golden eagles in earnest.

I was returning from Murcia with a new permit a few days later when I saw near the old monastery an animal running along an electricity cable by the side of the road. I leaped out of the van with the camera. It was one of the rare sub-species of Espuña squirrel, and it was using the smooth broad black plastic-covered cable as an easy route to get from place to place. It did not now have to leap from branch to precarious branch but could just go *hoppity hoppity* along the cable for considerable distances. Every time its long narrow aerial 'road' reached a tree, the squirrel froze and looked round for danger. Seeing none, it then hared along to the next post or tree, with no apparent fear of falling, and there stopped again. I followed it for half a kilometre where it leaped off into a pine tree for two more pictures.

It was 2.30 p.m. when I reached the Casa Forestal and found it closed, so I could not present my permit to José Miniano that day. When I saw the chain on the forestry track at La Carina was down, I took a chance and drove through. I decided to check the lower Eyrie 3 in the domed orange rock face above the great chasm first, though I felt sure it was now just an abandoned site. To confuse the guardas, for I did not want them hiking down to check my where-abouts, I went almost a kilometre past the trek-in spot and parked up near the pass. Then I clambered down through the woods and deep rocky gullies until I could see the eyrie face.

Just as I reached the rock-ribbed ridge above the twin pines on the edge of the abyss, which would make an ideal hide site, an eagle floated off the rock above the nest. I had no time to assemble the camera before it disappeared over the jagged shoulder ahead. I glassed the nest, and could hardly believe my eyes. It was completely built up, with fresh and yellowing sprigs of pine, and was almost two feet thick. At last, at last, five years after I had first found it, the ideal Eyrie 3 was being used for breeding. I had some hard and wonderful work ahead.

I hiked back up to the van and drove down the track, but now the damn chain was up and locked. I could not get out. I waited until dusk, but neither the guardas nor any other vehicle went past. I had no choice but to walk back to Red Villa, a distance I judged to be between three and four kilometres. It was soon obviously more than that, and after the five hard rocky kilometres already trekked, my knees began to hurt as I plodded down the steep hard roads. I kept taking short cuts across the tight bends by sliding down the treacherous shaley steeps between them and, oddly enough, the rough terrain and uneven movements eased my knee joints. I reached home in almost total darkness.

In the morning, to save my trekking legs for the hikes to the eyrie, I cycled back up to the van. Red Villa was almost 900 metres high, but it was still a hellish 400-metre climb above that to La Carina and the van, and the bike's English meter told me it was exactly five miles! It was bitterly cold and windy, and the van's bedding and cooking pans were all being used in the villa, so I could not even make a hot cup of tea. I ran up and down the track to keep warm until finally a white Land Rover appeared and I asked the driver to inform the Casa Forestal I was stuck behind the chain. In an hour, up tootled Pedro and Casimiro on their motor-bikes. They laughed as they let me out and urged me to borrow a key for the chain from José Miniano if I was going to work in that area for the week. I went straight to his home but had to wait three hours before he returned for lunch at 3 p.m. He was again charming and lent me the key, but by then it was too late to drive all the way back and hike down to the eyrie. A whole day wasted!

Up early next morning, I drove to the trek-in spot and hiked down through the woods. Although I now carried hide, tripod, camera gear, plastic foam to sit on, lunch and lengths of half-inch rope, I took a long route round the left of a knoll so as not to be seen from the eyrie. I cut about 50 leafy conifer twigs and sprays, tied them round the folded hide, and went almost to the edge of the trees to glass the nest. The female eagle was on it, her long tail cocked up in the air. I felt the old excitement, the surge of adrenalin, to be working once again with nesting eagles. She was probably on eggs, but in case she was not, and was just sitting on the nest, and would not return for days if disturbed, I belly-crawled to a thick black pine. I moved with aching slowness, keeping the tree between me and the nest, moving the camera and long lens carefully, little by little, so it did not make a tinny scraping noise on the rocks. On reaching the tree, I knelt up slowly, rested the camera against the trunk and took a few 'insurance' shots. She stayed on the nest. Leaving the camera by the tree, I shrank back until I reached the great bundle of the hide and its conifer sprays, and still she stayed put. Success, so far.

Now came the tricky part. I knew she would fly once I began erecting the hide, but it was hot, and with the sun shining on the eyrie, the eggs, if there were any, would keep warm for a good while. I had to do as much as possible *before* she flew, and try to make sure she did not actually see me. I began the long belly-crawl, towing the hide inch by inch by my side. I reached the camera and began inching it forward with my other hand. I used some short rosemary bushes as cover when going over an awkward rise, and reached the barrier screen of rocks and branches I had erected three years ago.

Glad as I was that I had built it, I realised it was not quite high enough to hide the big pack on my back. Afraid the eagle might see it moving, I went even more slowly. It was hell on my knees, hands and elbows now for sharp rock projected everywhere. At the last moment I had to crawl through a large rosemary bush in order to keep one of the twin pine trees between me and the nest. Quietly I sorted everything out, hid the camera by a tree trunk, tied anchor rocks to the ropes for the rear two poles of the hide, and not until I started to inch up the front poles from inside the hide did she take off. Swiftly I slid inside the rear flap so that she could not see me, waited a couple of minutes, searched the sky through a side panel, saw she was not about, and began to work with maniacal speed. The site was even better than I remembered. Two branches projected from one of the pines right across the front of the hide, yet they did not obscure the camera hole at the height the camera had to be on the tripod. I tied the two front poles to the top branch for rigidity, then disguised the hide's front by stuffing the biggest pine sprays between it and the branches. I set the rear poles with the rock-anchored ropes, weaved foliage into and round the top and side cords, spread more over the top, and in twenty minutes the hide was finished. I set up the camera and from inside worked a few more sprays round the viewing holes to complete the job. When I looked through the lens I could clearly see the tops of two whitish eggs in the nest. It was 11.26 a.m. I waited anxiously, for I knew I had taken risks, but after 13 years of working with eagles at the nest I thought I knew what I was doing.

At 12.23 I looked through the lens just as she landed back on the nest and I took the first pictures. Being a Spanish golden eagle, belonging to the smaller North African race, her plumage was of a lighter colour than her Scottish counterpart, but she was still a mighty impressive bird. She stood looking down at her eggs for a few seconds, as if checking that they were all right. Then she shuffled, face towards me, over them and shifted rhythmically from side to side, as if performing a rhumba, before very slowly sinking down. Not satisfied, she stood up again and enacted a slower and more jerky rhumba before finally settling on the eggs. Then she leaned her closed wings out slightly to the side and relaxed completely. She was obviously getting the eggs into her plumage, making sure her warm special incubating plumes were spread all round them. At 1.35 p.m. she stood up slowly, turned towards the front of the nest and settled down again with another rhumba. Four minutes later she stood, walked to the edge of the nest and took off.

What was wrong? Nothing apparently, for after three minutes she swept in again and went on to the eggs with very little ceremony. By now the sun had moved and was striking the bottom of the long lens hood, bouncing light up on to the glass so that good pictures were impossible. I would have to remove it. At 2.02 p.m. the eagle stepped to the edge of the nest and again flew away. I realised then that this one had been the male, for immediately the slightly larger female soared back, and the size difference was obvious. I was in the act of unscrewing the lens hood with a brown glove but she did not see me. This time she gently shifted the eggs into a different position with her huge hooked bill before another settling rhumba.

I had never used a square canvas hide for eagles before, yet neither eagle appeared aware of it, so perfect was the position. I had to use one here, not only to prevent a poisonous snake from slithering near my face but because in this sharp rocky terrain there was nowhere large and flat enough to use my lying-down hides. At 2.19 she took off again, and I got some flight shots.

A minute later I was startled by loud '*kri kri*' calls and the batter-whirring of big wings. I hoped it was not an eagle that had suddenly noticed the hide and was angrily about to rip into it. The wing noises seemed too fast for an eagle. Then I heard a deafening thudding, and through the side panel saw that a huge green woodpecker had landed on the pine trunk right by the hide, less than a metre from my head, and was the creator of all the racket. What a din!

At 2.22 p.m. the male eagle flew back. I noticed that he performed a very poor version of a rhumba on to the eggs, far more perfunctory, and not taking half as much care as the female. By 3.23 the sun was hazing up the lens even worse. I left all the camera gear in place, slid out and belly-crawled carefully up to the woods, delighted when I looked back to see I had not put the male off the nest.

I was camping at 1,350 metres (roughly the height of Ben Nevis in Scotland) and it was a bitterly cold night, well below zero. I shivered under the inadequate blankets, cursing the fact that I had left my sleeping bag at the villa. I was determined to put in a really full day recording the exact timings of the nest change-overs. I had never watched eagles on eggs from a hide before, and these birds were relieving each other far more frequently than Scottish eagles.

It was already hot and sunny when I reached the edge of the woods at 7.20 a.m. and saw that there was no eagle on the nest. I was 150 metres from the hide when the female sailed in, wheeled above the eyrie, then took off in a jet glide to the east. What luck! My hands, elbows and knees were scraped and sore from crawling over the rocks the day before, so I just ran down to the hide and got in.

The day's change-overs went as follows —

7.59 a.m. Male came in, looked at eggs, and left again.
8.18. Female returned, peered down at eggs, then settled on them. She looked up once at the male flying overhead.
9.05. She stood up, pulled nest twigs and fibres about with her beak, re-arranging them, then settled on the eggs again. Sand martins flew all round the nest but she took no notice.

9.30. She turned the eggs, tugged at more fibres, and rhumba'd down on to the eggs while facing the cliff wall.

10.58. She got up, turned the eggs, preened her right wing and sat down again.

11.18. After turning the eggs, she walked to edge of the nest and took off. Immediately the male flew in, walked to eggs and settled on them.

1.40 p.m. Male left the nest.

2.20. Female back, settled on the eggs with long rhumba. Forty minutes seemed a long gap, but during this interval sun was on the eggs. From time to time she made brief sideways wriggles on them.

2.50. She looked out and up as if she could see the male flying. She stood, took two steps to edge of the nest and flew out.

2.55. Male flew in, made brief rhumba on to eggs while facing away from hide. Preened his back feathers.

3.15. He stood, turned the eggs with his beak, then made a brief rhumba down again.

3.25. Adjusted the eggs again before moving to the edge of the nest. Female came in, also adjusting the eggs as the male flew off. Rhumba on to eggs.

3.40. She put her head forward on to the nest and dozed with eyes closed, occasionally waking to look around.

3.55. She stood up and flew away. Twenty seconds later the male flew in, settled on eggs facing out from the cliff.

4.06. He became more alert, stood up and departed. Half a minute later the female came back, turned the eggs briefly, and settled on them while facing the hide. It was obvious now that the two birds could see each other coming from a long distance. She rearranged nest twigs while still on the eggs, then kept still until 4.20 p.m. when she became very alert, looking around.

4.25. She stood, took several steps and flew off.

4.35. I heard little squeaks, apparently made by the female as she flew in. She inspected the eggs, made a long rhumba on to them, facing away from hide. She looked out, and I heard more squeaks, then she moved to the edge of the nest and flew off calling '*K'yew, k'yew*' quite loudly. She must have thought the male was coming in when she left before and was now expressing her annoyance that he had not!

4.40. Male came in, looked towards the hide, settled on eggs and spread his wings over half the nest. He nibbled nest twigs with his beak.

4.55. He looked out, squeaked, stood up and left.

4.57. Female back, settled on eggs, facing cliff wall.

5.31. She stood up, walked to the nest edge and glided away.

By this time I had endured nearly ten hours in hunched up positions and had had enough. I looked out of the hide, saw no eagles in the air and, leaving all the gear in position, walked quickly away. I felt it was safer to do this than to make a laborious belly-crawl to the woods when I could so easily be seen from the sky if one of the eagles returned while I was doing so. I found it fascinating that the eagles had exchanged incubation duties no less than nine times, far more often than at any Scottish eyrie I had known. As I climbed back up to the van, I saw dark clouds gathering above the peaks. It looked as if the weather was going to break.

Next morning there was thick mist everywhere and spatters of rain. I waited for two hours, but the weather grew worse and I was afraid I might not get out at all if the track became a quagmire. I drove back to Red Villa. I had no choice but to leave the camera gear in the hide, for I could not risk putting the eagles off their eggs for even a few minutes in such weather. As it was my last permitted day, I returned the key to José Miniano. After two wonderful days, rain had stopped play. Back at the villa, I gathered some pine cones and boiled up a cauldron of water to wash my hair and bathe away the sweat from my body. I was abed before dark.

One look at the yellow gold of the sun rising into blue sky next morning sent me roaring back to La Carina, permit or not. The chain was across the road, but with no gear to carry except an empty pack I stormed along the track and down to the eyrie. I had to collect my camera, after all, had I not? No eagles were on the nest or in the sky. I hurried into the hide. The female returned only eleven minutes later. For some reason, it took 4½ hours to collect my gear, in which time I saw three more change-overs and took the last of nearly 150 pictures!

I noticed the female always took about half an hour off in the warm afternoons, whether the male had returned or not. When she left the nest at 1.55 p.m. I took the opportunity to strike the hide quickly. I left the site pristine and made the laborious climb up and back to the van with it and all the camera gear. I now had to be sure the eagles were back on the nest, particularly as it was clouding over again and looked like rain. I rested over lunch, then drove to an old disused track on the far side of the canyon from the nest.

Light rain began to fall fitfully as I plodded down. Tired from carrying all the gear so far, I took only my binoculars. I hiked almost a mile before finding a tree-covered rocky spur that projected out over the great gorge opposite the eyrie. I climbed to the end of it and glassed the nest. Yes, there was the dark elongated form of an eagle on it. Good. Well, that was that.

As I walked back along the now wet track, I heard a gnawing, cracking sound — '*rack rack rack*' — like a rat chewing wood, though much louder, stronger, more powerful. It was coming from the woods below me. I looked down and saw between the foliage of the bushes a red-brown animal, almost auburn, like a pine marten, moving just 35 metres away. I could see another one, just behind it, also partly obscured by leaves. I waited, watching intently, then realised I had been mistaken — it was all one animal. I saw a 3-inch or longer tusk and a long snout, then the wicked little eye. It was a wild boar! And it was sharpening the other tusk on the bark of a tree, thoroughly enjoying itself, the eye half closed, making that racking din.

I did not know whether to run back for the camera or just run! Would it attack or run away? My heart was thumping, but this was too good a chance to miss. I stole away and, when lost to view, hurried to the van. I saw huge trotter marks in the mud of the track, then light patches on the trunks of two pines which the boar must have used as rubbing posts. I put a new film in the camera, hurried back and began stalking carefully when I reached the area where I had seen the boar. I had been ready to believe the wild boars of Espuña a myth; what I had seen was no damn myth! It looked about five feet long and heavily built.

Though I was scared, the short axe I carried in my right hand gave me a little Dutch courage. Gingerly I crept through the woods in a wide circle, but the boar was nowhere to be found. My first sighting of a truly wild boar in Spain and I had missed the opportunity to photograph it! I was so angry with myself for not obeying my own rule — ALWAYS to carry a camera in the wilds — that I hardly noticed the rain now pelting down. I had to be content with pictures of the tracks, of the tusking-tree where bark had been razed away, and of the two rubbing trees where the boar's rough flanks and neck had

103

made the bark of the black pines a smooth dull red. My clothes were soaked when I reached the van again. I had trekked 15 hard mountain kilometres that day, a third of it with 65lbs of hide and gear, and was so tired when I got home that I postponed my cone-fire bath until the morning.

For ten days afterwards I had to catch up with the desk work I found so tedious, but I enjoyed editing down some of the spools of my Scottish wildlife film on a little battery editor. I had resolved that if I failed to get any kind of television deal from that lot I would stop filming altogether. It had already cost me about £7,500 and I could not afford any more.

One Sunday morning, while I was at my desk, I was startled by the noise of children yelling and youths shouting behind the villa. Several families had hiked over from a Christian Community's permanent camp site almost 1,700 metres away in the woods and were having fun round my water reservoir. Children were gleefully scooping up water with their hands and poking sticks at the goldfish. They left politely enough when I explained that the villa was now occupied and that I was a writer who needed quiet in which to work. Within minutes another group followed the concrete irrigation channel down from the public picnic site above the villa and began the same hijinks. They too left when asked, but half an hour later I saw more families heading down through the trees. I could not spend all my time turning people away. I gave up and spent the rest of the day on the beach, camping out and returning on Monday morning when they were all back at home, work or school. This kind of disturbance did not happen every weekend, but it occurred often enough to make me realise that the Red Villa could be only a temporary home.

I returned to the high woods and peaks of Espuña on March 31 in search of boars. I trekked almost 700 metres down the steep, winding disused forestry tracks to the bottom of the gorge, where I found another cool earth 'bed' rooted out by a boar, but that was all.

After climbing back up, I sat on the edge of the high rocky spur which gave a magnificent view of the entire gorge and tried to spot one of the animals in the clearings between the trees, but had no luck. From time to time I glassed the eagles' nest. One of the birds was on

Nestling amid the pines below the Espuña peak, the Red Villa had 21 rooms but no gas, electricity or water supply, and no glass in most of the windows.

The golden eagles of Sierra Espuña exchanged egg incubation duties far more often than Scottish eagles.

The elusive greater flamingos are susceptible to harsh winters, and this migrant colony at Santa Pola has not nested here in twenty years.

After drinking from a water conduit, the fox stood on a small ridge only 20 metres away and looked back at me.

A pair of Egyptian vultures perch beside the road to Monfragüe, plumage bedraggled in the rain.

The gaudy hoopoes had four chicks in a tree-hole nest and flew in often to feed them.

The Egyptian vulture whistled close by on its way to the nest . . . where it landed by its mate, to take over incubation duties.

Two of Spain's most colourful birds – the bee-eater, which is being mobbed by cheeky sparrows and the azure-winged magpie.

it but I was not sure which until I saw the smaller male circling higher and higher above the eyrie on a thermal. He reached a height of about 2,300 metres and then went into a jet glide, his wings half back, and zoomed towards the Espuña peak at terrific speed.

I thought he was going right over the top, but no, his dark dot started diving down steeply below it. He braked with suddenly-opened wings and hit into something on the ground, or that is how it appeared. Although the distance was great, I could see something brown jumping about, probably a rabbit. The eagle bounced and ran over the ground, flapping his wings for speed and balance. Either he had missed with the first strike or he had failed to injure the creature enough to stop it. I saw him pull up after almost crashing into thick bushes. He just stood there for a while, probably feeling both disappointed and foolish. Presently he flapped away to the right and I lost sight of him because of the trees in the way.

On the way back I drove down a little track through the woods to an irrigation reservoir filled by a spring where I wanted to fill ten 5-litre containers with water for cooking. Suddenly I saw a large dog fox leap up on to the concrete water channel and bend down to lap water from it. He heard the van, looked back briefly, then leaped down and dived below a bridge over a gully. I pulled up, grabbed the camera and without any pretence at stalking, dashed to the bridge, knelt down and poked the lens round the side of the parapet.

To my astonishment, the fox was standing on a little ridge by a dead bush, looking back at me from 20 metres away! He was so close I could only see his head, chest and half of his back in the 640mm lens. He was much greyer than a Scottish fox. Somehow I managed to undo and pull out the close-work pillar, focus with the pistol grip of the Novoflex barrel, and take one picture of the fox with black nostrils and whiskers quivering before he dashed away. It turned out to be the best picture I ever took of a wild fox in Spain.

Now that I had truly cut my Spanish wildlife teeth on Sierra Espuña, it was time to get to grips with the really hard stuff.

_11_ · _Exploring Extremadura_

On April 3 I packed the van and set off for the wild bosquy mountains of Extremadura, treating myself first to a rare four-course blow-out of a lunch at Tino's, the Italian restaurant in Cartegena, for a mere £6.50 — to set myself up for the trip. The waiters were more than helpful. When I mentioned to them that I had been reduced to using candles in my home because I had been unable to find paraffin on sale anywhere in Spain, they produced a Spanish-English dictionary the size of a family Bible. After consulting it and discovering that the word in Spanish was not '_kerosina_' but '_petróleo_', I was given a street map with the place where I could buy some marked on it. I dashed round to a little red pump, which an old woman ran for her living, and filled a 5-gallon can. I could now run the little hurricane lamps in my van.

I took the scenic route from Totana which cut across country to Tallente. The road was very rough in places, but I was glad to have come this way when I chanced upon the most beautiful field of wild flowers I had ever seen — buttercups, purple bells, blooms like huge Michaelmas daisies with bright yellow petals and dark brown centres, and others I could not name among the host of poppies of a startling vivid red. I stopped and sat by the field, feeling I had entered paradise. It was a sight to have entranced the Impressionist painter Renoir. There was hardly a square inch without a flower head waving in the breeze and blazing in the sun. A choir of angels could not inspire one

106

more. If I had another lifetime I would write a book about the wild
flowers of Spain, which begin to bloom in the middle of January, for
here grow more than half of Europe's 10,000 known varieties.

While looking for a wine *bodega* in Lorca I saw a hide-tanning
factory, where cowhides, turned inside out and dripping blood, were
being wheeled about on fork lift trucks. The smell was appalling and
seemed particularly offensive to my self-righteous nostrils, for I was
trying to be a vegetarian and had not eaten meat for four months.
There was also a huge aluminium cement factory in the town that
exuded black sediment into the river and looked like a Fred Karno
imitation of Cape Canaveral.

Heading high into the mountains, I ran into a snow blizzard near
Las Vertientes, which boded ill for my van without 4-wheel drive. I
almost turned back. Then I thought — what the hell! Having driven
this far, I would try to fight my way through and down to Baza,
where it might only be raining. It was, and I bowled on up the
C323 towards Cazorla. I found a camping spot above the Embalse
del Negratin where the mud was not thick enough to bog down the
van. Just before sunset I looked out to see the clouds on the horizon
had formed themselves into the perfect image of an eagle sitting on its
nest. While I watched, the shape changed into the precise form of the
carved driftwood 'running rooster' given to me as a talisman by the
old log craftsman Ed Louette in the Canadian wilderness twenty years
before. As I took pictures, I could not help feeling that these strange
occurrences were a good omen.

Flocks of goldfinches greeted my awakening, and as I toasted bread
for breakfast I saw a peregrine fly from the top dead branch of a pine.
Towards Cazorla town I could see the high peaks covered by lowering clouds, and it was clearly snowing in the middle of the sierra.
Up at the 1,183-metre-high Puerto de Tiscar patchy snow lay everywhere. I saw griffons, looking hugely inappropriate as they soared
past the snow-covered rocks on the steep hills. There seemed to be a
denuded colony in some high orange cliffs 3 km further on and I
tried to approach it up a small track but the van began to waltz, the
wheels to spin on the snow-covered marshy ground, so I turned back.

In Cazorla I had difficulty finding the road to Burunchel, but once
past the village it wound steeply down to the valley. I went past the
lefthand turning to the Embalse del Tranco de Beas in order to take a
lovely picture of the birthplace of the Guadalquivir river. The water
was only just over a metre wide here, splashing down in many little

waterfalls. The road to El Tranco ran alongside the river in places, and I could see the silver sides of fish turning over. Some of the trout in shallow pools were a good two feet long, but notices saying that fishing was private enabled me to resist the temptation to have a go with the rod and line I always take with me. I went past the village of Torre del Vinagre, saw more griffons on the cliffs over the river and camped up on a little plateau in the forest. My only map of the Sierra was in German, and I was amused by the names of some of the animals.

'Tomorrow,' I muttered in my stage German accent, 'I vill go in search of ze vildschwein and ze damwild!'(wild boar and fallow deer).

Driving past the beautiful Embalse next morning, the air misty and a little drizzly, I saw three red deer grazing in an open firebreak above the banks. I parked in some trees, stalked back through them and got two pictures of their rumps. I had to say 'Hey!' to get them to look up and turn round for better photos. Just then I heard an odd snorting grunt but thought it just another hind giving a warning bark from somewhere in the bushes. To my great surprise, and intense dismay, a jet black wild pig, built heavy in the forequarters like a wild boar, came from behind a bush lower down in the firebreak and started trotting quickly − yes, trotting, not running − away to the right. I tried to focus on the wild sow but missed, and saw three little furry brown piglets running with her. Then two got up from where they had been lying in a thicket and also chased after her. I didn't get them either!

What with not having my camera when seeing the wild boar in Espūna and now missing the chance of these shots, I felt I must be losing my touch and that, at 59, my reflexes had slowed badly. I tried to stalk them and went down the very steep terrain to where it ended as small cliffs above the Embalse, but between the trees the wind was switching all over the place and of course I never saw them again.

Towards the end of the Embalse, I passed another firebreak and saw a thick post in the water. The top of it looked oddly aslant. I thought it might be a bird and glassed it with my binoculars. It was an osprey! I tried to stalk it, again going all the way down through the trees. When I emerged into the open, it had gone, probably having heard my footsteps.

I thought of putting up a hide and waiting the whole day, for this might be one of its favourite fishing posts, but soon realised I would be wasting my time. This was clearly a migrant bird. The osprey, or 'fish eagle', is now a very rare breeder in Spain, with only about 20 pairs nesting, mainly in the south eastern coastal areas. The decline in recent years is believed to be due to pollution of the Mediterranean and a decrease in its fish prey. Many ospreys, however, migrate through Spain in autumn and early spring, to and from their wintering areas in north and tropical Africa. The bird I had seen could well have been on its way to nest in Scotland. It was certainly pointed to the north! The only other birds I could see out on the waters were two swimming mergansers. I went over the hydro-electric dam near the end of the Embalse and turned left for Villanueva del Arzobispo. Vast, dramatic sandstone cliffs along here with many holes in them rose up but I saw no vultures. There were olive groves right up to 1,650 metres on the steep hillsides, so I supposed there was not enough dead farmstock or wild animals to support them.

The terrain changed near Arzobispo to rolling downland, and before I reached Villacarrillo the rain was pouring down like it does in a Scottish winter, and I could not see for more than a kilometre ahead. I saw the first white stork nest on a house roof just after Ubeda. The Guadalimar river before Linares was now running red from the sandstone washed down. Rain and dark stopped me before Córdoba, and I camped in an open spot up the country road between Villafranca and Adamuz.

It was lucky I did, for the first thing I saw when driving away next morning was a white stork stalking through a marshy farm field, and I took two photos. Nearing Córdoba, I stopped as I saw another on its nest on a beautiful baronial-style farmhouse with yellow bay windows. I backed up a muddy track, rested my lens on the farm wall and took many good pictures. I had to wait until the bird stopped preening, for while it was doing that it looked just like a bundle of old feathers on stilts. At Córdoba the signs quickly routed me round the town on to the N432, but after Fuente Obéjuna the road became so rough and filled with potholes that I thought I had ended up on a private track to a farm. A quick lunch at La Coronada (which sounds like the Spanish medical name for a heart attack) and I was in far greener, fertile and arable country. I saw five red kites before Azuaga but, by this time, a hard gale was blowing and they were moving too fast for good photos. Several white storks were stalking daintily in a field near the road, then I saw a huge bluish white bird with black tips to its long supple wings which were bending up in the winds.

It was a cock hen harrier, and I saw that it was hunting over the wheat fields with its drabber, browner mate. They too were being buffeted by the gale, in and out of focus in the camera in seconds. They were using the wind cleverly to help them to scour the land, allowing it to blow them along, then turning with wings lifted like giant moths and switching their long tails all over the place so that they could hover while looking down for insect and beetle prey. At Llerena a white stork was sitting on eggs in a huge nest on the bell-shaped church tower. I photographed her mate soaring in with food in his beak for her. Near the N630 turn-off for Mérida and Cáceres I saw another male harrier hawking along the verges of the road which, at that point, were ploughed up. It was a little smaller than the first and when I saw the beautiful dark brown bars on its underwings I realised it was a male Montagu's harrier — a rare bird in Britain, where there are only about 20 breeding pairs left. It too was being buffeted by the gale but it was working sideways with the wind. It could go to the verge, be blown back, then glide round again, in a semi-circle forwards, constantly travelling the way I was going. I kept trying to catch it up, stop, grab the camera and poke it through the window, but after one or two shots it would be a hundred yards further down the road. It seemed to be using the road as a boundary, not wanting to cross it. I hit on a cunning idea, reckoning that if I drove two or three hundred yards ahead I would have time to get out with the camera and be ready before it came close again. It not only did just that but repeated it three times, talking no notice of the van, me, or the camera. Although the sky had clouded over, making fast shutter speeds impossible, I took some fine pictures of it. I could see its yellow eyes, talons and its barred under-plumage clearly. What a wonderful road this was!

At dusk I camped down a blind turn-off by a railway tunnel just before Almendralejo. I woke at 4 a.m. with an uneasy feeling and saw the light of a dim torch shining on me through the window. I yelled '*Vamos! Marcharse!*' and gave two Alsatian-type barks while putting on boots and trousers. I leaped out with my axe. All I could hear was the sound of rapidly receding footsteps as the intruder made a speedy getaway.

Next morning it was sousing down with rain, and it took a long wet search in Mérida before I found the smart new office befitting Jesus 'Suso' Garzon's status as Extremadura's Director General del Medio Ambiente. Surrounded by a gaggle of secretaries and piles of documents, his huge form looked out of place behind a desk, but he crushed my hand and gave me an effusive welcome. I explained that I had just dropped in for a chat, and to give him my two latest books, as I was on the way to Cáceres to get a permit from the new Director of Monfragüe Natural Park. Suso astonished me by saying –

'It is not necessary for you to go to Cáceres. *I* can give you the permissions, for Monfragüe and for all Extremadura.'

This would save me a lot of trouble, and as I thanked him he instructed a secretary to type out the permits there and then. I asked him how he liked his new job. He shrugged, indicated his full desk and said he preferred to be like me, always working out in the field. I had the feeling then that even this prestigious job would before long prove too tame for a man with his extraordinary outdoor talents. Suso told me he had heard there was a wolf reserve just above the town of Oropesa. If I enquired in that town I would be sure to find it. I decided to look for it after I had been to see the new warden at Monfragüe, José Antonio, and find out the prospects for working with the rare nesting birds.

When I reached Monfragüe, I was surprised to find the Castillo completely rebuilt, the large wooden public hide on the river bank opposite the low vulture cliffs had been completed, too, and a house in Villa Real had been converted into an education centre. Busloads of youngsters from schools and universities were being brought in to learn about Spain's finest wildlife heritage at first hand. The system of summer wardens and part time 'vigilantes' to guide people round the public areas, and to accompany a few experts in the forbidden areas, had already been started. All the ideas Suso and I had discussed three years earlier were now being put into action, and the place was becoming a model for similar parks all over the country.

When I met José Antonio, he greeted me with unsmiling reserve. He remembered me as the expert at building hides and said he could probably help to photograph two species of vultures at the nest, but the rare black stork would depend on whether a suitable nest was being used. The imperial eagle, however, was definitely not possible. These birds, he told me stiffly, had suffered two bad breeding years and no licences had been issued during them. None would be granted this year either. I was deeply disappointed, but resolved to find my own imperial eagle nest outside the Park. Most of all, I wanted to enter my 60th year in a hide overlooking an imperial eagle's nest, just as I had spent every birthday in most of the last eleven years watching golden eagles in Scotland.

On my way out, I visited the observatory Suso had made below Penafalcon and photographed flying vultures. Suddenly a black stork came soaring down with nesting foliage in its feet. It looked like a long skinny arrow, a good six feet long from the tip of its red beak to the end of the trailing fronds. It banked rapidly below the trees and vanished round a low bluff. I hiked over the nearly sheer ground below the trees and found her on a nest in a rocky crevice some 30 metres above the river. The distance was really too great for decent pictures.

I drove along the country road to Jaraicejo in showers of rain, then was startled to see a huge orangey-coloured bird on the top of a cork tree. Was it an imperial eagle on its nest? As I drew nearer I saw it was a griffon vulture sunning its wings. I took pictures, then saw two more on trees on the right of the road. They too were holding open their great wings, shining like dark coppery beacons, drying them off after being drenched in the showers. A little further on I saw an Egyptian vulture perched on an old stump, then another sunning its wings while standing on the ground. I had just finished photographing them when an imperial eagle landed on a metal electricity pole, its silvery wing epaulettes showing clearly. My eye was caught by two smaller birds flying near it – a pair of black kites, flapping slowly but buoyantly along. I had seen all these rare birds in the space of just ten minutes. What a place!

Next day I set off to look for the wolf reserve above Oropesa. I had plenty of time, for the town was only 60 km away, and turned down a small road to take a look at the Embalse de Valdecañas. There was a fine stretch of water, a bulge in the Guadiana river, and I saw the cream and black form of an Egyptian vulture flying above it. I kept the glasses on the bird as it wheeled airily around before landing on a ledge in some small cliffs at the top of a hill, right beside another vulture which was clearly its mate. This must be their nesting ledge, and it appeared an easy place to work from a hide for there was a jutting flat-topped buttress only 30 metres away and at the same height as the ledge. I was reaching into the van to mark the place on my map when I heard a swishing sound above. A superb large creamy-speckled bird with a big hooked beak sailed close over my head. It was the nearest I had been so far to a booted eagle. I hoped it would show me its nest tree, but it was too early, for these eagles lay their two white and brown-patched eggs in early May, and it just soared on over the ridge.

After buying groceries and new film in Navalmoral de la Mata I was driving towards Talavera de la Reina when I saw three huge dark vultures in a field more than half a kilometre away. They were in a shallow dell and feeding from a white lamb carcass. I hiked up a long rise, bent double as I neared the top and managed to take two pictures of the black vultures before they spotted me and flapped away on their 9-foot wings.

In Oropesa my enquiries about wolves produced paroxysms of laughter from two men who told me there had not been any wild wolves in the *campo* round there for over a century. Nor had they heard of any special reserve. I wondered if Suso had made an uncharacteristic mistake. Well, he had said it was above the town, so I took the bumpy road up towards Candeleda.

After less than a kilometre or so I saw dozens of large birds wheeling over and landing on what looked like a rubbish tip by the side of the road. They were mainly red kites, white storks and ravens. I had never seen so many of these birds together before, especially red kites. I pulled into the dump, got out and was nearly sick from the terrible stench. Apart from normal domestic rubbish, it was also a repository for slaughterhouse carrion. There were hogs heads and legs, guts and rotting sheepskins everywhere. I braved it out for half an hour after tying a handkerchief over my nose and took fine shots of the storks sailing down in twos and threes, and of the great fork-tailed kites flapping around in that characteristic fashion where the shoulder bows of their wings are brought so far forward on each stroke that they look as if they are trying to shield their heads and eyes from your view. The storks seemed to be after insects and lizards but the kites were also taking the stinking carrion. Red kites were common scavengers in the streets of London before the Great Plague of 1666. Beautiful birds maybe, but they do not have the nicest of appetites.

Further up the road I pulled up when a huge red bird sailed past the windscreen and turned to circle over a large clearing in the cork trees. It was being intermittently mobbed by a small group of ravens, crows and red kites. I had never seen the like of this bird, looking similar to a huge kite, the sun gleaming on its bright coppery plumage. It dodged the dives of the smaller birds, turned over to rake at them with its talons and landed, bewildered and upset. I leaped out and took pictures, not knowing then that it was an immature imperial eagle which does not grow the dark adult plumage until it is three years old. When it flew out of sight, I drove on and stopped for lunch in a roadside clearing opposite the beautiful Tiétar river, which here was flowing through fertile green pastures and woods.

Suddenly I saw through the windows what looked like a small black vulture in the sky. Up with the glasses, and as it came nearer I saw it was not. There was the eagle shape, with longer tail and smaller size – then I saw the white shoulder epaulettes gleaming in the sun. It was an adult imperial eagle. I leaped out to take photos before she turned, dived down with talons out and landed on a flat-topped olive tree against the skyline on a ridge. Had she got a nest there? Surely the tree was too small, though its flat top was formed above three forks in the trunk. She launched from the top of the olive, flapped towards me, heading slightly to the right, extended her talons and sailed up into a huge eucalyptus tree on my side of the river. As she landed I saw the huge stick pile of a nest. How extraordinary! I had been worried about finding an imperial eagle's eyrie and here was one actually showing me her nest. The eucalyptus was clearly on private land, for there were horses grazing below it, but even so I decided to have a go at finding a hide site. I walked a quarter mile down the road, crossed a bridge and, after hiking almost up to the ridge, made my way stealthily through the trees unseen until I would be opposite the great eucalyptus. As I climbed back down I glassed the nest and saw she was not now on it.

I soon found a perfect hide site on the ground below a stunted olive tree which had foliage dangling almost down to the earth. From it I had a clear, almost level view of the nest which, luckily, was not obscured by any branches. Imperial eagles lay their two or three eggs at any time from the end of March, and in case she had already laid the first I resisted the temptation to set up my hide there and then. Quickly I marked the site with a small circle of stones and hurried back through the trees in a wide arc. I was crossing the bridge again when I saw an eagle return to the eyrie.

Although I had to return to Britain in a few days' time for publication of my second eagle book, *On Wing and Wild Water*, I now had a wonderful target to aim for when I returned to Spain in mid-May. I would spend my birthday with imperial eagles after all!

I never did find the wolf reserve that day, but after a hectic five hour search I finally located the man who owned it. A well-dressed policeman in Candeleda told me there was such a reserve owned privately and not by ICONA. He gave me rough directions to a track which led to an *embalse*, but I drove a long way without coming to the reserve. In desperation I approached a working party of five men in a jeep. The foreman immediately delegated one of his workers, a short pleasant young man called Antonio, to help me. Antonio led me to the home of an English couple who were known to be feeding the wolves. They were away, in the Pyrenees. He told me to wait by the main road while he dashed off to Candelada. He returned an hour later with news of a man by the name of Beltran who had something to do with the wolves. He then took me on a long jolting drive down bumpy sand tracks to the primitive stone home of an old shepherd. Apparently the wolf reserve was less than 2 km's hike further on, though the shepherd knew that Beltran was not there; we would have to enquire his whereabouts at a certain petrol station all the way back in Candelada.

I was ready to give up at this point, but Antonio was doggedly persistent and determined to find the man for me. I was sure that Beltran worked for the English couple and would not be able to give me permission anyway. We drove back to the town, where Antonio was directed into a bar. I was tired, it was nearing dusk, and I did not want to get trapped in a Spanish bar all night. Again he insisted, so reluctantly I followed. Campi, the barman, knew Beltran and asked my name before making a phone call. I bought wine all round, managed to persuade an unwilling Antonio to accept a mere 1,000 pesetas (£5) for nearly five hours of help, and after a few minutes went to get something from my van. As I turned back I heard a cultured voice say —

'Hello, Mike Tomkies!'

Before me stood a short but well-built and athletic dark-haired young man of about 27. Beltran de Ceballos, who it turned out not only spoke perfect English but actually owned the wolves and their reserve, smiled and extended his hand. Over a few *vinos* in the bar, I learned that he was a first class naturalist who had worked for ICONA and even at the wildfowl reserve at Slimbridge in England. The English couple, Richard and Julia Kemp, were making, in collaboration with Beltran, a series of Spanish wildlife films for 'Anglia Survival' television in Britain. They had filmed Beltran's wolves, wild bears at a mule carcass in Asturias, and even the mighty lammergeier dropping bones from a height in the Pyrenees, as well as many rare species.

Eventually Beltran invited me back to his home overlooking the town, where I met his attractive wife Chata and their two young children. It was soon obvious to me that this man knew almost as much about Spain's rare wildlife as did Suso Garzon. He said the reason he made films was to spread the conservation message, and to help rare species to be better protected. Full censuses were important and so was education, so that Spaniards realised that not just the major species need protecting but smaller, lesser-known ones too. Creatures like the imperial eagle, rare vultures, bear, wolf and lynx were glamorous and natural targets, but just as important were species like the red salamander, the Pyrenean tree frog, and the fascinating aquatic desman which, from his description, sounded a quarter mole, a quarter water shrew, a quarter mouse and a quarter seal! I let myself down when I admitted I had never heard of the desman.

When I showed him some of my wildlife books and said that my objectives were exactly the same as his, he told me he would help me all he could to get at close quarters with the species I wanted. But he was unsalaried, a professional freelance like myself, with little time to spare from his filming – I would have to pay for his aid. He told me that although it was commonly believed there were only about 70 pairs of imperial eagle in Spain, there were in fact more than 90 pairs, and he knew most of the eyries himself.

'By the way,' he said as I was leaving. 'There is an imperial eagle's nest in a huge eucalyptus near the road you came along today.'

It was a delicious moment that I should have resisted as I placed a hand on his shoulder and said –

'Yes. I found it!'

I promised to telephone him before I left Britain again, and we would make final arrangements then. I drove back down the road to Oropesa and camped in an open place below some evergreen oaks. I felt good. What with a little help from Suso and José Antonio in Extremadura, from Beltran in the Avila region, and with Imre in Madrid supplying background notes, covering Spain's wildlife might be an easier task than I had envisaged.

In the morning I woke to a sublime view. The great jagged snow-capped peaks of the Sierra de Gredos glowed brightly in the distance above Candelada, while below me the river Tiétar gurgled on its way to join the Tagus near Suso's home. The Tagus (*Tajo* in Spanish) was like a broad dark canal but this river moved with bright water, many splashings and flashing light. The rounded granite boulders made a peaceful haven from the wind for breakfast, and all around the oaks cast their gentle shade. I could live here, I thought. I drove hard that day on my way to pack up the Red Villa and camped in a little wood of umbrella pines near Pozohondo, south of Albacete.

At 3 a.m. I was startled awake by two slaps on the van roof, clearly made by a human hand. At first I thought it was someone fooling about, but then realised no-one fools around at that early hour. In case of trouble, I dressed − one cannot fight when naked − and got out. To my horror, all four tubeless tyres were going down. When I tipped water over them to locate the hissing sounds of escaping air, I found each had been punctured in four or five places with what must have been a needle-sharp point on the end of a stick. I dashed about with my axe and torch yelling vengeance, searching behind dark bushes, but the evil-minded vandal had escaped into the night.

I had a hard job in the morning to contact the Guardia Civil, but eventually they came, took particulars, then drove off and returned an hour later with a mechanic from Tobarra, getting on for 30 km away. Their little car was filled with a huge hydraulic jack and tools of all kinds. We jacked the van up on to four rocks and removed the wheels. Then off they went again to Tobarra where the mechanic put inner tubes into the tyres, returning fifty minutes later to put the wheels back on the van. At last I was free to move. Between them, they had driven a total of 135 km, the mechanic had done all that work, yet his charge was a mere £35, including the four tubes! They implored me not to think ill of Spain. I told them I loved the country and could never judge it by the act of one madman.

It was on my way to Santander, after packing up and securing the Red Villa, that I received a second and far worse shock. I wanted to have lunch with Imre and discuss a few things, and after a restful walk through leafy shaded squares of the lovely town of Aranjuez I decided to call from there. The phone was answered by a woman's voice and I asked to speak to Imre.

'I am afraid my father died two days ago.'

At first I thought I was speaking to Imre's wife and said how very sorry I was to hear it, but could I speak to Imre?

'Imre *is* my father!'

117

I realised then I was talking to his daughter, Elizabeth. I could hardly believe the bad news. Imre was two years younger than I was. Elizabeth told me that he had had a heart bypass operation some years back — but he had never told his friends about it. Three nights ago he had collapsed with stomach pains. His wife had called the doctor, who rushed him to hospital for an operation. Imre never came round from the anaesthetic.

His wife came on the phone and said she would look through his work and see if he had left any notes for me. I told her not to worry about it now, but that I would visit them on my return. I felt I had to do a little to help the family, for all of Imre's three children were severely handicapped. I camped in a high pine grove near the Puerto de Páramo de Masa and said my goodbyes to my friend below the trees there. How short and ephemeral is our hold on life, I thought, as I also recalled the recent death of my old friend, wildlife photographer Geoffrey Kinns, at the age of 63.

Next day, with a few hours to spare before the ferry departed for Plymouth, I set out a traffic-killed rabbit I had found in a field near the vulture cliffs at Escalada, some 70 metres from the van, which was half concealed behind a hedge. The birds were used to vehicles here, but while several griffons circled near, none came down during a three-hour wait. I took some pictures, however, of an Egyptian vulture which swooped low to investigate.

Back in England I got through all the radio, television and newspaper interviews about my new book and also signed an agreement which my publisher had been setting up while I was away for a film to be made about my Scottish life and work. It would include some of my own wildlife footage and be produced by Avie Littler of the Moving Picture Company. What pleased me most was that David Cobham, who made the feature film of *Tarka the Otter*, had said that he personally wanted to direct the film, based on a treatment that had been written by Brian Jackman. They needed to attract a budget in excess of £100,000 and seemed confident that they could gain the support of Andrew Neal (son of the badger expert Ernest Neal) at the BBC Natural History Unit in Bristol. I was less sanguine, for I knew there were others at Bristol who would be likely to block anything to do with me, and urged the film-makers to think about some of the independent television channels as well.

Imre's death following so closely on Geoffrey's made me look again at my own life. Perhaps the time had come to think about returning to my roots in Sussex, where my love of wildlife had begun, and to search for an isolated cottage there from which to launch a final assault on Spain's wildlife. My publisher had now given me a contract to write a book on the subject when I was ready. After that maybe I could revisit Canada and the grizzlies and then retire from the really hard stuff. I had to admit that in the past two years I had lost some of the physical stamina I once had for hard trekking in high mountains day after day, with heavy packs and hides.

I explored the country areas of my boyhood on the Downs from Worthing to Chichester and climbed Black Down near Haslemere, which at 280 metres is the nearest thing to a mountain in Sussex, but found little available at a price I could afford. One superb and perfectly remote house called 'Foxholes' was exactly what I wanted, but the sale price was £200,000. When I had first sought a wilderness life 20 years earlier, few had wanted the same, but now, with motorways in the south providing fast access from London and other cities and towns, many were the weekend cottages in the country where the owners were absent all working week. Even ruined old barns with planning permission, and an acre or so of muddy field were fetching extraordinary prices in the affluent south. Needing to get back to work on my Spanish studies, I abandoned the search.

While heading for the Plymouth ferry on May 17, I stopped in Tavistock to call Beltran de Ceballos. The telephone was answered by his wife Chata, who told me that Beltran was filming in the Coto Doñana for a Spanish company and would be away for a month. What a blow! That, along with Imre's death, meant I would now have no help at all. I would never have tackled the 77,180 square kilometres of Scotland when far younger. Now I had to try and cover all 505,020 square kilometres of Spain for its rarest species at my age and totally alone. If only I had more than the barest grasp of the language.

12 · *Imperial Protection*

As the camper van laboured up the long tortuous hill towards the 1,011-metres-high Puerto del Escudo my black mood lifted at the sight of a red kite flapping idly over the lush pastures and then two griffon vultures soaring high in the sky, the furthest north I had seen these great birds. This is the home of the Celtic Spaniards, and it is from this region that the Celts migrated first to Ireland and then to Scotland. Indeed the northern hay meadows which stretch right across the mighty peaks of the Picos de Europa remind one of parts of the Lake District and Scotland, for many are enclosed with dry stone walls to keep in the sheep and cattle. In autumn the farmers still cut their hay for silage with the traditional hand scythe.

Five kilometres past the Puerto a black kite landed by the side of the road, but swiftly took off again when I tried to pull up quietly. Beyond Quintanilla Escalada I stopped above the rushing Rio Ebro to glass the mighty range of sandstone cliffs that jut and rear above its far side. I had always felt that some of the natural oblong grottos in these escarpments must be used as nesting sites by the griffons that lived there. Sure enough, two of the nearest ones now were, and I could see the stream of white faeces stretching down the rock. I could just make out the hunched form of a griffon sitting on one nest, her head thrust into a dark corner, and beside her a gawky, greyish chick. I climbed up a hill on the other side of the road to about 100 metres with camera and tripod.

As I peered through the 640mm telephoto lens, now turned into a 960mm lens with a 1.5 extender, I saw another nest on the ledge, below the first one. This contained a well-fledged chick, which seemed odd, and just then a griffon sailed in to land beside it. I had my first pictures of nesting griffons but they were still too far away.

Neither adult made any move to feed the youngster, and I had the feeling that these birds were finding carrion less plentiful, as griffons were in many parts of the country now that the Spanish army no longer used mules for transport. Even farmers employ mules and donkeys far less than they did 50 years ago, so that today fewer of these animals are left, when dead, on the hills as food for vultures. Indeed, I discovered later that this colony of griffons had dwindled from 200 to fewer than 30 pairs.

I phoned Imre's family to keep my appointment with them in Madrid and was told by his daughter that it would be better to come the next evening when her mother returned from work. I knew that having been a freelance naturalist, like myself, Imre would probably not have left much money. I might be able to help in a small way by buying rights to use some of his pictures in my book.

Rather than dawdle around for a day I turned east after Boceguillas, where I again saw red kites, and headed for La Pinilla and the eastern edge of the Sierra de Guadarrama, where in April I had seen five griffons flying. I hoped to find some nests there and to put up a hide in the early morning for a few hours of work. The great range of the Guadarrama hills, when linked with the even loftier peaks of the Sierra de Gredos, forms the high rock-ribbed 'spine' of Spain virtually separating north from south. As dusk fell, I turned down a sandy trail where I could see no human footprints or vehicle tracks and hid the van among small pines, sure I would be safe for the night.

I was rudely woken at 4.30 a.m. by a loud human voice. Hell, not another mad tyre puncturer! I pulled on my trews, set my axe nearby, slung open the door and shouted '*Hola! Que pasa?*' (Hello. What's happening?) To my surprise, there was a gang of men outside. A light flashed, then four more high ones bore down on the van, accompanied by the thudding noise of a giant engine. I thought it must be a train. It was in fact a huge truck with wheels six feet high. The men gabbled and gesticulated that I was in their way. What they were doing there in the wilds with this enormous vehicle before dawn I had no idea, and I didn't stop to find out. I hauled out and camped down by the Rio Serrano 5 km away.

After two hours more of fitful sleep I rose to the sound of skylarks singing as they lifted into the air round me. The river bank looked promising with areas of reeds, marsh and open pools in which trout darted in the shallows. I sneaked down to the water's edge, camera at the ready, hoping to see an otter. I saw no otters, but a little whinchat in full courting regalia landed on a fence pole close by.

Curious to know what the gang of men had been up to last night, I drove back to the top of the track and walked down it. No-one was near my first camp spot, though I was aware of the loud buzzings of bees in the bushes all round me. I soon found out why. Where my van had been now stood 20 light blue square beehives. The men had obviously been to install these — and had done so in the dark before dawn when the bees would be blinded and dopey and unlikely to sting them.

As bees gathered round me angrily I suddenly felt extremely unsafe and walked away quickly. One bee kept pace with me, about two feet from my right ear, but then it suddenly swung off and had a mid-air punch-up with a wild native bee. I had never seen bees fight before. Maybe the newcomer was establishing territorial rights in the best way it knew. I reached my van safely and, while eating breakfast, made a Sony Walkman tape recording of nightingales singing, backed up by invisible choirs of finches, redstarts and flycatchers. Through the earphones I could hear the full beauty of early summer in wild Spain; cuckoos in the blue distance too, and the whir and zoom of insects' wings as they sped past the microphone.

With only 120 km to go to Madrid, I crossed the slow river at Buitrago de Lozoya, saw red and black kites wheeling in the sky, then turned up the C604 road to Rascafria, which turned out to be a mountain play town with brick cobbled streets that were terrible for the van. I wanted to head high into the middle of the Sierra de Guadarrama, but found I had to go back on my tracks to take the minor road up towards the 1,778-metre-high Puerto de Navafria, where I hoped to find eagles or vultures and maybe a nest or two. More nightingales sang from the bushy sides of the road, and soon I found myself in a forest of large pines and firs.

Near the top a plateau of rough land swung out to the left of the road, ending in an obelisk of huge white rounded rocks which perched above a great void overlooking an *embalse* of the Rio Lozoya far below. The top of this jumble of giant boulders would be an ideal place for lunch while scanning the surrounding terrain. No sooner had I alighted from the van than I saw a buzzard circling, then a white bird just as big soaring above it. Egyptian vulture, I first thought, but through the binoculars I could see it had a fully feathered head. It was some kind of light-coloured eagle, and it vanished over a far ridge.

I climbed to the top of the rocky obelisk and had just sat down when I saw a dark dot zooming down out of the sky towards the trees high above my van. As it drew nearer, the bird opened its wings, flapped them a few times, and landed on a dark blob in a flat-topped pine. I could see the silvery streaks on its wing glinting in the sun. An imperial eagle, once again showing me its nest. Even at that distance I could see the trees were too thick for me to sit on a higher part of the slope and view the nest clearly. Well, if the Candelada nest was not viable, and I could not work one in Monfragüe, I could always return here, find a helper somewhere in a local hotel and try to put up a tree hide. I took a photo and noted the exact location. Scanning the rock faces all round my high vantage point, I soon spotted a golden eagle eyrie in a small brown cliff a quarter mile below me. Unfortunately it was not being used – a pity, for it would have been easy to scramble down to a rocky ridge near it and erect a vegetation-covered hide overlooking the nest. Just then I looked up and, to my delight, saw the 'white eagle' heading back. It soared right over my head, and through the lens I saw the lightly-barred light coffee-coloured thick plumage – a booted eagle (*águila calzada* in Spanish).

Time was running out. I would come back here one day, but now I had to dash to Madrid.

I spent the evening with the Boroviczény family, sympathising with their tragic loss. Imre's wife had found no other notes left by Imre for me but I selected nine of his photos, and paid for them, before setting off for Sierra Espuña and the Red Villa.

I was thankful to find my rented home untouched, but there was no time to hang about. It was already late in the season, so I quickly unloaded everything I would not need and put into the van hides, more camera gear, bedding, clothes, gas bottles and so forth. Then I set off on a six weeks trip — the hardest wildlife task I had ever set myself! I was sure my best bets were the imperial eagles near Candelada, then to head for the Monfragüe Park area of Extremadura. I would try to get Suso to soften up José Antonio, and to catch Suso in his Monfragüe home I would have to reach it during the weekend. It was now Friday!

There was no time to take the more interesting route through Sierra de Cazorla, so I put my old van (the mileage on the clock now 71,739) through its paces on the faster roads to Murcia, Albacete and Quintanar de la Orden, then turned off up the rustic C402 towards Toledo, where the smooth rounded rocks in some fields looked like the bums of decapitated pigs. La Villa de don Fadrique was a farming village where ancient tractors wheezed up and down the street and all the men seemed small and wore black berets. It was like stepping back into the Spain of the 1800s. After Villacanas the road degenerated into a dirt track, dust blowing everywhere, as in a desert. After a bumpy ride I came on to the metalled road again, now dazzling my eyes like a shiny ribbon in the dying sun. The only flat place to camp in this treeless vineyard country was between two giant pitchers which some wags had painted to look like voracious open-mouthed sharks. One of the pitchers moved when I pushed it, and as it was uphill from the van I shoved a rock under it so that it could not roll into me during the night.

Just after Toledo next morning the sky turned black and it began to pour with rain, the whole landscape shrouded in gloomy grey. In Talavera de la Reina traffic was crawling through streets of muddy water. I wanted to be working with imperial eagles on my birthday in two days' time but I could not go to check the nest near Candelada now and risk putting the eagles off eggs or, more likely, young chicks in this awful weather. My luck improved when I took the country road from Jaraicejo towards Salto de Torrejón and Suso's home. I saw two Egyptian vultures sitting on a dead spar not far from the roadside, looking all bedraggled in the rain. Their wings were soaked and they could have flown only with difficulty, which enabled me to take two rare pictures.

I located Suso not at his home but over at Las Cansinas, the ICONA biological station in the woods of cork trees and evergreen oaks where I had camped before. He drove up in his red jeep and greeted me warmly. I showed him 50 of the best Spanish wildlife pictures I had taken and said I would give them to him tomorrow when I had captioned them all. He was pleased and put his long arm round my shoulders.

'Good. Come! You want to help me feed young imperial eagles?'

Would I! He led me through a farmer's cottage to a large shed where two downy white imperial eagle chicks were in box cages in front of a high window. One was 10 days old while the bigger was now two weeks. They had been taken from their nests because they were being bullied by their siblings and would not otherwise have survived the normal competition for food among eagle chicks. They were being handreared for about two weeks before the smaller one was to be put back in its nest fit and strong and at an age when young eagles no longer fight. The bigger one, which Suso said was a little stupid, would be put into a nest where the parents were trying to incubate infertile eggs, and they would rear it.

He took a quail from a packet of four, the sort one can buy in supermarkets all over Spain for the human table, snipped off morsels of meat, then tendered them to each chick from the end of a pair of scissors. They squeaked hungrily and took them with quick stabs of their thick blue-black beaks. The big one was certainly unco-ordinated and mistimed many of its lunges, missing the meat altogether. Suso said it had to go into a nest alone for even when bigger it might still not survive with a more aggressive nestling. He handed me the quail and let me have a go. It felt wonderful to be feeding imperial eagle chicks within minutes of arrival.

Suso was still pursuing a remarkable experiment he had originated in 1972, from which he had produced one of his many scientific papers. He had felt that the best way to help rare raptors threatened with extinction was to increase their reproduction rate, and this could be achieved by an artificial lowering of normal nestling mortality. That year he and a German biologist, Bernd-Ulrich Meyburg, monitored and controlled 13 active Spanish imperial eagle eyries, representing more than 25% of the overall population, then estimated at 50 pairs. Of these eyries eight were in central west Spain, the other five in Andalucia, including four in the Doñana National Park. I quote from the paper:

> Two of the pairs came to our notice too late for us to know the original number of chicks hatched. Two further clutches were completely or partially destroyed, by a storm in one case, by human hands in the other. Of the other 9 pairs, 4 had only one unfertilised egg each. Two others hatched 3 chicks each, and we took away the ones hatched last, those with virtually no chance of survival. One of these we put into an eyrie with an unfertilised egg where it was nurtured by the parent birds. The other, like one of the chicks from the only brood of two where the smaller did not appear to have a chance of survival, we put into eyries where there was only one chick in each of comparable size.

In this way the death of 30% of the chicks hatched by these 9 pairs was prevented, and the fledging success was increased by 43%. The paper concluded that this method was extremely suitable for the preservation of this bird which was threatened with extinction and that its application in the coming years would be appropriate. There was no fear of disturbing the present birds unduly owing to the very infrequent visits to the eyrie involved.

Suso told me that ICONA was currently sorting eggs and chicks of these rare raptors between about 30 different nests, using similar methods, to increase the survival rate. I was surprised and impressed. They were far ahead of any similar conservation programme I knew in Britain.

As we finished feeding the eaglets, I asked Suso if, when the chicks went back in nests, we could erect my kind of invisible hide at a discreet distance so that I could take photos while his biologists checked that they were being accepted by the adult birds. Suso smiled and said that the guardas usually kept watch through binoculars from half a kilometre or more away. No licences to photo imperials were being issued this year, but he would speak to the warden, José Antonio, about it when he returned from visiting his family home in the nearby town of Plasencia. I was afraid that Suso, who had to leave for his work in Merida the next night (Sunday), would miss him. With my poor Spanish, I might then have a hard task convincing José of the kind of help I both wanted and needed. Here, where I was simply not allowed to trek alone round the areas where rare species nested, I was far more dependent on other people than

I had ever been in Canada or Scotland, where I had worked almost always alone.

Suso led me down to my lone camp site in a glade between the oaks, near a pond which had been dredged out to attract frogs, dragonflies and the like. How long can I stay and work here? I asked him. He gave a genial laugh.

'A lifetime if you want!'

As dusk fell and I sipped wine while supper was hissing in my pressure cooker in the van, I heard strange singing and talking coming from the pond. About a hundred frogs had emerged from the water and were courting in the evening air. I could distinctly hear. '*Get back. Get back*' and '*Cut. Cut Cut*', as if they were advising me what to do with my wildlife movie, a print of which, along with a small hand-wound editing machine, I had brought with me in case I found time on my hands. Oddly, the cacophony of noise was not disturbing. Indeed it provided a soothing lullaby to send me to sleep.

Next day, Sunday, with José not yet back, I drove past the pond up a steep sandy track, parked in the woods and set off on foot to try and find some nests. I saw a pair of wheeling imperial eagles and watched them until out of sight. They did not land anywhere. I was walking beside the fence of a small reserve where ICONA was breeding red deer to release into areas where the deer no longer existed, and had just rounded a bend when I saw a few yards away beneath a large cork tree, a huge black fighting bull. I don't recall getting over the fence but I found myself on the other side in what seemed a split second. The bull, however, just looked up, amiably chewing the cud, as if wondering what this daft human was up to.

I then drove down to the new public hide near the huge hydro electric dam at the confluence of the Tajo and Tiétar rivers, and scanned the vulture cliffs across the water. There was an Egyptian vulture on a nest, too far away for good pictures, but the two griffon nests looked abandoned. One had almost blown away. It seemed they had failed this year. Suddenly I heard a babble of voices and a crowd of Spanish tourists filled the hide, the kids queuing to take a look through my telephoto lens. They were led by Suso's wife Isabel, who explained it was European Bird Watching Day, and more busloads were arriving to take a look at the great birds wheeling round and landing on the opposite cliffs. I stayed awhile, but this was not my kind of wildlife watching, and I drove back beyond the turning to Las Cansinas to scan some brown and yellow cliffs on the far side of the Tiétar river, where I had always thought there might be an eagle's eyrie.

I raked the jagged faces with my binoculars and suddenly saw something bright orange in a neat ledge high up between two grey rocky buttresses. It was the head of an Egyptian vulture on its nest, much nearer than the one at the public hide, and the nest was perfectly framed by a row of pink flowers. I climbed up the steep rocky hill beside the road for about 70 metres and found a perfect hide site, bounded on two sides by square boulders, with a sloping shale floor, almost level with the nest. Well, I may not spend my birthday tomorrow with imperial eagles but I jolly well would with Egyptian vultures, also increasingly rare birds.

Elated, I drove to say goodbye to Suso at his home and to give him the captioned pictures I had promised. He was surprised I had found the nest so soon. He told me it had been a bad winter between January and March and many of the vultures' first clutches had failed. The two Egyptians were both trying to incubate a second batch of eggs, which could well prove infertile. He confirmed that the two griffons had failed due to bad weather, as they were early layers. He told me José had returned but was busy with visiting schoolchildren at the Education Centre in Villa Real. I said I would not bother him now but would leave it until Tuesday, so that he could have a day off.

'No,' said Suso sharply. 'You see him TODAY. It's his job to help you – and any professional photographer. I will come with you now to see him.'

I tried to protest. Isabel was busy with people, he said, and so he had plenty of time, especially for me. He put me in his jeep and off we sped to Penafalcon, intending to intercept José on his way home from Villa Real. There was a group of bird watchers there, supervised by one of the green uniformed part-time vigilantes, looking down at the black stork nest at the foot of the immense cliff. I could see the stork on the nest, keeping her head low, as if afraid of all the watchers. Suso laughed at my question.

'No, she is used to cars and people passing by, has been for years. She is sitting tight because her first clutch also failed this year.'

Just then the male stork glided in, and she stood up to meet him. I could hear the odd squeaky cries and loud bill clapping of their greeting ritual. Then he disgorged a fish on the nest for her. I was taking pictures when Suso stayed my arm.

'It is too far away for you,' he said. 'There is a better nest for photographs, not far from the turning to Las Cansinas. José will show you.'

We chatted awhile to the vigilante who told us there had been a great storm an hour before I arrived. He pointed to some rocks which were blocking the spot opposite Penafalcon where I had previously parked my van. He had actually seen a shaft of lightning strike into the cliffs and smash out the rocks. They had not, as I had thought when first driving in, been bulldozed there to stop people parking. Suso looked at me with mock accusation.

'Señor Tomkies. If you do not bring rain, you bring storms!'

We had not seen José come past by dusk and returned to Suso's home where he wrote a note for me to give to José on the morrow, asking him to help me all he could because I was an expert, and to do his best to get me to work with imperial eagles. Again I felt a great debt to this man, to whom I was always reluctant to say goodbye.

As I sat almost naked in the heat at my camp site that evening I heard the thudding of an engine. It was José, who had driven down specially to see me after calling on Suso. His greeting was enthusiastic, his handshake firm, and he gave me a warm *abrazo Fuerte* (strong arm embrace). I realised then that what I had taken to be slowness, or laziness, or even surliness towards me, a foreigner, had been more the shy expression of a totally calm and relaxed man. Even with my poor grasp of Spanish I was delighted by what he said.

'Tomorrow, you come to my house at noon and we go to a hide I have set up on a hoopoe nest. And in the afternoon we set up a hide on a black vulture nest, you and me together. You are the first photographer here. I have Germans, Italians and French coming later, but you will be first in all the hides. It is good to work with you.'

The happiness I felt then stayed with me for many days. I did not know it at the time but ahead of me lay the finest, and hardest, month of my naturalist life.

13 · Little Old Monk

A harsh '*sqwawhl*' call, a rush of air, and — SNAP! There, by its nest hole in the trunk of the cork tree, a mere five metres away, clinging to the rough bark with two toes up and two down, like a woodpecker, was the craziest, gaudiest bird I have ever seen up close. It was clearly masquerading as a Red Indian chief! It had pinky-brown plumage, jet black wings with dazzling white bars, and huge bright cinnamon headcrest with black and white tips, which it raised and lowered, as if saying 'howdy'. In its two-and-a-half-inch-long black down-curved bill was a fat grasshopper.

I had often seen hoopoes, usually dashing away from my trekking form on their broad wings, for they are wary birds, and their lilting far-carrying '*Hoop poop poop*' calls are an integral part of the music of the Spanish countryside. Seeing this one so close, so suddenly, was a shock. After first looking at José's hide, which was like a medium-sized green tent, with no attempt at vegetation covering, I had not expected to see a hoopoe at all. Its loose sides flapped slightly in the strong breeze and there was a rent in the rear so that the birds would be able to see my backside resting on the stool. José had moved it by daily stages to within five metres of the nest hole. Yet, within seconds of setting the camera on its tripod, in she had come.

She hopped up to the hole, poked her beak in and kept weaving it about. Sometimes she jerked it back, as if she had been pecked by a chick. She spread her long black-and-white banded tail firmly against the trunk for support, obviously having strong muscles in it for she used it as a fulcrum as she weaved her head and beak sideways inside the hole. At times her belly quivered and heaved, as if she were taking deep breaths or regurgitating food to the young. Three minutes after she left, her mate, a slightly paler bird but of the same 11-inch length, landed with insects in his beak and did much the same. They came in so frequently, not a bit bothered by what seemed to me a crude hide, that I had taken forty pictures in less than an hour.

Now one landed, then another flew in and landed right on its back. It seemed like an attack. Whether the first bird was a stranger without chicks, and was fulfilling parental instincts by feeding this pair's young, I did not know. But they fell off together, squalling harshly, and there was a lot of wing flapping and thumping in the grasses. I tried to see what was happening through the side panels of the hide but could not locate them.

The feeding adults moved very fast and jerkily, especially when landing and taking flight. Snap – they were there. Snap – they were gone. On one occasion the pair came back together and performed an air dance near the hole, tumbling round each other like giant moths, uttering faint harsh drawn-out calls. Sometimes the female 'talked' to the chicks, making odd muted barking noises. I noticed the birds always made a soft harsh sound just before landing, as if to tell the young they were coming. Days later I was to find out why – in amusing circumstances.

It was hot in the hide and sweat poured off me. I resolved in future to take a very wet flannel into hides with which to swab myself down. Cold and wet had been the great problem in Scotland; now I wondered which was the lesser of two evils. At 2 p.m. I saw a whitish-blue beak emerge from the hole, followed by a well-feathered head, and sink down on the edge and stay there. The chick had a white patch at the base of its beak, probably to help the parents locate their young's beaks in the dark of the hole when feeding them. José had said I could leave when I liked, no need for him to walk me out, so after taking sixty pictures I was glad to quit the infernal oven.

I ran into a hot and dishevelled José near his home. After accepting my hoopoe success as no more than to be expected, he looked almost apologetic. We could not put up a hide near a black vulture's nest today after all. The nest he had in mind contained an unhatched, possibly infertile egg, and we could not risk putting the birds off it. He would consult a guarda called Toni, who looked after the best black vulture nesting area, and see if they could find a nest with a good-sized chick in it, where it would be safer to put up a hide. I told him about finding the Egyptian vulture nest across the Tiétar river and he said he would be happy for me to put up one of my hides on the rocky hill opposite. The distance was '*muy lejos*' (very far), he joked, so maybe I would not need a hide! True, the ledge was over 300 metres away, but all my shots of nesting birds so far had been close ones. It would be interesting and different to show part of the terrain, a good section of the cliff, and, if I was lucky, to photograph both birds in the air when they exchanged incubation duties on their two eggs.

After a quick omelette in the van, I drove to the place and hid my best canvas hide and tripod behind a bush on the little cliff at the bottom of the hill. I parked under the shade of riverside trees the best part of a kilometre away and walked back. Then I carried hide, tripod, camera pack, a foam cushion, and a soaked flannel in a plastic bag up to the site. I had the hide in place in twenty minutes, its poles tied by brown cord to rocks and thick stems of gum cistus bushes. These are well named, for at this time of year the leaves exude a sticky gum which can clog your clothes and hands. All this time the vulture stayed on her nest, though I could see her watching me with great interest. I wedged the tripod legs into the rocky shale and looked at her through the 960mm lens. After a while she lost interest and began to behave naturally.

She stood up, her long smooth white and fawn body and black-tipped wings showing clearly, turned the eggs over with her beak and performed an eagle-type rhumba back down on to them. The nest seemed to be made of small twigs, yellow hay and scraps of wool, though I could not see clearly because of the row of pink flowers. From time to time she kept pulling grasses in round her body and the eggs with her beak.

The Egyptian vulture, known as the *alimoche* in Spain, has a true carnival face, as if worn for a masked ball. It is bright yellow-orange and featherless. From a distance it looks like a wedge of cheddar cheese, its eyes like two currants stuck in the thick end. It is the smallest of European vultures, weighing a little over 5lbs, with a wing span of about four feet, but it is the most colourful. It is a fastidious eater, waiting until the bigger vultures have had their fill before feeding on the smaller morsels of carrion that are left. Some migrate in the autumn to winter south of the Sahara, and the bird is clever enough to break open large eggs, like those of ostriches, by picking up a stone in its beak and dashing it down on the egg. The younger birds copy the adults but often miss the egg; they have to learn to aim correctly.

Was I glad I had brought the soaked flannel! It was so hot in the hide I could only keep tolerably cool by swabbing my face, neck and armpits, and letting the breeze dehydrate the moisture. At 5.10 p.m. the bird stood up again, pulled grasses round the eggs, then sat down on them. Twenty minutes later the sun had gone behind the 7-foot ledge and the light became poor, so I left. I was just wondering where the black stork's nest was, the one Suso had mentioned, when I saw one of the birds gliding along the far side of the wide river. To my amazement, it suddenly looped up and landed on a huge nest, white on its sides from faeces, on a rocky shelf only 5 metres or so above the shore. I glassed it and saw there were three young chicks in the nest. She was now standing beside them, a long, dark red-legged statue. What luck! I could put a hide between two trees down on the shore on this side of the river and not be seen getting down to it, the cistus bushes were so high and thick.

Back at my camp site, I had a cold swab down naked, then recalled it was my birthday. I had not entered my 60th year working with imperial eagles, as I had promised myself for a year, but I had done good work for the first time with hoopoe and Egyptian vulture, and had found a rare black stork's nest. I could have no complaints. Then I found myself looking down at my legs. The firm muscles of my youth had dwindled, and they looked knotted, sinewy, grizzled, a pair of 60-year-old legs, and with a shock I saw varicose veins had begun to form on my right calf. Oh well, what the hell did it matter what they looked like so long as they got me up the Hill a few more times. I lay back in the dying sun with closed eyes, seeing only the blood-red colour of my eyelids. The bell-like notes of golden orioles sounded through the balmy air between the oaks, the frogs were starting their evening chorus, and the words of a favourite hymn from boyhood went through my mind. 'Time like an ever rolling stream, bears all its sons away. They die forgotten as a dream, dies at the opening day.' No, time is not bearing me away. I am not being borne away; I am feeling born again. I am on a new threshold. I am happy.

At 10.30 p.m. José drove down in the dark, and said that tomorrow we could put up one of my hides on the river shore to overlook a black storks' nest. I did not tell him I had already found it, just that I had seen storks flying there. I wanted him to feel good, to have the pleasure of showing it to me. It seemed, at last, I had reached the age of diplomacy.

We had a hard time breaking through the bushes with the hide and all the camera gear to get down to the Tiétar shore early next morning. In the end we manage it by a circuitous route without going back for a machete. There were fox and badger tracks in the soft brown mud along the river's edge. We set up the hide in front of one of the trees and between tall bamboo-like reeds. After helping me to disguise it with vegetation, which seemed hardly necessary while the stork stayed on her nest casually watching the whole operation, José left. I had a clear view of the female and her three chicks, which had orange beaks at this stage and looked like little semi-fledged pelicans, but I was surprised to find they were still over 200 metres away.

I soon found the rare black stork a hard bird to photograph well from a distance because it has a tiny head for its size. It appears to be all body, a long thick red beak and ridiculously long bandy red legs. She dozed on one leg for ten minutes, then flew off looking like a very long red-tipped arrow. Her legs, carried to the rear, resembled long pieces of drifting red wool. She came back in 11 minutes, and after a pause with her head held down, she regurgitated food not into the chicks' beaks but over the nest floor. It was then a free-for-all. The chicks all faced into the centre, heads down, rear ends lifted, wings half fanned out, grabbing for the food, sometimes out of each other's bills. I could hear them making odd booming '*ker-choom*' sounds as they squabbled.

At 10.10 a.m. she flew off again, returning 32 minutes later and landing on a flat sloping rock to the left of and above the nest. She stayed there for three minutes, then flapped down to the chicks and regurgitated three small fish, one after the other, with 20-second gaps between. Each chick got one. Then she returned to the rock and preened, and it was surprising to witness the versatility of that long beak. It could sort out the feathers of the neck just below itself and then be thrust right over the long greeny-black glinting body and preen the tips of the wing feathers on the bird's other side.

By now the chick's crops were bulging out white and I saw that they sat down with a sudden flop after a slow initial let down, as if their young knees could not take the strain of being at full bend. The stork flew back to the nest, dozed on one leg to 11.51 a.m. and then began to preen one chick's neck plumage. It kept dead still for this operation although it had been moving about a lot beforehand. By 12.20 all the chicks were sleeping and could not be seen at all. The parent then flew off.

Twenty-one minutes later a stork returned, and I took this to be the male for it looked slightly bigger and darker. He landed on the rock, stayed there until 1.34 p.m., then flew to the nest and regurgitated two orange fish. It took him 67 seconds to do this and afterwards he held his head down and shook his beak sideways, as if to get rid of slime, which sprayed about. (With black storks, both sexes share the duties of nest building, incubation and chick feeding.)

At 1.50 p.m. he flew off again, this time straight towards the hide and I hoped he would land right in front of it. However, he veered off and landed on the muddy edge well to my right, out of range of the camera which, of course, I dared not try to shift to a side panel. I watched him stand there for about five minutes before he dashed his bill into the water, struck the surface loudly with flapping wings, and flew straight back to the nest. He then immediately regurgitated what looked liked an eel, which one chick snatched and bolted down head first. The storks seemed to need a few minutes on the rock before regurgitating fish, but not, it appeared, the eel.

By 2 p.m. I had shot over 60 pictures. Despite my flannel swab, it was oven hot in the hide. The excitement helped me to endure it, for three times I saw black kites flying over and heard their shrill whistling cries, 'Pheeoo-kip-kip-kip'. Once I heard an imperial barking its usual 'Gak gak' calls as it flew overhead. What a place! All the time there had been odd sucking, splashing sounds near the water's edge up and down the shore. When I left the hide, I saw a fish's back like a big hump moving about two feet offshore. Two other fish with stiff thick light brown dorsal fins actually had a fight near the edge but took off when they saw me. It was obvious there were many fish in the river, which was why the black storks were finding it so easy to hunt for their young.

José had told me that when the dam opened, the surface of the river could rise two feet, so before leaving I lifted the hide higher into the reedy vegetation. I had only three hides with me and could not afford to have one washed away, not in a place so full of rare wildlife

135

as this. I drove to a shady spot under some trees further up river for lunch, and before typing out the day's notes, I took a walk down a wooded path to the shore, just in time to see a large brown and white speckled bird flying past. It looked like a huge osprey but did not have that bird's white throat and dark eye streak. (Later, from my description, Suso and José identified it as an immature Egyptian vulture, which does not get the light plumage and orange head until its second year.)

I dashed off to Torrejón el Rubio for food and petrol. When I returned to Las Cansinas, José told me the fish that the storks had been catching were *carpas*, a species of Spanish carp, common in the Tiétar. He was pleased with my success but said it would prove *nada* (nothing) compared with what I would experience the next day.

'You come to my house at 7 a.m. We have found the perfect black vulture nest for a hide, and you will be in it all day!'

Cripes, he was working this old horse a bit hard, I thought, but all I showed was eagerness. Slow he may be in speech and manner but, by heaven, José got things going, and he got them *done*! By the time I had finished my notes, sorted out camera gear for the next day and made a paella, I was ready for bed. This place was doubly good for me – I had no time for my usual evening drinks.

I was at José's home before 7 a.m. and found him in Suso's jeep, engine running, and in the back was one of the huge canvas ICONA hides. Surely, he was not going to set that up on a rare black vulture nest? I followed him up the road from Villa Real towards Plasencia. Then he pulled off to the right on to a tortuous gravelly grey track and headed up into a great range of hills and the 523-metres-high Puerto de la Serrana. Near the top he turned right again on to an even worse sandy track, where sharp ribs of rock stuck up at short intervals. After passing the stone hut vigilante Toni had built so that he could keep daily vigil over four tree nests of black vultures on the north side of the hills, to stop anyone disturbing them, my van could go no further. José told me to park and jump into his jeep, which then behaved like a real *caballo* (horse) as it jauntily bounced and bumped over the harsh jagged terrain for a further kilometre or so.

We then set off on foot, José carrying the canvas hide and its poles and I my camera pack, tripod, lunch, foam cushion, a litre of orangeade and the vital soaked flannel. We passed below some rugged white escarpments, with crags of limestone jutting out all over the place between the gummy bushes, then headed downwards. From here on

At nine weeks old an imperial eagle chick forms a 'tent' with its wings when mantling over prey brought in by its mother. (Photo by the late Imre de Boroviczény)

The male golden oriole flew to his nest with a great green grasshopper to feed his chicks.

Watching the rare black vultures at their nest was a wonderful privilege. The massive female folds her 9ft span of wings as she lands, then rearranges twigs with her beak. With outspread wings, she shields the chick from the searing heat of the sun. Later, the male regurgitates meat for the chick. He protects the little one with just his body, raising his rear feathers to form a heat shield for himself.

Finally, all three black vultures were on the nest together. The expression on the parents' faces seems to reflect the loving care they take of their quaintly dignified youngster.

The rare and graceful black storks had three chicks in the nest.

the jungle of rhododendron-type bushes, and madrona trees would have been almost impenetrable but for the fact that José and the vigilantes had hacked a narrow tunnel through it all with machetes. It was blisteringly hot and I was glad of the shade of this tunnel as we struggled on. I thought we were going right down the far side of the mountain, but after about 250 metres of sweaty progress we saw the light of a small clearing ahead. José paused and pointed out the nest tree. I was just in time to see the female black vulture glaring at us with her dark eyes before she spread the 9-foot span of her broad wings and sailed away. The nest, a broad platform of bare sticks and branches, was swaying in the breeze at the top of an *encina* (evergreen oak), and poking above it was the white and dark grey head of a small prehistoric monster pretending to be a chick, with a grotesque black-tipped beak, like that of a hornbill.

Because of the rising ground, the nest was level with the eye from where I would be sitting, and beyond it lay a superb view of the hilly woods and the *dehesas* (pastures) which formed the first carrion-foraging grounds of the vultures. These *dehesas* which cover the lowlands of the Monfragüe Park, and much of Extremadura, have been made by man between the ancient oaks and cork trees (keeping roughly 50 trees per hectare) where matted thickets have been eliminated to provide small fields for grazing grass, hay and cereal crops. The main aim of raising livestock – cattle, horses, pigs, sheep and goats – is achieved, yet the pastures also help provide food for the wildlife, including red deer, wild boar and rabbits, and prey and carrion for imperial, short-toed and booted eagles, all the vulture species, and the black and red kites too. The woods and thickets that are left give nest sites and shelter to goshawks, sparrow-hawks, a host of small birds, and refuge to lizards, badgers, foxes, genets, wildcats, and also a few lynxes. The two great rivers and their tributaries support some fifteen species of fish, otters, water rats, and many aquatic birds, including the rare black storks. No wonder Suso had fought so hard to conserve the area.

We worked as a team, with barely a word exchanged, and had the big hide installed between the trees at the clearing's edge in less than half an hour. José had clearly taken to heart my earlier idea of covering these bare hides with vegetation, for he and Toni had cut piles of sprays from the cistus and other bushes the previous day. I tied green cords round the top and middle, and we weaved the leafy sprays between them until the hide was naturally obscured. I was ensconced by 9.25 a.m., and having threaded leaves into an elastic band round the barrel of my 400mm lens, José left. After his footsteps receded, the chick began to behave naturally and I had a good look at it.

Its body, resembling that of a partly plucked turkey, was covered in a whitish fawn down. A few tufts of its first dark brown feathers were sprouting from the rear edges of its long pelican-like wings and the ends of its tail. Now and again its long neck reared up into the sky like a snake, and it swivelled its weird head and monstrous beak round in circular patterns that were oddly slow and comical. At first I thought it was following the flight of a parent in the sky, then realised it was just watching flies. Round the chick's neck was a hairless ring, and with the broad round dome of its almost bald head, this made it look from the back like a little old monk. Loose skin at the sides also resembled a pair of leathery ears. It preened the stubby feathers of one wing, stroking them with strange gentleness for so grotesque a beak, then it laid its long neck and head out flat over the sticks, again looking like a snake.

After 40 minutes I heard the faint sound of a car door slam, then what must have been José's engine as he drove his jeep away. Suddenly there was a noise like a storm passing above the hide. It stopped as quickly as it had started, and I saw the female black vulture had landed back on the nest. The racket had been made by the air rushing through her massive wings and pinions as she braked to land. What a sight she now presented, the largest raptor in Europe, well over three feet long and more than 18lbs in weight. As she gazed towards the hide, obviously not noticing it for she showed no alarm, her dark primeval eyes seemed to stare through the lens into mine with a sad long-suffering but patient look.

Unlike an eagle chick, which squeaks and makes a fuss when a parent lands, the young vulture behaved with oddly endearing dignity. It just looked up hopefully at its mother, seemed to realise it would not be fed, and gazed dolefully down at the nest sticks again. The mother thrust her beak below it and rooted about, as if hoping to find some fleshy pieces underneath, but there was nothing edible left there. She groomed the top of the chick's head with her huge beak, then carefully smoothed back the down she had combed up by pushing it back with the smooth curved part of the top of her beak, stroking it over the chick's cranium.

Twice the youngster gently grabbed its mother's bill, as if asking for food, but still it made no sound. Then it yawned. The vultures' world seemed one of infinite patience, of stoic acceptance that time passes with nothing much achieved, or achievable. The mother yawned too, appearing happy just to stand by her chick for long periods. Sometimes the chick dozed when sitting upright, then its head would begin to sink — down, down, down — and just as I would think it was about to topple over the edge of the nest, it would wake with a start and preen its legs instead.

At 12.03 p.m. the sound of sheep bells and the yells of shepherds came up from the valley far below, sounding as unnecessarily inane and alien as they had from eagle hides in Scotland, but the great vulture took no notice. Half an hour later the chick made several attempts to stand up, but though it kept its head down on the nest sticks for support and used its half open wings as a second brace, it collapsed again. Once I heard a barking '*Gak*' call as an imperial eagle flew over, but the mother just gave it a cursory upward glance with the great orb of one black eye. At 1 o'clock she began to look agitated. Then with her back towards me, she opened her great wings so wide that I could hardly get them in the lens. I took one dramatic picture, then another as she launched into the air, a third as she sailed away to the left, and a fourth of the chick staring after her in apparent dismay. Its face looked permanently sad, as if it knew even at this young age that it would often be disappointed in life.

Moments later I heard a brief flap. The male had landed with a small stick, which he dropped. He was slimmer than his mate, standing higher so that more of his tarsi and legs showed. He was also a paler colour, his head crown shining in the sun like light gold. I had heard another '*Gak*' eagle call, so maybe he had come in to guard his youngster. But a few minutes later he took off again. At 1.16 p.m. I looked through the lens and found the mother had come back, this time without making a sound. She now sought to shade her chick from the heat of the sun, first by holding her left wing over it. As the sun swung round the sky in the westward arc, she kept shifting so that her back was always to it, and then held both wings wide open to give it even more shade. She spent long periods just looking fondly down, watching as it lay on its side like a human child, with its head across the nest. It reached back with its gross beak to preen its underparts while still lying like that.

At first sight, or when one just sees a still picture of it, the black vulture chick appears ugly, almost obscene, but when one watches it in life, observes its natural dignity, its melancholy expressions and comical movements, it becomes an endearing even beautiful, little character. When its mother took off again at 3.50 p.m., the chick's agonised expression at being left alone once more made me chortle silently. At almost 4 p.m. the male came in with a great beakful of twigs and duffy debris which he put on the nest as my second film ran out.

Just then the female landed beside him. What rotten luck! I could have got both adults on the nest with their chick. By the time I had put in a new film, both parents had gone again. I hoped they had not detected my frantic but careful windings. When both birds were on the nest together, I noticed that the chick did make little chootling '*kuk kuk kuk*' calls to solicit food, for it was clearly very hungry. They sounded rather like the calls of a turtle dove but much deeper in tone. Ten minutes later the mother returned, again without food. Now the hungry chick pecked at her tarsal feathers and toes. At first she just shifted back her foot, but once she bent her head down swiftly and brought its head up sharply with her own beak, as if saying 'Don't do that!' She left the nest and returned twice more before 4.45 p.m., once with two sticks. A few minutes later the sky clouded over, the sun had gone for good that day, and she left again, as if knowing the chick could now be left without getting sunstroke on its bare skin areas. The poor chick looked dismayed, but I realised that in their world even young vultures have to spend days without food. The breeze grew stronger as the light died, the nest tree began to sway slightly, and this rocking motion soon sent the chick to sleep. At 6.30 p.m. I heard the faint slam of a car door high above, and before vigilante Toni arrived to walk me out I was all packed up and ready to go.

Although handsome and only 20 years old, Toni was a lad of few words. When I offered to pay him something, he shook his head and said it was his job, for which he was paid by the Park. Once he paused to see how the old guy was struggling along up the 250-metre rough rock-filled path with his heavy pack, surprised to see him moving easily and happily after his first day in a hide over such rare and magnificent birds. I just hoped I could spend another day there, for I wanted more than anything now to watch and photograph the chick being fed. I had grown oddly fond of that quaint little character.

14 · Griffon Heights

Next morning I was set up in the hide overlooking the Egyptian vultures' nest by 10.30 a.m. and saw that the male, which was not quite as big as the female and had a smaller white cowl at the back of his head, was now incubating the eggs. As I looked through the lens, he stood up, turned right round and sat down facing east. I very much wanted to photograph the changeover, when the female came in to relieve him, both birds on the ledge together. I felt I might have a long and boring wait, for vultures can fly great distances in search of food.

Owing to the steepness of the rocky slope, my position soon became excruciatingly uncomfortable. Although the tripod was at full stretch, I still had to scrunch my guts to get my eye down low enough to see through the viewfinder, producing pains in the region of my duodenum. One by one I dug out the little rocks below my foam pad and laid them round the tripod legs in an attempt to lower my seat so that I could see through the camera without strain. I was doing this, taking frequent looks, when I saw the female winging in and swooping up to the nest. The damn motor drive failed to work! I missed her landing completely, but by frantic hand winding I got them on the ledge together, then what may have been a jarred shot of the male leaving. Hell! I was bound to have a long wait now. I got the motor drive working again and took shots of her rearranging the eggs, settling down on them and pulling grasses in around her body.

The vultures could not leave their eggs to keep warm as eagles sometimes do in Scotland on a sunny day, for they would cook in this strong sun. But how often did they relieve one another? It was obvious to me, as I sweltered in the hide, that I could not put in a full day's watch to find out. Here, there was no shade from trees at any time and the heat of the sun beat down relentlessly. It was so hot that even my flannel dried out after two hours. At times I felt faint. I tried sitting completely naked but found I had to keep at least my trousers on. The trouble with sitting down for a long time with knees partly drawn up is that your legs want to fall out sideways, and to keep them upright produces great muscular pain after a while. Then I found a solution: I took my trousers down to just above my knees, where they held my legs the right distance apart without muscle strain. Even the vulture was feeling the heat. She was sitting panting with her beak half open, like a pelican laughing. I endured it until 2.20 p.m., when the sun went off the ledge anyway, then left with my backside aching all over. I found, too, that using my trousers as a leg holder had split the zip fastener of my flies. From then on I used a knotted scarf for the purpose.

I drove to a tapped spring at the Fuente del Frances for a swab down and to fill my water containers, then roamed about looking for more wildlife. I was in my van, perched above the Tiétar well over a kilometre west of the black stork nest, when I saw two black kites circling over a tree on a hill above the far side of the river. There were two bare brown spots in the branches where the leaves had withered and a dark blob between them. Then one of the kites landed on the blob which through the binoculars looked like a nest! Later I met José Antonio on the road and took him back there. He confirmed that the tree was right in the middle of a pair of black kites' territory and was delighted I had found the nest. When I asked him if we could get a boat and set up a hide there, and also use it to set up a hide near the storks' nest, he replied with a firm no. The stork cliffs were too steep for an *escondite* (hide) and no boats were allowed on any of the waters in the Park. Banning all boating was one reason why so many rare birds nested in the riverside trees and cliffs and the rule could not be waived, even for me!

Seeing my look of disappointment, José smiled, put his hand on my shoulder and told me to '*ánimese!*' (cheer up), for tomorrow we would put up a hide on a griffon vulture nest, and also meet the vigilante who controlled the banned area of the Sierra de las Corchuelas where imperial eagles nested, to see if I could work them too. I cheered up pretty fast!

I was almost late for my 8 a.m. appointment with José next morning. A flock of azure-winged magpies, called *rabilargos* in Spanish, had started coming to the rice left-overs I had been throwing out. These gorgeous black-helmeted, rosy-plumaged members of the crow family, which have bright blue wings and tails, are common only in Extremadura, and I had found them deucedly difficult to stalk in the wild. Now they were flying on to my rice in the early sunlight and, using the van as a hide, I took many photos of them without any stalking at all.

José, who had waited impatiently in his jeep, led the way back to the Fuente del Frances where we met two vigilantes. One was a young athletic man with a moustache called Felix, whom I assumed to be in charge of the imperial eagles. The other was a short, plump and talkative middle-aged fellow called Manolo, who did not look as though he would be much good on the Hill! The three men took out a large scale map and for half an hour jabbered away as they traced over the map with their fingers, apparently discussing routes by which I could be taken to a nest of these rare birds. It became clear eventually that the fat one, Manolo, was in charge of their area. As he spoke in a local dialect, I could barely understand a word he said but I did a lot of smiling and agreeing. That over, Felix and I jumped into José's jeep, which performed its usual *caballo* act over the tortuous rocky terrain until we were under the great cliffs getting on for a kilometre from the Castillo de Monfragüe.

Felix carried my tripod and foam cushion, while José, who had another brown ICONA hide under one arm, offered to carry my heavy pack. I thanked him but said that the day I could not manage my own pack I would give up this work. I almost changed my mind when the two young men set off on the hard 350-metre climb at a cracking pace. I was now carrying my biggest pack, with camera, lenses, lunch, a litre of orange juice, knife, cord, notebook, and a hefty tape recorder, and had a job to stay with them. There was a final hair-raising climb up almost sheer rock, which I thought might defeat me, until eventually I heaved the pack over on to the hide site, a perfect rectangle of grass, just a little larger than the generous proportions of the hide. It was bounded by three giant walls of limestone. The front was open to the nest which lay on a ledge slightly upwards only 25 metres away, and in it sat a huge almost fully fledged griffon chick.

We had the hide in place in minutes, tightly secured on all four sides with thin wire to rocks, a task made easier by the fact that the four poles went into pockets all the way up the sides and were not left loose, or with complicated tie-cords, as they are in British hides. One trouble was that we could not push the poles into the ground as it was so hard, and so a 9-inch gap was left between the canvas and the ledge. The three rock walls would take care of the back and sides, and I placed my empty green pack sideways across the front, with some greenery obscuring it so that my feet would not show. I also hid the shiny metal of the front poles while José cut and slung up some leafy green oak branches for me to tie on where I wanted them. He said that Felix would come to walk me out at 7 p.m., then the two men left me, all set up and ready for work at 10.09 a.m. The south-facing nesting fissure was difficult to photo as some of it was in sunlight, the rest in shade, and the youngster was crouching in a dark corner due to our disturbance. By midday the sun should be fully on the ledge and would remain so for several hours before it began to set in the west.

At 10.48 a.m. I heard the loud storm noise of air rushing through a vulture's feathers and just missed the landing of the female griffon. I took many pictures of her huge light copper and dark brown form as she preened her wings with the yellow beak at the end of her long short-feathered neck and head. Then she walked slowly along the ledge with head held down as if bent on some stealthy mission, flopped down behind a rock which completely hid her from my view and, I assume, went to sleep. After half an hour the chick emerged from the dark crevice and I saw it was fully feathered, though its head and neck were still all white. It stared towards its mother for a long time, not moving, as if knowing it was no good trying to wake her and get some food. At 11.15 a.m. the mother walked back on to the ledge, then very slowly, one after the other, picked up three sticks and laid them on top of each other. With the same deliberate movement she picked up a stray white feather and placed that on top of the sticks. The chick also did something comic: it stuck its left wing shoulder right out on the nest and performed a sideways roll over it before righting itself again.

At 11.27 a.m. the male swished in, so fast that I missed him too. The female went forward to greet him, and I took fine shots of the two together. By this time the chick had returned to the crevice. I still had not got an adult with the chick. At 11.45 the female took off and I got her going, mighty wings stretched out as she launched into the void. Three minutes later the male followed.

Now the bored chick began to entertain me with many comical actions. It reached right over its back to pull its tail feathers through its beak, scratched its head with its eyes shut for so long that it over-balanced and almost fell over. It squatted on its hocks, grey feet and claws stuck out in front, its huge wings held out to the side but bent in a bow so that the outer sides of its primary feathers were touching the ledge beside and under its tail. It looked just like a dog. All the time it panted with the heat, at about 75 respirations a minute. It was hard to believe that such heavy creatures nest on high sheer cliffs. If a chick fell off a ledge before it could fly, that would be the end of it. After a while it stood up, put its head down on the ledge, then lifted its arched wings right above its head in a delicious stretch. At 2.05 p.m. it looked round the scene for several minutes, then abruptly flopped down in a corner, with its wings stretched right out, and went to sleep.

All hides in precarious positions present problems, and this one was no exception. It was on hard level ground, and because the poles could not be pushed into it, the camera hole was far higher than usual. The tripod was almost at full stretch, and when I sat on the foam cushion the viewfinder was two feet above my head. To see through it for long periods I had to kneel up on the cushion, hold the remote control button in one hand and brace my body up with the other. The constant flexings of kneeling up and down, holding myself in half kneeling positions, produced excruciating pains in my knees, back and neck. With the chick now sleeping, I decided to take a rest myself and to lie out flat on my back. In order to do this my head and shoulders had to stick out of the back of the hide. I opened my eyes and saw great jagged boulders hanging over me. If one slipped, or a chunk broke off, I would be a goner. Those rocks had probably been up there for thousands of years but it would be just my luck . . . I experienced claustrophobic feelings and muttered a silent prayer.

At 2.29 p.m. I was back sitting on the foam pad when I saw through the hide spy hole that the chick was looking about with excitement. I heard a rush of air and just got to the camera in time to take two fine photos of the male landing on the outer rock of the ledge with a piece of sawn wood in his beak. Then his mate landed too as I

145

clicked away. He dropped the wood, turned and flew off, while the female once again crept behind the rock out of sight. Only then did the chick jump to its feet! Would I ever get them all together in one shot? The chick walked about the nest, flapped its great wings with loud swishes and made breathy honking noises, mixed with oddly thin cheeps. Once it stared out into the void, as if longing to go and get its own food.

The racket must have woken its mother, for she came out from behind the rock and started to preen, but the chick was now hungry and went towards her. She looked as if she was about to fly off, but the chick cried out urgently with odd harsh '*wheeoop*' noises. She turned to it and put her beak down to the ledge. This sent the chick into a wing-shivering frenzy. It began pecking and tugging at her beak until it opened and some red and orange meat began to slide out. The chick gobbled it hungrily. I was banging off shots for I could see clearly both heads and beaks, and the meat being transferred. It took 17 minutes for three lots of meat to be regurgitated in this way. Then the female took off, the chick flopped down in its dark corner, preened for a while, then went to sleep. It was 3.10 p.m., the sun was going off the far side of the crevice, and I thought that would be that for the day.

Only five minutes later a griffon landed, then had to get out again fast as the male was coming in on top of it, definitely intent on driving it away. Perhaps it was another adult that had not realised this was a nesting ledge. He stayed on the edge, occasionally looking down at the few vehicles creeping along like ants on the road far below, then took off after a seven-minute rest. From 4.01 the chick preened its wings, then fanned its tail up like a displaying cock capercaillie, so that it could reach each individual feather. Sometimes it put its left or right wing down on the nest, as a prop.

At 4.43 p.m. the female came in again. The chick gave the same harsh squeals, head down on the nest, wings shuffling in solicitation. This time she disgorged eleven lots of meat, each one of which the chick took from her throat just before it reached her beak. The mother's body quivered with effort each time the meat came up, and between disgorgements she just stood there, waiting for the next to arrive, taking until 5.01 p.m. to complete the feeding. Then she kept looking out into space, galloped comically to the edge like a fat child on sports day, and sailed away. At 5.05 the male came in again for another short rest, watching fondly as the chick picked up sticks and dropped them again slowly, as it had seen its mother do. When he left again, the chick went to sleep on the shady ledge for by now the sun was completely off it.

Just before 7 p.m. I heard a whistle and realised it was Felix coming to walk me out. I was almost packed by the time he arrived. He was glad to hear of all the feedings but surprised me, once we were well away from the nest area, by trekking upwards towards the Castillo. My van was down by the road, I was tired and hot from the week's exertions and the strains of the day, so I began a slow traverse down over the rocky ground. Suddenly I scented goat, which was odd, for I had heard the shepherd and the bells of his herd go past well below the hide an hour earlier. Sure enough, I found an old she-goat in the bushes, clearly on its last legs, too weak to walk, and it let me stroke it and nuzzled my hands. I shouted to Felix who came halfway down, but he said there was nothing to be done for it – it would die and become '*comida para los buitres*' (food for the vultures). I wished the poor animal a better deal in the next life and reluctantly left it. Felix then explained that he was trekking up because he had (thoughtfully) brought his car to the Castillo so that I would have a far shorter trek out, upwards or not. There were great cliffs between me and the van on the route I had wanted to take.

He drove me back to my van and, like Toni, refused to take any payment for his trouble, saying he was paid by the Park.

I had a swab down at the spring. Vigilante Manolo drove up to say that I would be working with imperial eagles in a few days but it would involve '*mucho andar*' (much walking). He gave me an odd look. I thanked him and said I was used to hard walking. I did not think I would have much trouble keeping up with him.

Even after my cold water bathe, I was perspiring again by the time I reached my little camp site by the pond at Las Cansinas. It seemed to be getting hotter with every passing day, and as the heated engine was under the bed at the back of my van, and took so long to cool down, I had to leave doors and windows open for the interior to be endurable. This was the invitation for all kinds of bugs, biting flies and mosquitoes to wing in and take a bloody feast from the first part of my naked body they could reach. Once I went down to the pond and briefly dangled my feet, to cool them down again. I felt that if I could just get the imperials, visit the storks and Egyptian vulture hides again, my work here was just about done. I did not mind the little flies that landed on me to lick up my sweat, but being constantly bitten was not on. There was one little sandy fly with a high pitched buzz that had a bite like a crocodile. The orange-bottomed horse flies here were so big that if two or three landed on a horse at once they would probably break its back. As I ate my supper late that night I felt a sharp pain on my right ankle. A big flat black bug was biting away and next to it was a black leech! Their lives ended.

Some Spanish insects and beetles are enormous. You can be driving along when there is a smack on the windscreen, which is briefly filled with the vision of flailing hairy black legs, then *swish*, it has gone, and a sickening thump tells you its body has landed in the mud or on the road behind you!

The heat seemed to be scrambling my brains, for I tried to pour a glass of wine into the pipe I was smoking instead of my mouth. One evening I spent ten minutes searching for my glasses — until I realised I was wearing them. I lit a cigarette when another was still burning, half finished, in the ash tray! (I should explain that I do not smoke during the day, and NEVER out of doors, or on treks, or in hides, but I like to relax with a few smokes at night, or at my desk or in the van.) I also found I kept losing and misplacing things. Even though I had the van's little gas fridge fully on to keep meat, butter, milk and my bag of films cool, the ice box never froze. In the end I put all the meat into the pressure cooker, boiling it up each night and just taking the little I wanted for each meal. Somehow, I managed to avoid serious stomach problems, swigging down British-made kaolin and morphine mixture when I felt the slightest pain.

All Saturday I spent in the van typing out 5,000 words of notes made in the hides, my gut again aching from being cramped up for so long. My only recreation was to watch the beautiful rabilargos which were coming to my scraps in increasing numbers. Suso, now back, visited me in his jeep and was again a fund of helpful information. He was surprised by how these usually wary birds were coming so close for my titbits. He said there were two theories about them: one that they originated in Spain, Japan and China, the two populations being separated by the schisms of the Ice Age; the other, and more likely, he thought, was that they were brought to Spain as pets by Spanish and Portugese sailors in the seventeenth century from Japan and China. Many escaped to form the wild breeding populations of today. They had small nests for their size, and although they nested in colonies, these were hard to find because of the birds' wary cunning. They were late breeders, so their eggs would be hatching about now. I hoped I could find such a colony.

Suso also explained more about how the Monfragüe Park was working. There were now ten wardens employed all the year round, and ten part-time vigilantes from March to October. The latter guarded the reserved areas and rare birds nests so that they would be left alone by humans. Increasing numbers of photographers and bird watchers from all over the world were coming to Spain, especially to the rich wild life of Extremadura. It was better to concentrate them all here, where they could be controlled, than to have them working on their own, sometimes taking foolish risks, all over the Province. Most wanted birds and animals which were rare elsewhere, and if they were common here, the system made even more sense. He felt every biotope in Spain should have an area like Monfragüe where wildlife photographers and students could be controlled and helped at the same time. And, when he had had enough of being Director General del Medio Ambiente of the Province, that is what he would set about achieving. He had already surveyed some 60 other areas of Spain for this purpose. What an extraordinary man he was, so visionary, so efficient, so relaxed, so much time for everybody. If I had had a perfect grasp of Spanish I would have been happy to trot along at his heels, as unpaid assistant.

It was after he had left, and I was trying to take better shots of the rabilargos, that I came to a terrible realisation. As I looked at the camera on the tripod I saw that the manual button was not on. And now, I could not remember ever having switched it on at any time during the entire rare work in Monfragüe so far. Was the heat indeed affecting my brains? Of course, I had varied the speeds of my exposures in the tricky blinding light, to ensure *some* perfect shots, but did these speeds change if the manual button was not on? For the life of me, I could not remember! How could I have forgotten, become oblivious, to so simple a thing? My heart sank. I would have to do the whole lot again. Jośe Antonio would surely be furious.

15 · Rarest Raptors

As I was still not sure that I had wrecked everything I said nothing to José, and next morning I was at the black stork hide by 8.30 a.m. While I was setting it up, one of the birds flew to the rock beside the nest and stayed there, showing no fear at all. On the walk down I had seen the pair of black kites that often flew over, circling above a tree high to the left of the stork's nest, and one of them had flown into it. Wondering if they had a nest there, I decided to keep using the hide anyway. I noticed that the three stork chicks, now more fully feathered, liked to all stand facing inwards, towards the rock face behind the nest, as if wanting to present their backs to the early warmth of the sun.

I finished the film, took it out, then tested the camera. Not trusting the sound of the shutter speeds, I opened the back to watch the shutter closing as I varied the speeds, first with the manual button on and then with it off. It was disaster! The speeds did not vary unless I had it on. I had surely wasted the entire time: very few of the shots would be exposed correctly. I had no choice but to do everything again.

At 10.10 a.m. I saw the stork had gone, so kept my eye to the viewfinder. The chicks began to dance excitedly, and I knew she was coming back. I made no button mistakes this time and got a great sequence of her flying in, landing and regurgitating fish for the young. I could hear them all clapping their bills with anticipation.

When the sun went off the nest, I left the hide and drove to

150

Plasencia for more supplies. The place is utterly Spanish, a real carnival type of town, and I had lunch at a cafe pavement table.

On the way back I photographed a flashy bee-eater being squeaked at by a cheeky sparrow on a dead spar. The bee-eater is Spain's most colourful bird, with bright blue breast, bulging yellow throat, a black eye stripe topped by brilliant kingfisher blue, and head and back plumage of orange, chestnut and yellow. Several black kites flew obligingly near the road too. Well, I would work the Egyptian vultures again tomorrow – and also the hoopoes, if their young had not flown. Then all I had to do was to ask José to have me put into the black and griffon vulture hides once more so that I could rectify my ridiculous mistake.

Wanting to start early, before the sun became really broiling, I was in the Egyptian vulture hide before 8 a.m. The female was on the nest and got up every half hour to turn the eggs, pushing them about with her beak. At 9.30 the metal girders, which protect motorists from the sheer drops along the roadside, began to crack and ping as the rays of the sun made them expand. She obviously heard this, walked to the front of the nest and peered down. When another cracked, she flinched as if it was a gun. I thought she was going to fly and switched on the manual button, but she decided the noise was harmless and went back to the eggs.

For the next four hours I endured hell in my haunches, watching her turn the eggs, draw hay round them with her beak, and preen her feathers. Once she walked to the edge of the nest and looked all round the sky, as if expecting her mate to come and take over. He did not, and she went back to the eggs and banged her beak on the nest debris all round them, as if in vexation! Several times the black kites came circling over the hide from the tree near the storks' nest, and now I could definitely hear faint cheeps coming from there. I was almost sure now that they had a nest with young in it. At 1.29 p.m. the vulture stood up, walked purposefully to the front of the nest, and I took shots as she opened her creamy wings wide, closed them, opened them again, then sprang into the air.

I knew the male was coming in and banged off many fast pictures as he looped up, passed her so that both were in shot, landed, and started to turn the eggs before sitting down on them. There had been no mistakes this time; it had been worth the long hot wait. At 2.20 p.m., with the sun off the ledge, I packed up.

After a swab down at the spring I was typing my notes when little plump Manolo drove up and said we would be going to the imperial eagles on Saturday, the only day he could get off. I thanked him, and again he said it was a long hard hike. He gave an odd short laugh. Later, when I told José I wanted to do the black vultures again, as I was not sure whether my camera had been working that day, he said languorously, of course! When I told him I would like to do the hoopoes again, he said go in *now*! So I did. The young had not yet flown, and the adults came in and out as often as before.

Congratulating myself on hauling back my stupid mistake so easily, I thought it would be nice to have a look at young hoopoes close up. The hole was too high to see into, so I fetched a rock on which to stand. I put my hands on the tree trunk and raised my eyes to the hole, expecting to see an array of four or five beaks pointing at me. I did not. I had a brief glimpse of what looked like young birds' backsides and SQUIT — I was half blinded by hot sticky white liquid splashing into my face. They had all squirted their shit at me! It might have been coincidence that they all wanted to go at the same time, just as my face appeared, but to me it seemed a definite defence reaction. I did not tell José about it for he might have disapproved of my going so close. I hurried to the van to get cleaned up.

Early next morning I had just photographed the black stork flying in with a new stick for her nest when the black kite pair came over from the south, calling to each other. The cries sounded like the high-pitched whinnying of a horse in the distance. They soared above the river, then a third kite came along and the first pair attacked it, making it turn over in the air to protect itself with its talons before it beat a hasty retreat. One of the kites then flew into the tree above the storks, where I had thought there might be a nest. No doubt about it now, for I could hear the shrill trilling cries of chicks as they greeted their parent. Through the long lens I could just see a bit of the nest and the kite's head. It appeared to be looking downwards. Something moved beneath her, under the tree itself, something reddy-brown and large. It was a *cierva*, a red deer hind, and she was swollen like a barrel, heavily pregnant. She was reaching up with her head, apparently chewing at the holm oak leaves. Although she was only about two metres from the kite, the bird did not seem perturbed. Not until she moved away, as I tried to get pictures unobscured by foliage, did the bird leave the tree. It swept out across the river, dived in display, circled over the nest tree again, and was then set upon by two azure-winged magpies which dive-bombed it, dodged its thrusting talons and temporarily forced it down into a large bush. Twice more the kites went into the nest during my four hour stay.

All that time I was clicking away at the black storks too; feeding their chicks at 9.41 a.m. and 11.21 a.m. on *carpas*. The youngsters still had the exasperating habit of facing inwards, to the rockface behind the nest, so that they looked like skittles in a ten pin bowling alley from the back. I had the deuce of a job trying to get all their orange beaks showing at once in a picture, or of them shaking and swallowing the fish. Once the chick on the left began tugging, then pushing, at a stick. The mother watched, gangled over on her absurd red legs, took the stick in her beak and weaved it under another at the edge of the nest, showing the chick how to do it.

When I told José about the kites, he said he knew of the nest. A hide had not really been necessary for the black storks but he had helped me to put up mine, so as to avoid disturbing the kites. I did not think black kites were too wary of humans, for that very morning one had swooped close over my head near his farmhouse, making the sparrows wheel up in clouds and sending his chickens scurrying for shelter.

I went back next morning to take flight shots of the black kites and storks while sitting just behind the hide. Both kites appeared to my right and gave a dazzling display of aerobatics, diving on each other, one bird doing a complete forward roll in the air. When the stork landed on her nest, she began jerking her long red beak up and down before disgorging and this made all the chicks squeak. She appeared to be conducting a small choir, with her beak as the baton! When the kites went in and out of their nest, their chicks called shivering '*schree*' sounds. At midday the two black storks winged over, landed on a rock and dozed together for more than half an hour.

When I was ready for lunch and a rest from my hunched position, I went further up the river, put the camera on its tripod at the water's edge, and took some shots of the kites flying into their nest. I was just turning away when the heavy camera fell forwards against the tripod — the holding screw must have come loose — and the whole lot overbalanced and fell into the river. Stunned with shock, I was slow to react. The camera must have been underwater a full two seconds before I fished it out. The insides were soaked. Nothing worked. Here was disaster number two!

153

I had no choice but to open up the complicated inside computer workings — a job only an expert should tackle — and dry it all out as fast as possible. I left it in the sun after drying every bit I could with a chamois leather. Having repeated the process in a three-hour struggle, I got it working again. Phew! How would I have acquired a new camera in time for the black vultures and imperial eagles if I had failed? The constant heat was definitely affecting my brains.

Because my van could not go so far as José's jeep, we had a longer walk than before to the black vulture nest. Toni danced over the huge rocks like a chamois, carrying just my tripod while I stumbled along with the 30lb pack. The female vulture was on the nest as we neared the hide, and Toni reckoned we could set up without putting her off. I said it was better we *did* put her off for if she saw anything suspicious at the hide, such as the big lens being poked through, she would always be suspicious of it. Also, the greenery round it was dying and needed replacing. We worked as fast as we could, and I was all set up by 10.05 a.m. Obviously we had not scared her much for she zoomed back only 16 minutes later, a very fast return, and I got a sequence on motor drive of her landing.

As I watched the chick preening its wing and tail feathers, which had grown a full two inches since last week, with its mother fondly watching, I thought there were advantages in being a vulture. It eats one good meal, stuffing itself, and then does not have to bother with food again for a week or more. I took photos of her shielding the chick with just her left wing but, when changing the film, I inadvertently hit the side of the hide with my elbow. Suddenly I noticed dozens of huge 3-inch spiders running down the walls of the hide and across its roof. They had been clustering together in dark corners at the top, having found the hide a good shelter. Some dropped on to my head, others scuttled over my legs. Panic! I swiped them off with my hands in a shiver of revulsion, trying not to betray the movements or make any noise. I broke a rule, lit a cigarette and blew the smoke at them. Luckily the vulture did not notice. The smoke shifted the spiders but for an hour they kept trying to come back in, marching towards little gaps and probing with their long front legs to see if it was safe to return. *Horrible!*

At 11.55 a.m. a butterfly fluttered over the nest. The vulture jerked her head back in surprise, pecked at it irritably, but missed. She could get quite ratty! I took photos of her holding up both wings against the sun, the chick pecking up at them until her head bent down quickly as if telling it off. The chick stood up, flapped its wings, and then stood next to her, also looking out over the vista like a little old man. At 12.25 p.m. the mother became alert, looked round the sky, stepped to the edge and flew.

Suddenly I heard the *bam bam bam* of great wings hitting the air, and the lighter-coloured male landed from the left. After three minutes he put his head down, shook it violently until his throat swelled up, and then regurgitated four pieces of meat. The chick, now making little chootling '*kuchuk kuchuk*' sounds, pulled them from his beak. A minute later he produced another piece. At 1 p.m. the male disgorged two more chunks, this time on to the nest itself, and the chick picked them up from there. Was this to help teach the chick that in later life its meat would not come from a parent's beak? Five minutes later he fed it again from his throat.

The male also shielded the chick from the sun but not with his wings out. As the sun moved west in its arc, he shifted with it, so that during four hours when the sun was behind the hide I could not see the chick at all. His body bulk alone hid it from my view. When he had shifted to the left and I could see the chick again, twice it pecked at his feet. When it did it a third time, he darted his head down and hit it on the top of its cranium with his beak. Stop that! At times he lifted out a wing, reached under it with his beak and zipped up the primary feathers. When he shut the great wing again I almost expected to hear it slam! At 2.10 he was standing so still that I saw a spider making a web between the top of his wing and an upright nest twig. Four minutes more and he produced food for the ninth time, standing patiently as the youngster pulled it from his beak.

I noticed at the sun's height he raised his back feathers high, with many air cooled gaps between, as a sort of heat shield for himself. I had not seen the female do this. Maybe her plumage was thicker than his. At 3.05 they both began looking round the sky, and I heard the chick making little breathy '*swilly*' squeaks. There was a swishing rush of air above the nest, obviously the female passing over, but she did not come in. At 3.37 the male regurgitated four times more. When a morsel was dropped between them, he picked it up and fed it to the chick like an eagle feeding its young. He also put a larger chunk under his feet, rended off morsels and proferred those to the chick. Occasionally the chick sat on its bum, feet stuck out to the front, leaning back on the elbows of its wings. Hilarious!

At 5.06 p.m. I heard a wing flap and saw that the mother had landed from the far side. At last I had all three together on the nest. My tired body quivered with nervous tension from being braced up to the viewer for so long as I tried to ensure I got good pictures. After half a minute the male left, then the female fed the chick five more pieces of meat.

While the act of regurgitation looks rather repulsive, as if the bird is being sick, it is not the same process at all. Vomit is unwanted, half-digested, smelly food which the body has rejected, and is brought up to be expelled. In regurgitation the meat comes out more or less in the same state in which the vulture ate it. Only when chicks are very small do vultures bring up semi-digested food. It is a very convenient way of carrying heavy amounts of food from up to 100 km away. At 6.30 p.m. she brought up the chick's nineteenth feed of the day.

When Toni arrived to walk me out, I was happy but exhausted by the tension and the heat. And tomorrow I faced not only a hard trek but endurance all over again at the imperial eagles nest.

After seven hours fitful sleep on the hot van bed, I was inconvenienced in some bushes at 7.30 a.m. when I heard hooting: Manolo had arrived half an hour early. He kept his car radio blaring and said it was better we went when it was *'templado'* before the sun was high. I swallowed half a mug of tea, choked on some dreadful Spanish muesli, slung my gear into his tiny Renault and off we careered. On the south side of the Sierra de las Corchuelas, we swerved through the gates of a *finca*, drove up an awful rocky track and parked by a yard of smelly goats. Then we set off on foot.

Had I been wrong about this man! Small he was, but not fat, nor even plump. Manolo's body was just thick, and very strong. He went off like a Spanish ibex, carrying nothing of mine, just his own rations and a walking stick. With my 30lbs I doggedly followed his fast-stumping legs up a steep stony route, sweat pouring and blowing hard. He looked back and asked if I wanted a rest. Of course not, I replied. I always blew hard for the first five kilometres, then began to move. I shouldn't have said it, but I knew what he was up to, trying to give me a real hard time. He looked at me differently after that and reduced the pace slightly. I kept with him easily enough as we forced ourselves upwards for over 5 km, and we had covered half the top of the Sierra before we came out at last on a high ridge covered with obelisks of limestone and pines.

At first Manolo could not locate the nest and seemed embarrassed, annoyed with himself. I said I understood, for in such rocky ground with trees escarpments could look different from day to day. I had done it many times in eagle terrain. He seemed pleased by that. Eventually we located the nest on the side of an escarpment, a black triangle in a madrona tree a good 400 metres away. José had said it would be about 200 metres. At first I thought the nest was empty. As I looked around for a good hide site amid jagged rocks which rang hollow when I hit them with the tripod, I saw that there was a chick in it, for suddenly a great red wing flapped out over its surface. It was well-fledged, about 8 or 9 weeks old. I reckoned the eagles would be just dropping food off for it now.

To my surprise, Manolo had no hide there. I had not thought to ask. He tore up and threw over a few fronds of gum cistus, told me to arrange them how I liked, and said he would keep watch from a hill further away. He was clearly not an eagle hide man and I was amazed.

'Hey, I need help to construct this *escondite rápido*,' I said.

'*Sí?*' – and then he set to work with a will.

He tied three large dead branches into a wigwam frame, then we covered this in with cistus fronds, the leaves down for the lower half, and leaves up for the top half. It was flimsy, with many gaps, but he thought it would screen me from the eagles' view. I did not think it would work at all, but after the tough trek, better make the best of it. I was set up by 9.40 a.m. and Manolo left. I took three photos of the young eagle, but there were many leafy twigs round the nest and I could not see all of it.

Twenty minutes later an imperial eagle flew past the nest but did not go in. I refrained from moving to photograph it in case it did. Presently the eaglet shifted to the left of the nest and I had a good view. It was coppery red all over, and I could see a white patch on its throat and the large yellow sere of its beak. I pressed the button and the damn motor drive banged off five shots madly, on its own, before I could stop it. I was sitting on a rocky shelf on the foam pad and felt a pain in my left hand. Huge wood ants with heads like golf balls were swarming over the rock round me. I knuckled the one that had bitten me, and a few others, then hit on a better scheme for keeping them away. I fed them! I put cheese, buttered bread, egg crumbs and bits of fruit cake near their earth citadel and they left me alone to go after the food.

I soon realised that the eagles had built cleverly, for when the eaglet wanted shade, it just flopped down behind one of the leafy screening twigs that protruded round the nest. There was no need for the eagles to shield it, like the vultures did. At 2.31 p.m. I saw one of the adults beating towards the nest from the west, sun shining on her silvery wing epaulettes. I waited with bated breath, finger on the button, but dared not move the camera on to her flying form in case she saw the movement. She did not go in. Eleven minutes later, I heard her call to the eaglet from high in the sky to the east — '*howlk howlk*', and it called back to her '*Gak, kerchuck kerchuck*'. Yet again she did not fly in. I was sure she knew I was there. The eaglet had a sleep, stretched out, and I got photos of it flapping its long red, yellow-tufted wings. I heard the eagle calling twice more after that but could not see her through the fronds.

It seemed no time at all before Manolo arrived to walk me out at 6 p.m. I realised then that I should have photographed the eagle flying past the nest, for it was my only chance to get her in the whole day, but there it was. Manolo was impatient to get going, no doubt back to his family, for it was Saturday night. I dismantled everything in a hurry, finding later I had left my remote control cord behind in my haste. Towards the end of the long stony trek out, he seized the folding chair José had lent me (which I had been unable to use because of the rocky ground) and we chatted away. As I saw his perspiring face I thought he had probably done his best for me. It was, after all, one of only four imperial chicks to be fledged in the Park this year and at least I had been able to photograph that, a chance no-one else would get. He too would accept no payment.

I was so tired as I drove back to Las Cansinas that my mind played loud tunes as the tyres whirred over the road. The van had been so hot during the day that the little fridge had not worked at all, and I was sure none of my films would be any good. I put them into a wet towel to keep cool in a slight breeze.

At dusk saw a huge white mastiff dog moving about under the trees, presumably one of the Spanish *mastíns* that ICONA were breeding in enclosures at Las Cansinas. I went out to make friends but it swerved away, looking weak on its legs. This seemed odd, and why was it running loose?

On Sunday, naked while typing notes at camp in the shade of cork trees, I noticed that my skin was covered in insect bites, some already with yellow heads. My urine had been bright yellow for days and I felt, to put it bluntly, knackered. But if I managed to avoid collapsing, I was determined to put in another ten days at this marvellous place.

16 • *Orioles, Italians and Other Rivals*

From where I sat in a small rocky arbour some 250 metres high near the Portilla de la Higuelas, I could see right round a spectacular bend in the Tiétar river. I watched the black kites circling slowly over the water, as if they were hunting for fish on the surface, and going into their nest. In the distance the black storks also glided in with food for their chicks. I had endured enough of cramped oven-like hides for a while and had found an ideal perch between two gum cistus bushes where, because I was wearing full camouflage gear, I reckoned no bird would see me unless it flew very close. Here the slight breeze was so refreshing. I was hoping for flight pictures of the immature Egyptian vulture that I had thought might be an osprey when I had first seen it flying in this area.

Presently three herons came wafting round the bend far below and landed on a flat rock. They lined up on it, heads shrunk into their shoulders, clearly just taking a rest. There was a brief rush of air behind my head, and a cheeky rabilargo landed on a cistus sprig, craning its neck to look at the suspicious hunched form it had seen sitting in the bushes. The merest swing of the camera on the tripod had it in full view for a good shot before it flew away again. I heard a series of flute-like calls as a small rainbow of bee-eaters flashed by, occasionally diving after insects in the air. This time I was too slow.

I was munching a sandwich when I saw a large creamy bird outline gliding towards me from the direction of Las Cansinas. It was an adult

159

Egyptian vulture. I whipped the camera up, tripod and all, and took three pictures as it whistled by, quite unperturbed by my nearness. Then it glided down, down, to my left and sailed into little cliffs above the river. It seemed to go into a crag which protruded beyond the trees and bushes, only 13 metres or so high. Surely she can't have a nest there, as low down as that, I thought.

I kept watch, and soon she came out again, circled over the river opposite me, then landed on a beach 300 metres downstream to my right which was used by bathers at weekends. She walked towards the water. I thought she was going to take a drink, but she stopped less than a metre from the edge and started picking up little objects and jerking them back down her throat. Five of them, in about five minutes. Was she swallowing pebbles, insects or picnic refuse? I could not see at such a distance. One of the black kites came along and swooped down low over the vulture's head in a mobbing attack, but she took no notice. The kite turned as if to have another go but changed its mind when two azure-winged magpies shot out of the bushes and began to mob it, diving round its fleeing form with '*cheese wheez*' calls. The vulture watched them go, then leaped into the air, flew upwards and behind me, as if checking whether I was a threat, turned and sailed down into the little cliff again!

I felt excited. There *must* be a third Egyptian vulture nest there, and it looked as if it might be easy to work. I would go now and see if I could set up a hide for some really close pictures.

After shoving all gear except the long-lensed camera into my van, I worked my way down the steep rocky ground and round the head of a short creek which cut into the land between the cliffs and me. The far side of the creek consisted of 7-metre high sheer rock faces and large snaggy boulders below them. Clinging on to little spurs of rock with my hands, holding the lens of the camera, which was strapped round my neck, upright with the crooks of my elbows, and trying to find purchase with my boots on the sharp boulders, I worked my way along. Twice I nearly fell off into the deep river. Finally the faces fell sheer into the water, with no places for my feet, and I had to climb up and go through the *matorral* (thicket) itself. With so much thorny, spiky undergrowth it was like a jungle, and without a machete I could not clear a way. I had to fight for every yard, placing the camera before me under the dense festooning creepers and bursting my way through to it, time after time. The bushes scratched and spiked me even through my camouflage jacket and the twiggy debris on the ground choked me with dust.

Eventually I reached what I thought were the right cliffs. I lowered myself over various projecting boulders, holding on to trees and leaning as far out over the drops as I dared, to see if there was a nest below them. Finding none, I gave up and fought my way back. The whole journey was no more than 150 metres yet it took me an hour and a half. I drove to the bathers' beach for a better angle of view and saw there were in fact two little cliffs above the shore where I had been – and blow me if the vulture did not fly out of the second lot as I watched. Obviously I had reached only the first. The second cliffs were only some 20 metres past the first, but in that thicket one could see no more than three metres ahead.

Next morning I spent three hours in the rocky arbour and saw a heron fly on to the land spit opposite. It walked into the water of a small lagoon, waded about 30 metres very slowly, picking its feet up with exaggerated care, and then stood by a stump, as if waiting for fish to pass by. Eventually it flew to my side of the river and landed out of sight. Of the Egyptian vultures I saw no sign.

I drove to the Castillo and was greeted in a friendly way by Felix, who was keeping vigil on the roof, and took pictures of a flying griffon that looked so pale it appeared almost white. I asked Felix if it was a young bird. No, it is *'viejo'* (old), he replied. When griffons grow old, they go grey, like humans. I had not known that before. He told me the old she-goat had died and that they had put it out in front of a permanent rock hide for a French photographer who had spent six days in the hide and got nothing. Hours after he had left in disgust, the vultures had come down and scoffed the lot! I could see the site far below us, and there were a few griffons flying above it right now. On the way back down I parked the van, stole through the trees, and in minutes had taken my closest ever photos of these birds flying.

I returned to the rocky arbour shortly after 5 o'clock and was just in time to see an Egyptian vulture fly out of the second set of cliffs and land by the line of bushes on the far side of the river. It walked about, again picking up and swallowing small objects, then it flew up to join its mate and they disappeared down river. A few minutes later they returned, circled opposite what seemed certain now to be their nest, then sailed off to beyond Las Cansinas.

Suddenly I heard a car door slam. Two men walked down to me

wearing trainer shoes and bright white shirts. They turned out to be Luis Angelo Gandolfi and Marco Pavese, two celebrated Italian wild life photographers who were making a film in Monfragüe and wanted to use the black vulture hide José and I had built. I suggested that they should freshen it up with new vegetation and wished them well. They also asked if they could film me taking photos with my long lens, so I obliged with a little acting job while Pavese used a hand-held cine camera and a 150mm lens. I was surprised by this, for the BBC had once criticised me for filming without a tripod, yet Pavese had won a BBC Wildscreen award that very year, for a film about kingfishers.

While we sat chatting on the rocks, a black kite flew down towards the river and plunged its talons into the water, snatching up a small fish and flying back to its nest with it. Of course we were all too late to get on to it, even Pavese with his hand-held movie camera. After their black vulture session they were going to film vultures at a carcass in the permanent hide beyond Las Cansinas. Since I had seen the Egyptian vultures fly down there just an hour before, I wondered if José was at this very moment baiting the place with a dead goat, but I said nothing. Marco told me he had once taken good film of an Egyptian vulture trying to crack a false ostrich egg with a big stone. It had also eaten eleven of the twelve hen's eggs he had set out, not by hitting them with stones but by cracking them on stones instead. After eating them it had not found it easy to get into the air. Hmm, I thought, I'll have to try that! When the two men left, the Egyptian pair returned and flew into the second cliff.

I carried a hide half a kilometre to the Tiétar river in the afternoon and set it up in bushes overlooking a broad stretch of dried mud. After fruitless hours trying to tempt the birds down to take two eggs, I went to Las Cansinas to meet Mario Alvarez Keller, the young biologist who was looking after weak and injured birds. He had eleven griffons, four black vultures, eleven buzzards, several red and black kites, and three imperial eagles, all living in special high net-ting enclosures. The birds that were not injured had all been found weak from hunger in various parts of the Province. They were being fed well, and wing exercised, until strong enough for release. They were often sent to other parts of Spain or any other suitable country that asked for them. Eighteen vultures had been sent to Sardinia in this way last year.

When I reached the new hide early next morning, the eggs had gone. It seemed as if I had a good chance of seeing the Egyptians cracking and taking them — until I spotted faint fox tracks in the dried mud, indicating *el zorro* had probably taken them during the night. I put out two more eggs and returned to the hide. Half an hour later I heard woofing wings. A pair of ravens flew over the eggs without looking down. Moments later I heard scratching noises. A large lizard was climbing up the outside of the hide. It had a brief snooze on the sunny top, climbed down the far side, then leaped off into the grass while still 18 inches above the ground. At 11.20 a.m. I decided I was wasting my time. Surely all the vultures would be at the goat set out beyond Las Cansinas for the Italian film-makers. Suddenly it dawned on me — so, probably, would the griffons nesting near the Castillo! What better opportunity could I possibly have for going solo into the hide near them and so correcting my mistake in leaving the manual button off when working them earlier? José had said I could do that . . .

After great swigs of water, to avoid carrying it, I made record time over the rough ground with camera pack, foam, lunch and tripod, covering the half-hour trek in just ten minutes. Assuring myself there were no vultures in the sky, I was in the hide and set up by 1 p.m. Forty minutes later the chick honked and in came one parent, followed immediately by the other. It is always said that griffon sexes look alike, but I now saw that the slightly bigger bird, which I took to be the female, had a more reddish tint in her head and neck. After a few minutes she left again.

For three and a half hours the vultures performed as well as before. I photographed the chick putting its head low and making '*bee-op*' sounds to solicit food, of it squeaking and leaping angrily towards the male when it did not get any, of him opening his wings wide twice and the chick copying the action with its own. It preened, sat in dog-like poses, and trampolined about the ledge beating its wings. At 4.45 p.m. the female returned and, after the male had left, fed the youngster five pieces of meat, both their beaks well in view. She flew off at 4.53 p.m. with the chick still soliciting for more. When it stopped looking round the sky and went to sleep, I left.

On my way back to camp I saw another sick goat in the road near Penafalcon. As I stopped, up drove the Italians in a white camper. With a theatrical gesture, Gandolfi handed me my lost rear lens cap, which he had found in the black vulture hide. He said they had had a terrible hot time in the hide by the goat beyond Las Cansinas and not a single vulture had come down! They had found the remains of a big dead white dog lying there, eaten by the vultures the day before, so they were not hungry. I realised it must have been the sick mastiff I had seen in the woods.

'Did YOU put it there?' Gandolfi suddenly demanded.

'Of course not!' I replied, adding that I had all the pictures of vultures at a carcass that I needed.

I thought I had better grab the dying goat in case they did, and went behind the van to pick it up. The Italians had not seen the goat and were amazed when I emerged with it in my arms. They asked suspiciously what I was going to do with it. I said it was sick and needed veterinary attention. When I saw Felix further up the road with the local shepherd, I handed it over to them.

I spent next morning in the rocky arbour, watching the Egyptians going in and out of their low crag nest, and even saw the far pair flying over the spot where I had placed my eggs, but they did not go down. Several vultures flew from Penafalcon towards Las Cansinas. I was sure the Italians would be able to film them today. It was odd that they should have thought I had put the dog out for the vultures for I felt no sense of rivalry with them. I had my own targets, and hoped they made a marvellous film.

Several times I heard the melodious calls of golden orioles near by, but despite their bright yellows they were elusive and hard to see as they skulked in the middle of bushes like warblers. I glimpsed them only briefly in flight, as if someone was flashing golden mirror reflections of the sun over the trees and shrubs. A big green lizard came from between the rocks, staring up as if trying to make out what I was. It moved one leg after the other in broken, delicate, disjointed movements, like a creature in an animated cartoon where not enough drawings have been made.

After lunch I was about to trek off to the eggs hide when a German photographer and his wife drove up and asked where I had been and what I was doing this morning.

The cheek! He was trying to pick my brains. I said, 'Oh, just photographing vultures, anything I can.'

'Vee have been doing orioles zis morning.'

'Orioles,' I repeated in surprise. 'What orioles?'

'At ze tower in ze woods, vere you saw my van zis morning. Italians have done zem too.'

Apparently José Antonio and his helpers had put up a tower hide overlooking a golden orioles nest without telling me about it. At first I felt peeved, especially as I had shown him an oriole nest I had found.

Then I realised that José did not tell every photographer where every hide was, or he would have been worked off his feet. The German, who was clearly a kind old fellow, told me where to find the tower, and in return I showed him the black storks' nest, the three chicks now almost fully fledged. As he left I thought — to hell with the eggs hide, I would take a look at the orioles NOW!

I drove to the woods and soon located the metal tower among the cork oaks by a small dry stream bed. It was 40 feet high, the struts far apart. I did not fancy climbing up there under the weight of my heavy pack with all the camera lenses and the tripod, but if that old German could . . .

I got up with a muttered prayer, shifted the loose floor boards aside and gingerly crept over them into the hide. It was hotter in there than a boiler room. I set up and found I could use only the 200mm lens for the nest was a mere five metres away. When I peered through the view finder, I was both surprised and amused. One windy morning I had lost a length of loo paper in the woods and later, feeling guilty, had gone unsuccessfully in search of it. The orioles, it appeared, had taken a fancy to it for nest building, and there it hung, waving merrily in the slight breeze from the bottom of the nest! There also were three well-fledged young, bulging over the sides, their broad pink beaks open as they panted in the heat.

Ten minutes went by before I heard a flute-like cry, '*oleo oleo*', and suddenly the male oriole was on the nest, a huge green grasshopper and some flies in his beak. He was 9½ inches of gorgeous colour, with a bright saffron yellow body, orange eyes and dark white-fringed wings. He seemed oblivious to the clicking camera as he reached across the nest and stuffed the grasshopper down the throat of one chick and gave the flies to another. He returned twice more in the next hour, always announcing his coming with the '*oleo*' calls, which was a great help to me, and brought the chicks to their feet in a frenzy of squeaks and wing shiverings.

I shot off two films before hearing cars go up the road near by. I felt it was probably time to leave, in case José should be annoyed to find that I had gone up the tower without his permission. In my haste, the tripod fell out of my hand, zoomed down and hit one of the cross struts with a great clang. Not until I reached the van did I realise the disaster. The vital top platform of the tripod and the camera-holding screw had broken off in the collision. There was only a half-inch strip of metal left, on to which somehow I would have to tie the camera in future. Hell! I could not go back to look for it, in order to stick it back with Superglue, because at that moment another photographer drove up, got out his gear and headed for the tower. When I did search later, I could not find it.

There was a heavy rainfall overnight, the first since my arrival. When I set off in the morning to hike to my riverside hide with three new eggs, I found the water had risen so far that it cut off my usual route of high sandy mud, so forcing me across a bog. I threw a baulk of wood into the middle of the bog, and after a ponderous but fast hop, skip (on the log) and jump, got over it. Even so, my left leg went in to the knee before I was clear. I saw that the fox had gone before me, floating over the soft mud, its prints broad and deep and the claws showing clearly. It had taken the eggs again, for there was no sign of broken shells. Or else the rising waters had washed them away. I set three new eggs out and spent five hours in the hide. I saw the black storks flying with food to their young, watched the black kites circling near their nest and heard their chicks crying out, but nothing came to the eggs except a pair of cheeky azure-winged magpies. Even they did not take or eat the eggs, but just moodily rolled them about with their beaks before flying off again.

When it began to rain again, I left and went to stock up with supplies in Torrejón el Rubio, where I told two friendly shopkeepers that I would like to live in the area. I asked them to let me know if they heard of an isolated *casa* near one of the rivers. They wanted to know if I was married and had a family, and when I said no, that I was a *soltero* (bachelor), they both looked sad and gazed at the floor. Of course, they assured me, it would be *possible* for me to live in the area, but they knew of no such house for sale. It was a final statement. In later travels I came to realise that Spanish society is predominantly a family society. A middle-aged unmarried man is an oddity there, suspected always of having something wrong with him. With an attractive wife I would have been invited to take part in social life much more than I was, and there is no doubt it would have helped enormously to secure a property.

I was in the tower hide overlooking the orioles' nest by 9.25 next morning and found I could not have cut it finer. I did not know it then, but young orioles leave the nest before they can fly, dispersing among the tree branches and keeping in touch with their parents by making loud double '*Kiu-Kiu*' calls. There was now only one youngster left in the nest, and it too climbed out and perched on a nearby twig. Four times in the next hour the bright-coloured male (the female has dowdier plumage, with no blazing yellows) came in to feed it insects. Once the male pecked gently at the chick's anus, below the short yellow tufts of its tail, clearly to stimulate it to defecate. In a few moments the vent opened, out came the white blob, and he took it in his beak and swallowed it before flying off. When I moved the floor boards to leave, I saw a young Spanish photographer waiting patiently below. Queuing up to watch nature getting on with life seemed a touch absurd to me — certainly not my style — but I helped him to carry his gear up to the hide.

I felt drained of energy, due partly, no doubt, to the sense of anti-climax from knowing I would soon have to leave this wonderful place. I had pushed myself really hard during these past three weeks. I went to the Tiétar and took down my two hides, which were about to be lapped by water. When I called with a bottle of whisky for José at his home, he was talking to the Spanish photographer and wanted to share it with us there and then. I said it was for *him*, for his birthday, or for Christmas, with my thanks.

Sitting there in the sun at 6 o'clock, glasses charged (with some of my own wine), José told me that the Italians had gone away for a few days in order to recover from their ordeal. They had spent five sweltering days in the hide opposite two dead goats (and the white dog) without any vultures at all coming down. I had a sudden idea. If the goats were still there, beginning to get high, why not have a go myself? I mock-boasted in my cups that I would get the vultures down in two hours!

José shook me then by saying — 'Okay, we go NOW. We put up one of *your* hides and you go into it at five in the morning.'

Away went the wine, and we careered along the two kilometres of sandy track between the gum cistus and scenty shrubs to the site. The Italians had built a wall of rocks, presumably hoping the vultures would perch on them, and in front of it lay the corpse of their newer goat, only 25 metres from their hide. It seemed to me that by altering the look of the landscape too much, and having the goat too close, they had guaranteed their own failure.

In less than an hour we had my best hide up between bushes, with vegetation tied round it. Then I dragged the stinking goat, its flesh almost all consumed by maggots, 60 metres from my hide. The guts fell out on the way. José laughed with approval as I covered up the guts with rocks so that the vultures would not go to them, out of my sight behind bushes, rather than to the goat. I said the goat was really no good, but José thought that the Egyptians might come to it. As I had not photographed Egyptian vultures at a carcass, I felt it was worth trying just for that. I drove him home, cooked supper at the camp site and fell into bed at midnight, feeling that I was a glutton for punishment. I did not rise until 5.40 a.m., and even then it was still pitch dark. I gulped down tea and cornflakes with milk gone sour, made a lunch sandwich, tramped down the track and was in the hide by 6.45. It took half-an-hour to tie the camera to the broken tripod platform with elastic bands, cord, camera tape and a pencil forced in as a wedge to make it all tight. I must be CRAZY!

The goat was now almost totally consumed by the maggots, its skin and hair sunken in like the cheeks of a man long dead. Stinking air from the decaying flesh of the goats and the dog wafted into the hide. After a while my nostrils got used to it, and it smelled just salty sweet. I was certain nothing would come down to this rotten lot.

At 7.46 a.m. I took a look through the side vents of the hide and was amazed to see an Egyptian vulture standing 20 metres away to the right. It was just looking about. I could not photograph it for there were two thick cistus bushes in the way. It would also have seen any movement of the long lens and flown off. Moments later I saw two griffons standing beyond the carcass but the ground drop was such that I could see only their heads and shoulders. After ten minutes one of them flew to the carcass, stood still for a while, bent its head down for a closer look, then grabbed a bit of fur and skin with the tip of its huge beak and gave a couple of disinterested tugs. I did not bother to take pictures as I had scores of griffons at a goat and was running short of film. I was waiting for the Egyptians to come in. The griffon evidently decided that the little flesh left was too putrid to eat, for it let go again, stood for a few seconds, then suddenly took off, followed by the second. I looked through the side panel and, dammit, the Egyptian had gone too!

I spent nine more tortuous hours in the hide but apart from a lone griffon circling low over the goat with loud *sigh sigh sigh* swishings of its great wings at 4.11 p.m., no more vultures came down. My spine, hips and scrunched up guts were hurting badly and I could bear it no longer.

Next morning I said goodbye to José Antonio at Villa Real and thanked him for the most hectic and marvellous three weeks of my naturalist life. He laughed louder than I had ever heard him before

Sometimes a griffon flew close, as if curious about what I was doing.

High in the nest cliff, the griffon chick sits in one of its many comical poses while its mother looks for her mate.

The jagged snow-capped peaks of the Sierra de Gredos glowed brightly beyond the beautiful Tiétar river.

Two female Spanish ibex cross a slippery slanting rock high in the Gredos peaks with the sure-footedness of the true mountain goat.

when he heard that the three vultures had come in just over an hour of my entering the hide, never mind the two which had been my daft boast. He was sure the Italians would like to know that! He made me promise to return, and I was deeply touched.

I felt sad as the rolling hills and great rivers of Monfragüe receded behind me but as the old van bowled along the beautiful C501 road towards Candelada and the mighty snow-capped peaks of the Sierra de Gredos appeared to my left I felt a new excitement mounting, and not a little fear. After checking the imperial eagle nest near that town, I would have to perform some very hard treks indeed up there, for among those jagged granite crags, some over 2,000 metres high, roamed the elusive *cabra montés*, the mountain goats of Spain known as the Spanish ibex.

17 · On High with Ibex

Rounding a bend just before Jaráiz, I saw an empty old farmhouse by the side of the road. On her nest on the roof stood a white stork with two almost full grown youngsters. I pulled up and climbed on top of the van to get more level with them. The storks just stayed there, twisting their great red beaks this way and that as I took photos. To have these huge black and white birds nesting on your roof is a symbol of good fortune in Spain, and many folk put artificial platforms out in the hope of attracting them.

The white stork has long lived close to man and once nested in many mediaeval towns throughout most of Europe, including Britain. To the Romans it was the symbol of filial love, because the young were so well looked after by their parents until well grown. To the Arabs it was the symbol of spring, and they held festivals when it returned from migration flights. In Europe, of course, enquiring children were told the stork brought babies and left them under a bush in the garden. The white stork is becoming rare in western Europe and even its highest concentrations in Spain have been in decline for many years. They migrate in late summer through Gibraltar to their African wintering grounds, and flocks up to 3,000 strong can provide a spectacular fly-past in a day. Before 1939 it was estimated that more than 100,000 storks migrated in one season, a figure which dropped to 38,900 by 1974. A census carried out by Professor Francisco Bernis in 1948 counted 14,500 occupied nests in Spain, but by 1974 the number had dropped to 7,341. Reduction of habitat (even town birds need the proximity of water and countryside for food supply), drainage, poisoning from pesticides in wheatfields, death by crashing into power lines, eggs stolen by illegal collectors, and eggs stolen for human consumption – these hazards all make life difficult for the white stork.

I had just climbed off the van roof and put the camera back into its pack when there was a swish of great wings above my head and the second adult swept in. To my surprise, it opened its beak wide and regurgitated a spray of clear water around the nest. At first I thought it was to clean the chicks, or to give them a cool bath, but later I discovered that storks do this in order to refresh the nest. They eat an extremely varied diet – fish, water snakes, crabs, molluscs which they catch in shallow waters, small animals and insects, as well as some vegetable matter – and so the nest can become rather smelly, hence the impromptu water showers.

I left these graceful creatures and continued on my way through Jaráiz, Jarandilla and Villanueva de la Vera in the foothills of the snow-capped peaks of Sierra de Gredos, and then Madrigal de la Vera and Candelada close under the great ramparts high above them. I was making for a place called El Raso which, according to my map, lay at the foot of the highest peak in the whole mountain range, the mighty 2,592 metres high Pico Almanzor. Tomorrow I would trek up there.

By 7.45 p.m. I was parked opposite the towering eucalyptus tree in which the imperial eagles had their nest. There were cars at the bridge near the farmhouse and several groups of men, stripped to the waist, were walking up and down the banks of the river with forked sticks, putting bowl-like nets into what remained of the shallow water. Perhaps they were looking for eels or fish trapped in the shallows. The tree looked deserted except for a few starlings flying in and out of the nest. At 10 p.m., with dusk falling, some men were still within 70 metres of the tree so that a definite check was impossible. I drove towards Navalcan, found a track to the right and camped below some holm oaks. As I cooked supper, red-legged partridges called to their chicks in the thickets '*chuck chuck – chuckar*'.

Early in the morning I hiked with a hide over the bridge and back through the trees to the hide site which I had marked with a circle of stones. From that open spot it was clear the nest was empty, with no chick faeces to be seen. It had either failed or not been used at all this year.

I drove up towards El Raso, took a sandy track to the north, passed a few small farms and parked at the end. I set off on foot through the sparse trees and soon saw that there were two slightly lower peaks to the south east of the Pico Almanzor, and I went up the broad shoulder that led to the one on the right. The air grew refreshingly cooler as I climbed the rocky ground between bushes and trees, glad to get the old cramped leg muscles working again. At the end of the tree line, I descended into a short valley, then turned left and headed up most of the righthand buttress. There were still little pockets of snow, or heavy frost, lying in north-facing dells near the top of the two main peaks and I paused in a dark rocky arbour to glass the crags and granite cliffs all around. Knowing that the grey-brown colours of the ibex would mingle with the rock, I worked slowly, carefully. I had read about the Spanish ibex in a book called *Wild Spain*, which was written as long ago as 1893 by two naturalist hunters, Abel Chapman and Walter J. Buck, and in parts it is evocatively written.

> No trophy is more dear to the big game sportsman; few so hard to secure . . . If a man's heart swells with the pride of strength, if he flatters himself he is master of all the beasts of the field and of the arts of fieldcraft, let him try a campaign with the wild goats. Verily, there is no sub-lunar undertaking calculated better to take the conceit out of him. Mere figures give a poor idea. To say the favourite haunts of the ibex lie at 8,000 ft or 10,000 feet altitudes is hardly any real criterion of the difficulties or hardships of their pursuit . . .

They were right. That day I saw no ibex at all before I climbed back down to the van, my legs beginning to quiver with fatigue, for they had not suffered such exertions for many weeks. The trek with Manolo had been a mere jaunt in comparison. I drove back to my favourite camp site above the Tiétar river on the Candelada-to-Oropesa road, where in April I had thought of buying a plot of land. Almost every flat bay beside the river was filled with cars and tents and happy families splashing and shouting in the waters. Generally the Spanish prefer to live communally in towns or villages, so the ancient rural populations have been depleted. But in recent years, as happened to the British before World War Two, the car has liberated them, and they return to their beloved *campo* on every holiday or fiesta day they can, especially waterside places.

I clambered down to the river between large rounded boulders and found a secret quiet place. I was about to strip off and plunge in when I had a most unusual experience. A few large wood ants were running over the sandy mud near my feet and in the middle of them a black sand wasp was dragging along a spider which was far bigger than itself. The spider was still feebly struggling, the wasp having paralysed it with a sting to render it harmless but keep it alive and its tissues fresh. It was now clearly trying to get the spider back to the hole in a dry part of the bank where it had laid its eggs and where the body would provide food for its hatched young. When any of the big ants came near to within four inches, the wasp immediately dropped the spider and dive bombed the ant, pumping its lower abdomen on to the ant's body, trying to sting it. Sting — and off. Sting — and off. Sting — and off. The ants tried to fight back but always, after two or three skirmishes, they fled as fast as they could go.

The wasp then flew back to the inert spider and continued to drag it on. It overcame twigs and other obstacles by hauling the spider up to them, pausing, and either going round to pull it through from underneath or heaving it around them. The wasp also kept running down to the water's edge and back to the spider, as if to check exactly where the water was. Then it dragged the spider *into the water*!

The wasp must have known that the wind was blowing in the right direction, for it jumped on to the floating spider and, using its wings as sails, navigated the ruffled waters for almost three feet until it reached the opposite shore of a miniature bay. Then it pulled the spider out again and started hauling it towards the undergrowth some six feet further on. The wasp continued to chase away ants by diving on them, but it also ran about every so often as if checking exactly where it was going. At first I thought it was looking for its egg hole, but soon it became clear that, after leaving the eggs to go and look for prey, it had left scent posts along the route so it could find its way back to them. Following this previously marked overland trail, the wasp dragged the spider to one post, left it and dashed about to locate the next, then repeated the process until it disappeared into the undergrowth and out of my sight. All its movements were quick, fidgety and determined. How had it known it could SAIL across that stretch of water to save itself much hard dragging? I had seldom seen so much individual intelligence in the insect world.

After my bathe I drove round the beautiful lake-like Embalse de Rosarita where many people were out in the sunshine on this fiesta day. The only wildlife I saw was one great crested grebe out on the blue waters. I looked at the map and saw there was a road from Candelada to Arenas de San Pedro and Mombeltran that led up to the Gredos peaks and the 1,352 metres high Puerto del Pico. Surely there would be *cabra montés* somewhere up there! Then I had an idea. Maybe Beltran de Ceballos was back from filming in the Coto Doñana; he might help me to find the ibex. I phoned his Candelada home and found that he was not only in but would meet me in the garage bar in ten minutes.

He brought with him his lovely wife Chata, and also his charming parents, who were visiting from Madrid. Since his father had once run the Spanish office of *Reader's Digest*, and writing wildlife stories for the *Digest* had paid my way in the wilds of Scotland for four years, we had much in common and the talk was good. Over drinks Beltran told me it would be easy to locate ibex, and he marked on my map a place called El Refugio, which I could reach by turning off the C500 road at Hoyos del Espino. Then I could hike up towards the lagoons and, if lucky, I would find the big goats on the high rocky hills before I had walked two or three kilometres.

'You camp up there tonight, see the ibex in the morning and be back here in the afternoon. Then we will do black kites taking fish, and you can photograph wolves and wild boar too,' Beltran said with a chuckle.

The last two were animals he kept in his own reserve and used when working with the British television film unit. But surely it would not be possible to drive so far, successfully trek after the elusive ibex and be back in Candelada the next afternoon? I said I would meet him on Saturday evening.

Beltran was a freelance who, like myself, made a living from his knowledge of wildlife. I quite understood when he suggested a fee – so much if he helped me to set up hides on rare birds, and half that fee if he just gave me a verbal tip-off and I found the species on my own from that. He was surprised at how much work I had completed in Monfragüe in so short a time, and laughed when I told him how the young hoopoes had squirted their faeces into my face.

'Young hoopoes always do that to an enemy,' he said. 'That's why the parents always give that harsh call before landing with food, so they don't get it in *their* faces. When we ring hoopoe chicks, we always scratch round the hole with a stick first, so they have no shit left when we put our hands in!'

I camped in the holm oak glade above the Tiétar again and in the dark saw an odd glimmer on my leg. It was a female glow worm, and when I gently put her out she elevated her rear on my hand, shining her light for all the males to see.

Woken at 7 a.m. by the bells of a flock of goats being driven by, I set off early for the ibex. The road to Arenas de San Pedro wound up through lovely pine woods, and from Mombeltran it was all slow, second gear work as the jagged grey face of the Puerto del Pico loomed high to my right. I soon found the turning to El Refugio. It was high here, with masses of yellow flowering gorse bushes, short bracken and a kind of bell heather sprouting among the granite boulders – just as in Scotland! The sky had clouded over and it looked like rain. The peaks high ahead were shrouded in mist – just my damn luck!

I was dismayed to find a car park at the end of the little road, filled with scores of cars containing hikers, climbers and tenters who used the hills round the lagoons for camping. A man who ran a soft drinks stall said I would probably see some female goats on the far side of the ridges above the car park, but if I wanted the big males – the *machos grandes* – I would need to hike up to the peaks above the lagoons.

After lunch I set off in full wildlife tracking gear, green trews, camouflage jacket, bush hat and camera pack. At first the path was paved like a Roman way, and hikers wearing bright reds, blues, yellows and whites were tramping all over the place. I was sure I was wasting my time; the *cabra montés* would be miles away from this lot!

I climbed on, until the paved path ran out and there were just worn tracks in the grass. I came to a huge horseshoe valley, filled in at the far end by hills. On the right, above some small lagoons, reared a vast escarpment of bare greenish rock slabs, and I realised that not far beyond these rose the Pico Almanzor. I had been in the right area after all. Judging by pictures I had seen, I was sure the goats would be up on that precipitous escarpment. Then I saw a tent halfway up those cliffs, and another in the valley bottom by the lagoons, both bright blue! The wind was coming from my right, so I decided to head for the ridges on my left and work round the top of the horseshoe against the wind, about eight really tough kilometres. I had gone about two, feeling despondent about the bad light and with rain about to fall,

175

when I spotted a goat in the valley bottom, only 500 metres ahead, before the lowest tent. There was another beside it.

I thought they would be just *embras* (the females with small horns) but then I saw a much bigger beast with a magnificient horn spread. Through the binoculars I realised it was a *macho,* a big male. I would stalk them.

Dodging back out of sight, I half ran, stooping low, to the start of the ridges on the left which I started to climb, blowing hard. I was below the skyline when I saw two men walking towards me from the low tent behind the goats. Surely the goats would see them, or get their scent, and head across the valley, away from the lagoons and up towards me? I wriggled on my belly a long way to a small rock and set the camera on it. I now saw that there was a flock of about 50 ibex, some among them with huge rugged horns.

Sure enough, the herd began to work their way up to where I crouched, moving perfectly downwind where they would not be able to pick up my scent. My heart pounded with excitement as the big *machos* headed nearer, moving through gorse bushes where I could see only the tips of their horns. They browsed several other kinds of bushes, then began to emerge into the open, so close that I could not get both their horns and their feet into frame! The first to come out was a huge old fellow who looked towards me, apparently unable to see if I was a man or not. I crouched still, clicking off marvellous shots. Ending one film, I put in another with slow snake-like movements of my hands and shot off most of that on some 20 ibex, all looking my way. I varied the shots — the biggest beast on its own, a group, two standing together — until I had enough. I stood up, my knees aching, fully expecting them to bolt.

They did not! They just stood there, completely unafraid, gazing at me with glowing amber eyes, calmly chewing the cud. Quite clearly these animals were used to humans, and my hard, elaborate, professional stalk had been quite unnecessary. I bent down to put the dismantled camera and lens into the pack, thinking how ludicrously easy it had been. One of the big machos walked towards me and, for a moment, I thought it intended to charge at my posterior, just for fun. Instead it crouched low at the rear, making gyrating pumping movements, and I saw that its penis was out. It was staring hard at me all the while. Not wishing possible ravishment by a sex-crazed ibex, I decided it was time to take off. As I walked away, the two men from the tent came up to the rear of the beasts which, now that

After an elaborate stalk the big male ibex proved unexpectedly easy to approach. When one glared hard at me and made suggestive gyrating movements, I felt it was time to leave.

A young white stork practises in a high wind before its first flight from the nest on a farmhouse roof.

By setting out dead carp on the river bank I attracted a black kite to come down and feed.

A male Iberian wolf starts his summer moult. Lifting his lips to reveal his teeth is enough to maintain ascendancy over another male in the pack without fighting.

Two wild boars feed on the flesh of a dead mule.

This fairy-like insect, far from common, has no English name, so I called it the 'ribbon-tailed lacewing'.

There were always red kites at the refuse dump near Oropesa; in mid-February they were courting in the air.

A white stork sails into the rubbish dump.

Thousands of grey herons and night herons nest communally in the evergreen oaks of the Coto Doñana, spangling the trees like jewels.

A scared red deer hind herded out of a forestry compartment by a horseman.

they were sandwiched between the walkers and me, began to show alarm. The herd ran between us down the valley to cross the lagoons. Some of the males fenced with each other, bashing and crashing their horns together, as if a brief punch-up on the run down was a fine thing to have!

I was back in my van less than two hours after leaving it with all the pictures of Spanish ibex I could ever want. I raised a brief toast to Beltran; and to Chapman and Buck. Beltran had been right. It *had* been easy. I would have been less pessimistic had I known at the time that the Spanish mountain goat, or ibex, enjoyed a population explosion in recent years. Their numbers were estimated at 11,657 individuals in December 1970, a figure which rose to 28,190 by 1980. Today there are well over 9,000 in the Sierra de Gredos alone, a similar number in the Sierras de Cazorla and Segura, and over 4,000 in the highest parts of Tarragona, Castellon and Teruel. Curiously there are believed to be no more than 20 or 30 individuals in the Pyrenees, in the Ordesa—Huesca area. This success story is largely due to rigorous hunting control and the support of government policies by owners of private hunting estates.

I drove Beltran to a small farm 800 metres from the *finca* which he ran for a wildlife foundation. The track was too bad to take the van any closer, so we had to walk in. Beltran kept seven Spanish wolves (five females, two males) in a two hectare enclosure there. They were still wild, though tame towards him and his young blond assistant Miguelito, who fed them. They were not as big as the Arctic wolf of Canada, had tawny brown coats, which were now in the first stages of the summer moult, and earned their keep by taking part in a number of films, including two made by the British TV company. They were fed once every three days on dead deer or mules or donkeys given to him by local farmers.

But first we decided to try the black kites taking fish from the shores of the Embalse de Rosarita which ran along the bottom of his *finca*. It was a beautiful spot with reeds, dead spars and humped rocks jutting out of the water. We set up my best hide, near a bush for extra cover, and I tied on a top and middle cord from which to prop up and hang vegetation. Beltran said he had never done that before but thought it a good idea. Miguelito had prepared the way by putting two dead *carpas* on the shore there yesterday and the kites had taken them. We set three out today, two I propped up on their bellies as if they had run ashore by mistake, and one lay on its side with its tail just in the water. I was in the hide and all set up by 12.40 p.m. Beltran and Miguelito left.

At 1.19 p.m. I heard a swish of wings and saw a large shadow fly over the fish. It was a splendid black kite but it landed on the farthest rock to my right and began eating the remains of a carp which it must have taken there yesterday, and which we had not seen. There was some foliage in the way but by tipping the tripod to the left, a movement luckily it did not see, I took pictures of it and then some of four bee-eaters which landed on a branch bent into a superb natural bow. The kite looked down gloomily as the remains of the fish slid slowly off the rock and into the water. Then it jumped down to a lower rock, just out of my sight, and must have flown away low for I did not see it again.

Two hours later another swift shadow shot across the hide. I thought it might be a bee-eater, but then something landed on the shore to my left. Through the lens I saw it was another black kite. I clicked away as it walked to the fish that was lying on its side and began pecking holes in it and eating. It then moved to the biggest fish, lying upright on its belly, and looked down at it, as if asking itself how on earth it got there in that position. The kite then strode into the water up to its knees and took a drink! It grabbed a beakful, reared its head upwards and swallowed the water down. It did this quite quickly, three times more, and I could photograph the drops falling from its beak. After that it flew off. I could not follow the flight without breaking the camera bindings to the broken tripod. It flew back to my right, calling 'king . . . ing . . . ing . . . ing' — again sounding like the distant whinnying of a horse. After only ten minutes another shadow passed over, and I was just in time to see the kite landing. This time it went to the farthest fish, turned it on its side, and pecked meat from the soft belly area. It ate three helpings, then flew off, allowing me to change to my third film.

The heat in the hide was almost unendurable. My wet flannel dried out completely. When I could bear it no longer, I tied the flannel to garden cord and, with a quick movement, threw it into the water from the back of the hide. Then I hauled it back, soaked, and swabbed myself down. Oh, what a relief!

I thought that would be that, but at 4.43 p.m. I was amazed to see the fish on its side sliding down into the water. Clamped on to its tail was a glistening khaki-brown helmeted head. A terrapin, about 18 inches long, was stealing my fish! I had not known there were any terrapins in the river. The fish was towed a short way out, bobbing under twice due to the terrapin biting chunks out of it from underwater. A slight breeze then blew the fish back to shore. At 5.24 p.m. a magpie arrived, landed in a bush beyond the three fishes, flew to the farthest one in short wary bursts and pecked out its top eye. Then it waddled to the fish in the water, and pecked at the eye that was under the surface. There was a distant peal of thunder, and the magpie exited left. Minutes later I heard a black kite calling and one flew to the left of the biggest fish, ignored it, waded into the water and took three drinks. I tried to improve on my photos of this activity.

For a while I had been puzzled by a loud '*rat rat rat*' noise, often repeated. I searched round through the lens and found they were being made by three bee-eaters on the bowed branch. They were beating to death some insects (maybe bees, to nullify their stings) with sideways blows of their beaks against the branch. How they failed to knock themselves out I did not know.

It had been a day of wonderful action, but I was glad when Beltran came to take me out of the torture chamber. I took the fish away and asked Miguelito not to put out any more carps. I would do another stint in the hide tomorrow and wanted to ensure that the kites would be hungrier than they had been today. I was surprised they had not carried the fish away.

We repaired to a primitive stone hut, which was headquarters for the two men when tending the wolves and working at the *finca,* and Beltran produced two young Spanish wolf cubs, which he allowed me to photograph. Every time we put them on the ground they instantly scattered in opposite directions, and it took some time for me to get them both together in the grasses. They had been part of a litter of four born to one of the females in a rocky den in his enclosure. Because he was doubtful that all four could survive, Beltran had taken these two away before their eyes had opened. He explained that at one month old they were imprinted on man and could not be released to the wild for they would turn to humans for food. He would have to find good owners for them and asked if I would I like one. If I could find my own isolated wild place in Spain I most certainly would! Beltran said he had heard of a Spanish writer who wanted to sell a cottage up in the Gredos hills above Candelada – he would make inquiries for me. Ever since my beloved Alsatian

179

Moobli had died nearly five years earlier, I had refrained from getting another dog; perhaps taking on a wolf would not be letting his memory down. After dinner, cooked by Chata, I went to my camp site above the Tiétar.

Again I was woken early by bells, on a herd of cows this time. I met Beltran at the garage bar for coffee and *churros* (chocolate covered breakfast cakes) and we again hiked into the *finca*. As we sat around on rocks, planning the day, I realised I had heard nothing more of the wild boars I understood Beltran was going to show me. I asked him where they were. He smiled and said —

'*Miguelito . . . jabalí!*'

Miguelito went round the end of the long stone hut and I heard him opening what sounded like a heavy wooden gate. All of a sudden, round the corner of the hut came two great wild boars, charging towards us. The bigger one, which was growing 1½ inch tusks and weighed about 200lbs, came right up to me and sniffed gently at my ear with its wet velvety snout. A wild boar! Just then, up came Miguelito's golden retriever and snapped at the boar's snout. The boar snorted, lunged to his right and banged into me. I just got out of danger in time. After two more snaps from the dog, which the boar returned with defiance, they crashed away to my right before the dog obeyed Miguelito's command to leave it alone. Beltran explained that they were two young brothers, whose mother had been shot by a hunter, and had been brought to him when they were still very young. The best way for me to photograph them was at a mule carcass he had set out several days ago to attract red and black kites and imperial eagles. The kites had come but not the eagles, which he had found came to only about one in twenty carcasses, and then only in winter.

He took me over to the mule carcass under the shade of an oak trees, with the Embalse in the background. It lay, rib-cage upwards, the bones staring starkly up at the sky. The two wild boars went at it, ripping great slabs of rotting black and green meat off the bones. I climbed one tree and took pictures of them with the sun in their eyes, snorting and tearing off the meat. I walked round them, taking more close pictures, hoping they would not decide that I was too near their food and get nasty. Beltran told me they were tame towards humans, a statement he was to rue the following year.

To get the boars back into their pen, Miguelito came down with two big carp, which he dangled and shook temptingly. The boars

clearly preferred the fresh fish to the rotting mule and as he ran back
to the pen they chased after him to get the carp.

It was then time for the wolves. Beltran thought it prudent for
me to wear his old Barbour jacket, showing me teeth marks in its
sleeves. The bigger dominant male, Alex, could be bad tempered,
and it might be better if the wolf believed I was part of him. I said it
would be unnecessary, for I had never been hurt by a wild animal yet,
not even by grizzlies in the wilds of Canada, and I would be careful
not to give Alex any reason to attack me. I waited outside the double
gate of the enclosure while he and Miguelito familiarised themselves
again with the wolves. (Beltran said that even they had to be careful,
for if one wolf did attack, the whole lot would follow, operating as
a pack.) Then I went inside too, with Miguelito standing near me.
One of the big males kept trying to sneak up to me, but I was not
too scared for I thought the other one, further away, was Alex. Then
Miguelito said, '*This* is Alex!' and got between the wolf and me.

As Alex kept pressing and dodging to get closer to me and
Miguelito fended him off with his body, I asked him to let the
wolf come. It would not hurt me. He moved away and Alex had his
chance. He came padding up suspiciously, hackles raised, and sniffed.
Slowly I lowered my hand, the back of it to the wolf. At first he
shied off. But he came back and sniffed my hand again. I tried not to
show fear, told him in a quiet voice he was a nice wolf, a good wolf
and I would not try to hurt him, but wanted to know him better, and
so forth. He showed no aggression — but Beltran came up and took
him further away, showing me the wolf's canine teeth as he did so.
They were about half the size of Moobli's! I asked him to let the wolf
go again, so that I could photograph him coming towards me, which
is exactly what happened. Miguelito came near me again, and it was
clear both men *were* afraid that Alex would attack me. When Beltran
told me to leave the enclosure, I did so.

Of course, it was not the same as photographing wolves in the
wild, but I would get around to that one day. Beltran later said it
would be better to try this in autumn or winter, when the animals
were hungrier and I might tempt them to a bait. I would also have to
be in a hide covered with cow and sheep dung, to prevent the wolves
picking up my scent.

At 12.30 p.m. the two men installed me once again in the hide.
The black kites did not come down this time, but I took more photos
of bee-eaters and terrapins stealing the fish. It was even hotter than

before, and when I took the hide down and carried it with the camera gear to the van, I was grateful I would not have to go into another one in this sweltering summer.

Beltran invited me to take a shower at his house, and I can remember no finer pleasure than standing under that cool spray, shampooing my hair and scrubbing away five weeks' accumulated sweaty grime from my body. Bathing down with a flannel at various camp sites or in cold rivers does not do the job properly. Afterwards I felt as if I had lost two inches all round. When I stepped on his bathroom scales, I found I had lost nearly a stone and was down to the middle weight division!

Although Beltran tried to kid me he expected the full fee for each species – black kite, wild boar, wolf, bee-eater and even terrapin – we amicably agreed a compromise sum and I paid him. He was interested in my Scottish wildlife film, and we discussed the possibility of filming Spanish wildlife together, for I still had all my movie equipment. All I wanted to do now was to escape from this remorseless heat for a while. When Beltran phoned Brittany Ferries to book me on the first boat from Santander to Plymouth, he was told that all the ferries were full for the next two weeks.

To hell with that, I decided next day. I would go straight to Santander and, by hook or by crook, get the van on to a boat. But my adventures were far from over.

I pushed over the mountains to Avila, switched on to the small N403 road towards Valladolid, and camped early in a pine wood before Mojados so as to allow the engine to cool down before it was time to sleep. I did not notice that I had parked near some rubbish discarded by picnickers – and in Spain where there is rubbish there are flies. Within minutes a swarm of over 500 were inside the van, buzzing, flying and some little zebra-striped ones biting. I tried to clear them out by driving fast up and down the road with all windows and even the elevating rear door open. The draught was terrific and blew away some valuable documents, which I had an awful job finding again, scattered hundreds of yards apart. As soon as I stopped, out came half the swarm again from draught-proof corners of the van where they had hidden. I had to belt around with a tea towel, with all the windows open, to drive most of them out. Then I camped in a rubbish-free area of the wood.

Next morning I saw a strange and large lacy-winged insect flitting about the woods and took some photos. It had long semi-transparent light green wings framed with dark brown, and two long drooping tail plumes with brown zebra stripes in them. I had seen two on the slopes below Monfragüe Castillo, but not as close as this. It looked like a fairy! Later I found out it was a member of the striking and beautiful lacewing family of nemopteridae which dance up and down in the air at dusk when looking for mates, rather like mayflies. They occur in southern Europe but are uncommon. Their 'tails' are in fact elongated hind wings, and when I discovered that they have no English name, I dubbed the insect the ribbon-tailed lacewing.

On the journey I noted that there were white stork nests in trees before Avila and on church towers in Piña de Campos and Alar del Rey – all with rivers near by. These birds like to be near water if possible so that they can fish and drink and bring supplies back to the nest. The Rio Pisuerga opened out here with fine places for swimming flanked by lush fields, and after Reinosa the road wound down through beautiful green canyons, the steep slopes lined with fir, beech and larch, all rather like Scotland.

At the Santander booking office I was told by a charming Spanish lady at the counter –

'There has been one cancellation. You can go tomorrow!'

I have never put down cash faster. I camped up in the hills, the van's clock now showing 74,300 miles.

As the ferry steamed out for Britain on June 30 I realised it was exactly 21 years to the day since I had first flown to Canada to start the wilderness life. Even the fact that all the cabins were full, and I had to sleep on the floor with my boots and pack as a pillow, could not reduce my happiness.

183

18 · No Peace Anywhere

There was really no pressing need to return to Britain for the rest of the summer. There was no new book to promote, no finished manuscript to deliver to my publisher, no news of progress on my wildlife film for television (from the Moving Picture Company or anyone else) and no home to go to. I wanted a respite from the relentless heat of Spanish sunshine, but otherwise my return was to prove an abortive hiatus. I stayed with friends here a week, there a few days, or camped in my van in the gloom and the rain. It was impossible to settle to working on the book about Moobli.

I took a fancy to a round tower folly I found in woods near the summit of Leith Hill in Surrey, the highest point in south east Britain, but not to the price demanded for the ruin. A delapidated cottage and 29 acres of Cornish bog, in which I found buzzards nesting on a cliff, gained my enthusiasm for a couple of days but, mercifully, it soon evaporated. An avid reader of my books stoutly refused to sell me even one of his 240 acres of woodland on the Sussex coast where I grew up. I was adrift. Promising my publisher (goodness knows why!) that I would be back for *Wildcat Haven* when it came out in November, and would bring with me *Moobli* finished, I set off again for the Red Villa in early September. I had an uneasy feeling, as I motored down from Santander, that the villa had been burgled. Taking a new route which by-passed Albacete, I hurried through the mountains to Ayna, which was built on a dramatic 700-metre cliff face and deserved more than my apprehensive glance. I saw men flailing almonds from the trees as I approached Espuña and bet myself that would be going on under my window when I tried settling at the typewriter again.

When I reached the house the first thing I saw was that one of the window guards had been torn out and the shutters forced open. My heart sank! Had all my gear gone? The only things I really cared about were my diaries, photos, film projector and precious old oars. To my astonishment, the intruders had failed to break through the stout oak doors of my study and of the bedroom upstairs. All they had escaped with were a mop, a brush and a bucket, and two plaster effigies of Jesus on the Cross from the chapel room. Not much of a haul! Even so, they had unbolted the back door and left it wide open. I felt the place was no longer safe.

It was also as hot here now as it had been at the end of June. After carrying in everything from the van, I could not sleep for the heat and lay sweating all night, naked on the bed, without even a covering sheet. As I struggled to get the primitive water system going again for a cold shower, and wrestled the huge water jars into better places, I heard voices and children yelling. Some new groups had walked over from the Christian Community camp to play around my reservoir. While I was talking to them, feeling guilty about putting a stop to the children's fun, several young men in shorts ran past. When I called out that the place was private, they said they were soldiers from the Espuña encampment and were on a training run, following map references given to them by their superior officers. The three nearest and usually deserted farm cottages also had families in them and I could hear dogs barking and folk shouting to each other.

I had found no peace in Britain, and there was no peace here. How could I tackle the hardest part of *Moobli* in this sort of racket? I took out my frustration on a hard bike ride through the mountains, not returning until dusk.

For some time I had been in touch with an estate agent near Tremp in the southern Pyrenees, who was scouting out and selling old abandoned *casas* and *fincas* in that area. When he wrote to say he had a few likely places to show me, I arranged to meet him, praying that at last I would find the New Wild (and quiet) Place. Hammering a stout wooden bar over the broken shutters, I loaded everything of value to me into the van and set off with 78,665 miles on its clock.

The heat was unrelenting. A blue haze hung over the land so that

185

I could not see clearly for more than a kilometre or two, nor make out any details in the distant mountain landscapes. The palm trees near Alicante were sprouting great pineapples of white blossom between the fronds. Instead of the motorway to Valencia, I took a short cut up the N340 through the mountains to get away from fuming, snarling traffic. I stopped for refreshment in Xativa, for it was such a beautiful little town, filled with shady trees, flowered squares and lovely old buildings. After enduring the traffic stench of Valencia, I cut up the N234 road near Sagunto and camped behind a huge and smelly old water works. I hoped it was not a sewage works. Despite the unpleasant thought of inhaling methane gas all night I left the rear door of the van open, to help cool the engine, and in came the mosquitoes. But there was a wonderful carpet of gorgeous blue columbine flowers growing near by and I took a photo. Weeds maybe, but they were as pretty as any bourgainvillae.

Up the motorway to Tarragona and on the N240 to Lerida, the ancient capital of Catalonia, which the Catalans spell Lleida, I passed through white and black grape country. After the mountain range, olive and almond trees were growing together. I took the C147 towards Tremp and by late afternoon was through Camarasa, and into country as dramatic as I had seen anywhere in Spain. Great canyons stretched as far as the eye could see, vast gloomy walls of rock rising 700 metres or more on either side. I drove on through this frightening splendour until I came to an even greater sheer wall of green-grey rock that towered into the sky on the far side of the river. Stopping to make tea, I was amazed to hear voices coming from halfway up the rock face. Two young men at about 400 metres were climbing that terrifying cliff, clinging like spiders, carefully putting their hands and feet into tiny crevices and tapping in pitons. It made my head swim just to look at them. Later I was told the wall is known as the Terradets, and is one of the most famous and testing rocks in the Pyrenees. Not for a million would I have attempted to go up there.

Soon I came to the scenic Embalse del Terradets and stopped at the Hotel del Largo. In the bar were photos of six wild boars shot in the area, three of them little more than piglets. It seemed wretched hunting to me. I was told they had been shot before the law was changed, making it illegal to shoot piglets and sows with piglets or in the breeding season. I sipped a beer on the terrace and admired the view. This was certainly superb country.

186

Next day the agent drove me to see the three isolated properties he had in mind. The first, really out in the wilds, was a huge old barn filled with straw and animal dung upstairs and downstairs. The only water supply came from a spring half a mile away, and the 24 acres of unfenced land was just steep rocky ground above a gorge. The pines on it were dwarf stunted trees, though they had lost none of their tops, so it did not appear that there were deer in the area. I thought the place overpriced at £33,000, especially as it was at a height of 1,500 metres and would be very cold, even snowed up, in winter. The second property was a hay loft, too near a farm building that was in frequent use. After I bought him lunch at the hotel, the agent drove me almost to the village of Amettla, on the road to Ager, and stopped at a curious little square stone building. I was amazed when we went inside for it had been built back into the rock. There were nine rooms, three with red-tiled floors. The views were spectacular. Straight ahead was the 1,677-metres-high peak of the Sierra de Montsec, flanked on either side, for as far as one could see, by the great ridges of the central Pyrenees. There were some useful outbuildings, and these and the basic furnishings were included in the price, which, at £16,000, seemed a bargain.

My initial excitement was soon damped. The solar electricity was not working because the two young men who owned the place were in dispute with their supplier over price and had hidden the panels. When buying property in Spain, one is landed with all the previous owner's property debts, so I could have been in trouble here from the start. The water system was not working either because the pipe had split somewhere and the supply had been turned off at the village, where only two or three families remained. The agent did not know the exact boundaries of the property, but if I walked round with my neighbour he would tell me where they were. I'll bet he would, I thought.

Even so, I was interested, and I decided to look round the area for two days and camp by the house to see how peaceful it was. I went down to the lake, which was lined in places by quiet pine forests, and was delighted to see many fish near the surface — rafts of carp gulping down insects, huge black bass, and what I was told later at a local bar were rainbow trout. The owner said there were other species of fish, including barbel, and all fishing there was FREE! You had only to pay to fish in the rivers and even there the permits were cheap. I returned to camp by the house at dusk but my pleasure evaporated when I was suddenly invaded by the noise of bells and a flock of over a hundred sheep and goats. They walked right through what I felt must be 'my' property and out of what would be 'my' front gate! The shepherd was a big plump man, and when I held up my arms in query, he said I should shoo them away from the van, which I did. He laughed and went on up to the village with his flock. That night I could see no fewer than twelve houses lit up, and for a time I could not sleep for the cacophony of barking dogs.

Next morning a car with GB plates went down the track beside the house, parked below the ridges, and two men walked up with a hang glider. I learned that an Irishman had just started a club at Ager and the gliders often soared along below the ridges to the left. This did not seem to be good for local eagles or vultures, not that I had yet seen any.

Later, while driving towards Ager, I spotted a booted eagle flying above the van. I leaped out and got two pictures before it landed in a clifftop bush far ahead. I drove on towards it, but it flew back the way we had come. I turned and chased after it and took two good flight shots as it zoomed across the fields, passing below a leisurely flapping red kite.

Next morning I was woken by a Land Rover going down the track. A man got out and started digging with pickaxe and mattock at rocks on each side, as if marking out places for road improvements. Then a farmer began working with a power saw in a field 300 metres away, felling old olive trees and cutting them up for firewood. When I discovered that the water could be turned off by the shepherd's house, and imagined what might happen to the supply if I asked him not to bring his sheep so close, or I fenced them out, I decided sadly that the place was not for me after all. Maybe the old abandoned farmhouse which I had seen isolated among trees on the far shore of the beautiful Embalse de Camarasa would suit me better.

I asked the agent, who lived in a magnificent house that looked like a castle, and which he ran as an hotel, what he thought about restoring the old farmhouse, but he was not encouraging. It would cost a fortune to take building materials across the water. Besides, all the lake shores were owned by the Catalan hydro-electric company, which did not allow people to live there or any kind of new development. But he said that he now had a clear picture of what I wanted and would continue to look for something suitable.

The idea of living in Catalonia appealed to me for the Province is strong on conservation and animal rights. When half a million signatures were collected for a petition on animal protection recently, the Ministry of the Interior introduced new legislation which imposed fines up to £12,500 on anyone convicted of causing suffering to any animal, wild or domestic, and Catalonia implemented the regulation immediately while the rest of Spain (up to the time of writing) was still thinking about it. A large wetland reserve in the Gulf of Roses near Figueres, where 289 species of birds have been sighted, was created when local ecologists and bird lovers put pressure on the Catalan government, so saving the area in the nick of time from speculators wishing to push urbanisation of the Costa Brava further northward. Pleasure boats have been banned from the two largely pollution-free rivers that feed the marshes of the Aiguamolls de L'Emporda Reserve. New lagoons and scrapes have been created, and water levels are now controlled by biologists instead of by farmers who would flood their grass fields in the dry months, so denying nest sites to many birds.

With the approaching deadline for delivery of my new book I could not venture so far north on this trip, but I decided to make a small diversion on my way back to the Red Villa to look at the Ebro Delta, second only to Coto Doñana in importance as a Spanish wetland. Lying about 160 km south of Barcelona, the mouth of the great Ebro river (which drains almost a sixth of Spain's land surface) comprises long sand spits and sheltered bays, chains of fresh and salt water lagoons fringed with reedbeds, sand dunes and scrub bushes with silt deposits that spread over a huge area. Of the 260 species of land, sea and freshwater birds found in the region over 90 breed there. Some 300 avocets and terns (gull-billed, common and little) nest here, and the colony of sandwich terns is the largest in the country. The 1,600 pairs of red-crested pochards is the largest breeding congregation of these gaudy ducks to be found in western Europe. Little bitterns 'gruff' in the beds and climb the thick reeds like parrots. Little egrets, dazzling white, stalk fastidiously and snap at prey in the shallows, and a few peachy-pink squacco herons can startle a human being with harsh crow-like calls. Yet, despite the establishment of a National Park, the delta is still under threat − not only from intensified agriculture in the buffer zones but also from development for tourism.

I turned off the N340 south of Tarragona and took a small road leading to La Cava through maize and rice fields. The place was almost deserted on this autumn Sunday, with fewer birds to be seen than in the breeding season. Heading towards Amposta on a sand road, I saw a marsh harrier quartering the wet fields, every so often missing a beat of its broad, almost black wings. I counted myself lucky to get photos of it, for twelve years earlier the number of marsh harriers on the delta had declined from 20 pairs to just a single pair. Indiscriminate spraying of poisonous insecticide from aircraft, lethal to the birds as well as rice-boring grubs, was banned just in time.

The Red Villa was untouched when I returned, though I found a large scorpion on the floor of my primitive hosepipe shower. I picked it up in a cloth and watched its huge sting go right through the fabric, fortunately ending up against my thumb nail. I put it outside and took its photo. Too weary to unload everything from the van that night, I slept in it yet again. It was after 10 p.m. when I heard a series of explosions that made me wonder if World War Three had broken out. Then I discovered that the noise was coming from a nearby farmer's bird scarer. Something must have gone wrong with the timing mechanism for the racket kept going at intervals throughout the night. Dogs barked too. In the morning I was woken by the sound of a tractor and the shouts of men harvesting almonds. Then came even louder bangs as workmen blew out the site of a swimming pool at a nearby house. Was there no peace anywhere?

I spent the next two days writing letters and getting in supplies. It was still insufferably hot. I took frequent cold showers and kept a wet flannel by the desk to cool my face. The truth was clear: I was funking the Moobli book, afraid that I could not write about his death without sentimentality or breaking down.

A violent storm helped to put an end to the torment. I stood outside in the deluge while thunder banged round the peaks and lightning flashed, not caring if I was struck, and returned to the house exhilarated, cooled down at last by lovely, life-giving rain. I had not appreciated how much I missed rain after living for so long in Scotland. If I were to set up permanently in Spain, I knew that I would not survive the long summer heat unless I lived close to the water — river, lake or sea — so that I could swim every day.

After the air had cleared I disciplined myself to week after week at the desk in order to get the book done. Loneliness was accentuated by the constant need to recall the companionship of the remarkable Alsatian who had shared my life in Scotland and who had gone for ever. Now all I had to raise flagging spirits was a great spotted woodpecker banging away at the iron-hard trunk of a dead spar and a pair of feral cats that came from nowhere to scoff the scraps I was leaving out to attract foxes and then disappear again.

Towards the end of September I was puzzled by odd thumps and scuffles outside the villa at night. I shone a torch but could see nothing. When Greg's workmen came to repair the torn-out grating, I mentioned the noises. They laughed and took me down to an almond terrace to show me trotter marks in the soil.

'*Jabalí!*' (Wild boar.)

They told me that boars came down from the Espuña forest in the dark at this time of year for the almonds that lay on the ground. Boars also liked the pink fruits of prickly pear cactus, and I could see the scuff marks made by their cloven hoofs all round the largest cluster of the cactus in front of the end window.

That night I opened up the far room and set the camera and flash unit on a tripod in the half-open shutter of the glassless window. I waited in the dark for two hours, but no boars came. For several nights I watched without result. Then, at 4 a.m one morning, I heard scuffles again from my bed and crept downstairs by torchlight to set up the camera. After half an hour I heard more thumps and could just make out three dark forms near the cactus. They were not large — sows rather than the bigger tuskers — and I could smell them. I waited until one reached up for a prickly pear and pressed the remote control button. The flash did not work, but the click sent them scurrying away, and they did not return. After working all day I was too tired to keep watch all night, and before long the rest of the cactus fruits and the fallen almonds had gone.

I was sitting very still at my desk one night, imbibing too much *vino tinto* while listening to records on my little 17-year-old battery player, wondering where in hell I was going to end up, when a spider built a web from my hair down to the desk. I noticed nothing until I stood up and broke it. At this time of year many long-legged spiders came into the house from outside and spun webs in the kitchen, in the bathroom, and in other empty rooms. Few of them ever caught anything, and after many patient days they just slimmed down, wasted away, died, and became part of their own webs. When a wind soughed through the rooms, they blew away, drifting in the air,

191

wraiths of their former selves, then floated slowly down to become mere dust on the floor. It was as if they had never been. Much the same happens to us all, I mused.

More entertaining than the spiders were the geckos, medium sized lizards that like to come into occupied houses in southern Spain and which pay their 'rent' by catching insects on which they feed. They come in various shades of green and brown, measure up to eight inches long, and although heftier than any British lizard, they run comically over smooth vertical walls without ever falling off. They are harmless, and do not attempt to bite when you pick them up. I had five of them, all quartered in the room below my study, where they could hide, or sleep, in crevices in the beams.

One evening, while I was cutting my back hair by feel, pulling out the longer strands and trimming off the ends with scissors, I saw that a gecko had climbed up from below and stationed itself on the wood frame outside by my plastic window. It had clearly worked out that moths came to the window at night, trying to get through to the light of my paraffin lamp, and caught them more by the feel of their whirring wings than by sight. It would wait, dead-still, until the moth came near and was fanning its head, then make a short fast leap forward, usually grabbing it by a wing. It gulped the poor moth down in a series of jerks after short pauses. I have seen them catch mosquitoes that land on the walls. They stalk nearer with deliberately slow movements of their legs, glaring with their big dark round pupils, then pounce and snap it up with open jaws. Geckos were welcome in my house!

One morning I was woken up by curious whistly fast '*whee-yu, whee-yu*' screeches, which I taped. I looked out and saw a little owl fly across the valley of almond terraces and land on a rock above a stone recess. Then another followed, landed near the first, and both started *dancing* about, making these strange sounds at each other. Pulling on trews and a sweater, I crept out of the front door and stalked to a thick pine − but one flew off. I took a photo of the other before it too went away down the valley on flickering barred wings and apparently landed somewhere near the first. I slid back, hurried sixty yards further down, using the rim of the valley to hide me from their view, then stalked up to a big rock and slid the camera carefully over. These dumpy little owls, only 8½ inches long, but with wing spans of 21 inches, are found all over Spain and are perfectly camouflaged against their rocky and sandy habitats, and it took two minutes to locate even one. I took its picture, not realising until it was developed that I had actually caught the two! The owls stay together as pairs on their territories throughout the year and nest in steep rocky crevices. They are also noisy, and if I was not woken up by mistle thrush, a blackbird, a crested lark fluting, or rasping jays, these little owls were my alarm clocks. Sometimes the jays mobbed the owls with harsh calls, the owls responding with screeches, until there was an appalling racket.

On two mornings a vixen walked past the van, giving unearthly ringing '*Kai-ee kai-ee*' shrieks, as if trying to locate a mate. I taped them and put out a slightly-off chicken as bait. At dusk one of the feral cats was at it. I cut a bit off for the cat then nailed the rest seven feet up a pine, hoping to get the jays at it. In the morning twilight, with the owls screeching nearby, I peered out to see, not jays but a huge feral ginger tom cat, a good three feet long, at the chicken. He was clinging to the trunk with his claws and tucking in. I would never get that fox now.

Later I put twelve 5-litre containers into my van and drove to the spring in the woods half a mile up the mountain for water pure enough for cooking and making tea. When I got back, what looked like a huge female sparrowhawk came soaring up, saw me, made a quick about-turn with powerful beating wings, glided down my track and landed on a dead pine. Only then did I realise it was an *azor,* a goshawk. She stayed for a few seconds, glaring with piercing marigold eyes, and I cursed at not having my camera with me. One should, at *all* times.

By November *Moobli* was almost complete, though I still had to select and caption the pictures. I returned to Britain at the end of October with the script and did some television, radio and press interviews to promote my book *Wildcat Haven*. My publisher urged me to drive to Scotland for some of them and I ended up in a wintry Aviemore where the BBC television 'Animals Roadshow' was asking me to be filmed in the Highland Wildlife Park. The producer wanted to see if I could make friends with the Park's wildcats, which I did by by rubbing raw liver round my trouser bottoms and holding some in my hand. A big tom wildcat came to me twice, almost feeding from my hand, and also let me put meat close to his head on a branch. As far as I know the sequence was never shown. I was not sorry, for it seemed a trivialisation of all the extraordinary experiences I had enjoyed rearing three litters of these beautiful and untameable creatures and releasing them into the wild.

I missed the last pre-Christmas ferry to Santander, so took a later one to St Malo and drove back through France to winter at the lonely Red Villa. After the 1,000 mile drive the van, my old *caballo* which had never let me down, showed 85,342 miles on its clock.

A lonely Christmas Day was just a prelude to the period that followed. Suddenly I had run out of all motivation. I ought to go after the lynx, the wolf, and get better observations of bears, but felt I did not want to trek *anywhere* any more. Both writing and tramping over hard hills were such lonely occupations. And still my film had not been sold. At 800 metres high, it was now as cold at night here as it had been in Scotland, and the small paraffin stove only took the chill off the air. For days on end I was unable to get any British programme on the radio, and spent the dark evenings reading a newspaper while the wind howled down the open chimneys, sipping whisky to help me sleep at night. I buried myself in little chores to dispel the lethargy — typing my diary, marshalling notes for a new book, mounting photos and re-arranging my Spanish and Scottish slide shows, yearly accounts and correspondence with readers, and so on. I went for hard bike rides to exhaust myself so that I could sleep, for now I was beginning to worry about the future. On Sundays, when it was fine, I sat alone on the beach near the Puerto feeling that even hope had come to an end, that nearing 60 I knew I would be alone for ever, would never fall in love again. Frequently there were pains in my head and in my guts, and once more that strange migraine blindness I had suffered before leaving my Scottish home for good came over my eyes — a sure sign of both depression and stress. I realised I did not even know a doctor here. When I went to consult Gregorio Parra, I found he had gone to Madrid for the winter.

On January 30 a hurricane hit the villa, ripping out my new plastic windows. The tied shutters above my bed blasted open with a crash, showering me with broken glass. I felt the place itself was trying to kill me. Later I found the house full of dust and crumbling plaster, and the top of a tree snapped off and swept the hosepipe bringing water from the reservoir away into the woods.

For the first time I felt fear at living alone in an isolated wild place.

19 · Wild Boar Marsh

After spending two days in mid-February in Madrid with a publisher that had bought the Spanish language rights in one of my books I decided not to return at once to the Red Villa and drove instead to Extremadura to seek out Suso. Just to talk to someone of like mind would help to set me right again.

Near Oropesa I was surprised to see a white stork on a huge nest at the top of a tree only 20 feet tall, quite close to the road. At least eleven red kites were in the air over the rubbish tip when I passed that way again. Some pairs were already performing their courtship displays, wheeling and diving on each other, presenting talons and giving shrill, ringing cries. There were also crows, starlings, seagulls, pied wagtails, and cattle egrets by the score standing around with yellow-billed heads hunched into their necks − all vying for the pickings.

There were dozens of white storks at the dump's far end but they were hard to see because their plumage mingled perfectly with the whites, greys and multi-colours of all the rubbish. Some were courting, throwing their heads and long bills back on to their shoulders. Occasionally there were brief fights as males jabbed at rivals with their beaks, to drive them away from their mates. One flew up with something in its beak from a green mound beyond the dump and five kites went in pursuit, mobbing it, as if trying to make it drop its morsel. Only by vigorous flapping and swift dodging did

195

the stork manage to evade them. The kites seemed to be in perpetual flying motion, and several times I saw them dive on grounded gulls, which leaped to one side and allowed the kites to take their food. When I reached my old camp site above the Tiétar river, a hoopoe landed close by the van and began probing its long beak into the ground, as if posing for my camera in the setting sun. The whole day had lifted my spirits. I was far happier out in the field, making observations, than sitting alone at my desk.

Next morning I went to look at the Egyptian vulture nest on the far side of the Tiétar river, and was astonished to find it had been taken over by a pair of griffons, one of which was incubating an egg in the flowered crevice. It is clearly first come, first served, in the vultures' world and they had nipped in before the Egyptians had returned from wintering south of the Sahara. A Land Rover drew up and I was hailed cheerfully by two of the Monfragüe guardas. They told me that Suso was no longer running the Reserve. Hell! Had it been a wasted journey after all? I would go to his home anyway, and leave a note if I did not find him there. I did not reach it before, at the last bend, I heard a loud whistle from the woods — and there, waving to me, stood Suso beside Isabel and two of her sisters, with José Antonio and Mario Keller.

I was taken home for wine and given a great welcome. The three men were delighted with the large coloured prints I had made for them, and Suso told me why he had resigned after three years as the Province's Director. He felt he had done enough organising of conservation on the political level. He had appointed wardens and guardas, who now knew how to protect rare species, and had procured walkie-talkie radios and cars for them. He had set up the structure for protection and wanted to leave it to others to carry on the work so that he could return to his old job of surveying new wildlife areas. He put his hand on my shoulder.

'I am like you, a man of the field!' he said. 'I am not happy at a desk!'

I told him I had not been happy isolated at my desk in the Red Villa this past winter and had thought of moving to his area. He looked at me keenly and told me to meet him at Las Cansinas at midday. He said I should camp on a little *camino* high above the residences so that I could see imperial eagles in the morning. The three women escorted me there.

It was indeed a fine spot for I saw a female imperial soaring along the ridges of the Sierra de Corchuelas. She lurched through the air for its entire length without going down to a nest. Some minutes later the male followed her path, and I could see his silver wing epaulettes gleaming in the sun. He landed on a dead spar atop the crest.

When I met Suso at noon next day, he gave me the name of one of his friends, Señor Belarmino Galindo Martín, the Mayor of Majadas de Tiétar, who he was sure would help me find a new home in the area. He also asked me what other species I wanted. The hardest of all, I replied — wild lynx! Suso wrote down the names of two men, Dr Javier Castroviejo, Director General del Medio Ambiente of Andalucia and head of the biological station at Coto Doñana National Park, and Dr Miguel Delibes, who was running a lynx radio collaring project. He had worked with both men who were not only leading scientists but excellent field workers.

'Your best chance is in Coto Doñana, and these men will help you. Now is the best time as the lynx will be rutting, and also going to sun themselves on open sandbanks between the marshes. So — go NOW!'

I did not relish another drive, 350 km south, but pursuing the elusive lynx was a far better option than returning to the frustrations of the Red Villa, so I did as he bid me.

The beauty of Seville was subdued as I tramped round the town for over two hours in the rain. No-one seemed to know where the 'Casa del Peru' was. I felt tired, dispirited, alien, and almost gave up and headed for home. Eventually a kindly import agent telephoned the place, the Pabellon del Peru, and directed me to it. I climbed the marble steps and passed under the high arches of the elegant palace. The girl at the reception desk said that Dr Castroviejo was not in, but, without calling up on the internal phone, she led me along marble corridors and ushered me into the presence of Dr Delibes.

When Miguel Delibes, short, dark and energetic, heard I was a friend of Suso's and glanced at some of my wildlife books, he became helpfulness itself. He spoke fair English and said he would give me the maximum three day permit to visit the very heart of the Doñana reserve. If I would come back at 3 p.m. I could go there that very day with biologist Juan Aldama, who was radio tracking wild lynxes.

'Of course, it is unlikely you will see a lynx in the wild,' he said. 'But if you drive round with Juan and the man who traps them, that will be your best and perhaps *only* chance.'

I took a taxi back to the van and ate an omelette in cheerful anticipation. Once more my spirit had been lifted. I felt sure Miguel Delibes was right, for the Spanish lynx (Lynx pardina) is a seriously endangered animal. In 1979 there were estimated to be between 600 and 800 pairs. By 1986 the estimate was down to some 400 animals. That year two new laws were passed, adding to the original protection law of 1973, which indicated measures of protection and also set the minimum 'replacement' value of a lynx at 120,000 pesetas (£600), so providing a guide to the kind of fine to be imposed on anyone who killed a lynx. Out of the 17 autonomous regional ICONAs, 10 have actualised the laws. These are the areas where lynxes are known to exist — Andalucia, Aragon, Asturias, Castilla-La Mancha, Castilla-Leon, Cataluña, Extremadura, Galicia, Murcia and Valencia. Six of these regions have set the maximum fine at a million pesetas (£5,000).

The decline of the lynx is due not just to hunting and trapping (which are illegal) but also to the destruction or transformation of its habitat by planting pines and eucalyptus, and using heavy machinery to remove the natural vegetation. The spread of myxomatosis which reduced the animal's main prey — rabbits — has also taken a heavy toll. Even lynxes themselves get caught in traps and snares set out for rabbits; they are killed by cars on the roads, can be drowned in deep wells, and also die from illegal poisons. Of 87 dead lynxes from the mountains of Toledo and the Sierra Morena studied since 1974, it was found that 65% were killed in traps or snares, 16.6% by gunfire, 3.4% were knocked over by vehicles, and 11.6% perished from unknown causes.

I returned to the *pabellón* just in time to see a stocky handsome young man climb out of a Land Rover. Juan spotted me immediately, we shook hands and went into the office so he could get my permit, which Dr Delibes had already had typed out. Miguel told me to drop in on my way back as he would have some useful papers for me. He also wanted to photostat my books' appendices on species like grizzly bear, cougar, golden eagle and wildcats. He offered the opinion that, as in Scotland, Spanish wildcats (*gato montés*) were heavily hybridised. They had a radio collar on a tom wildcat in the Reserve and it was often located haunting the homes of female domestic cats on the edge of the Parque!

As Juan led the way to El Rocio, the last village before the Reserve, I saw steamy water splashing on to the road from his bonnet, and he pulled in. His radiator had boiled dry. The fan belt had become loose due to the dynamo coming adrift. He had no tools with him so I grabbed mine from the van and, after a short oily struggle, secured the dynamo back in place. I was glad of the chance to help a biologist before he could help me for it got our relationship off to a good start. As we set off again Juan, who spoke good English, warned me that El Rocio was a real cowboy village, like something from a western movie. It was! The 'streets' consisted of a series of sandy potholes, all filled with water from the recent rain, and I nursed my old *caballo* over them with care.

He took me to meet trapper Rafael Laffitte, who told me that they had caught and radio-collared 15 lynxes. A professional trapper had worked the first year but had caught only one, and it was then that the slim moustached Rafael, who had studied wild animals all his life, had taken over. He caught the other 14 in the last four years so he was clearly no fool as a trapper. While five of the lynxes were presently wearing collars, the batteries in four others had gone dead, so those animals would have to be re-trapped.

At first Rafael was a serious, unsmiling fellow who seemed to dislike the idea of this old grey-bearded amateur traipsing round with him for three days. He treated me to a scathing look up and down. Miguel Delibes had told me I could not wander about the Reserve at will, doing my own thing. That would require a permit from the Ministry of the Interior, which could take weeks to arrange. I was left in no doubt that I would have to do strictly what Juan and Rafael said. I tried to be self-effacing, showed him my books, and said modestly that I had trapped wildcats. When I told him I had taken part in a cougar radio-collaring project in Canada, and had a few ideas about traps, his interest perked up considerably. He even smiled, shook my hand, and told me to meet him tomorrow at 8.30 a.m.

I drove two miles out of the village and camped deep in a pine wood, feeling a mounting excitement. Would I succeed in photographing a lynx in the wild? Miguel had told me he knew of only two men who had achieved it, so it seemed a forlorn hope.

After unlocking the huge and guarded metal gate that bars entrance to the secret heart of the Coto Doñana reserve, Rafael took me through to meet Carlos, the station governor. Carlos then ordered me into his Land Rover and drove us at bouncing speed over eleven kilometres of deeply rutted sand tracks to the elegant old Palacio de Doñana which now houses the biological station and laboratories. As I stared down at the reedbeds from an upper room and then over miles of open water that stretched as far as the eye could see, I thought I was looking out over the Atlantic – until I saw the position of the sun. Rafael told me I was looking north, over the vast *marismas* (marshes) which reached halfway to Seville and made this the largest wildlife reserve in Europe.

Carlos then drove us to the two hectare high-fenced enclosure which held the wild male lynx. Rafael said I could go into the observation hide below the top fence, but despite being in an enclosure there were so many shrubs and trees, the lynx would still be hard to spot. I had no need to do that for the lynx was out in the open, and impatiently waiting for us. It had on a radio collar, from which projected a piece of plastic pipe. I took photos through the wire. Rafael then opened the gate, stepped inside and told me to do the same.

The lynx stood its ground, clearly expecting food from Rafael, for it growled deeper than a wildcat and seemed angry that we were not feeding it. Rafael held up a dead rabbit, so the lynx could see it, as I switched my camera motor on to Sequence, then dropped the rabbit on to a patch of grass I had indicated. The lynx, smaller than the European lynx *(Lynx lynx)* and weighing about 35lbs, glared with bright green-grey eyes at the rabbit, its tufted ears pointing forward and its short stumpy tail held comically up in the air. Then it stalked slowly forward, suddenly charged towards us like a streak of orange lightning, grabbed the rabbit by the neck and dashed off with it. The blasted Sequence button on the camera did not work! All I could do was to click off one shot, slightly out of focus, as the lynx seized the rabbit. Rafael, who spoke no English, just smiled and said we could do it all again tomorrow. The lynx was fed one rabbit a day, or about 4lbs of fallow deer meat.

We drove about 2 km along the sand tracks, turned right to the *marismas* again. I was told I could wait for a wild lynx under a tree a good way off from nesting trees where herons and spoonbills were already assembling. I thought the place was far too low for, if a lynx did come close, I would be unable to see into the dense bushes for more than 25 metres. There was a tall metal tower with a wooden hide on its top 40 metres nearer the trees – could I use that, I asked? Rafael said the hide was locked and neither of them had a key. I said the only place in which I could possibly work in this flat area was that tower, which was leaning to one side and shaking visibly in the wind.

Rafael looked confused for a moment, then took a pair of long handled pliers and began to climb the tower. Before he reached the top, a gust of wind shook the structure and he clung on tight.

Looking down with white face, he said: '*muy alto*' (very high). To my surprise, he slowly climbed down again and confessed he had no head for heights. He handed me the pliers and said that I could try. I told him I too had problems when working on eagle nest cliffs, but I would make an attempt.

I climbed up with heavy pack, feeling none too safe. As I cringed over the top edge the tower moved in the wind. It was decidedly shaky. I gave a curse, clung on to a metal bar with one hand and moved the pliers over to the padlock which was looped through two flimsy staples. One yank, a staple came free and the door was open. I called down that all was well and dropped the pliers to Rafael. He was looking not altogether pleased the old guy was up there after he had failed. He said he would be planting young trees in the lynx enclosure about two kilometres away and that I should meet him there at 1 p.m. I scrambled into the wooden hide and started setting up the camera with the whole thing on the tilt, and shaking with each gust of wind.

Once again I seemed to be looking at an open sea, but before the marshes began there were three large cork oak trees, each filled with large nests and scores of grey herons and smaller night herons with dark patches on their shoulders. The birds were in constant motion, some flying away to feed, others winging in to the trees, flapping and quarrelling, their harsh squawks and '*kraink*' calls mingled with the quivering, ringing cries of red kites hunting near the hide with typical downward flaps of their wings.

Here I was, in the place which I had subconsciously avoided for so long. The Coto Doñana National Park, Spain's best-known wildlife refuge, is a complete marshy wetland of 192,700 acres where the mighty Guadalquivir river brings its silt and phosphates before emptying into the Atlantic ocean. It is one of the most important sanctuaries for rare wildlife in western Europe. Over half Europe's bird species live or breed in the Doñana, or visit the region during their migration flights. It also contains a dozen pairs of the endangered imperial eagle, one of the five rarest birds in the world.

This vital eco-system of sea, dunes, marshes, grassy shrubland and forests was owned for centuries by noble families and used as a hunting reserve. Spanish kings came here for stag and wild boar. In the second half of the last century naturalists and egg collectors arrived, and through their articles, diaries and books the world became aware for the first time of Doñana's wild paradise. A young Spanish ornithologist, José Antonio Valverde, who in ten spring days in 1952 ringed over 2,000 young herons in Doñana, spearheaded a programme of conservation in the region. When a plan was put forward to cut down the remaining pines and oaks, to drain the 'useless' and allegedly disease-spreading marshes, and to plant eucalyptus for the paper mills, Valverde fought it with a fund-raising campaign all over Europe. The most important donation (of a million dollars) came from the newly founded World Wildlife Fund, and a further $700,000 was contributed by the Spanish government. When landowners agreed to sell part of their properties, the eucalyptus idea was abandoned. The area was still threatened by an agricultural drainage plan, but in 1964 a biological reserve of 15,320 acres was established, with Dr Valverde as its director, and in 1969 a government decree created the first Doñana National Park, taking in the reserve and increasing the area to 91,500 acres. Ten years later it was increased again to its present size — 119,000 acres of park, 61,300 acres of land buffer zones (where visitors could see the wildlife without disturbing it, and some farming could be done), and 11,900 acres of marine buffer zone. The fight by leading Spanish naturalists and a few landowners to establish the Park was not won easily, and mass tourism, the possibility of some drainage, of development and road building round the buffer zones, still threaten parts of Doñana. In recent years the struggle to preserve the area has been led by Valverde's successor, the dogged Dr Javier Castroviejo, who has sought publicity and enlisted the aid of international conservation societies.

Drought and an increase in poaching (due, to some extent, to economic recession) brought a new threat to the region ten years ago. Fodder crops failed, and in 1981/82 about 9,000 grey-lag geese perished, almost the same number as were taken by hunters. The hunting was finally stopped in 1983. There was a scandal two years later when 30,000 birds died (including hen and marsh harriers and peregrines) after the banned pesticide *methyl parathion* was sprayed on fields to destroy a plague of crayfish.

Today Doñana is thriving again, with multitudes of little song birds now safe from clap and mist nets, bird lime, traps and guns. All owe their futures to this migratory refuge, and many nest in the cork oaks and umbrella pines that grow between the marshes. Red deer are found here too, and flocks of up to 15,000 huge pink flamingos feed along the river and many stream edges. Sometimes foraging wild boar wreck their nest sites, and foxes steal chicks, so occasional hunting to control these species is allowed. Other birds include the flashy bee-eaters, egrets, Kentish plovers nesting on the beaches, rare spoonbills, ducks of many kinds, and the grey, night, squacco and rare purple herons. There are booted and short-toed eagles, azure-winged magpies, great-spotted cuckoos, avocets, godwits, and black-winged stilts, which look as if their black and white bodies are miraculously suspended above the water, so hard is it to see their long slim legs.

I was indeed gazing at a wildlife paradise through the left view hole at the top of this rickety hide when I suddenly spotted a wild boar a hundred yards away – a sow actually, with a row of dangling teats, and a youngster with her. They grubbed perpetually in the earth, seldom lifting their heads. Then I saw another wild boar, a tusker this time, far off and under a tree. A cattle egret flew down and landed right by his nose, but he took absolutely no notice! As the boar dug into and turned up the earth, the egret looked down with its head on one side, then grabbed whatever grubs, beetles or insects the pig was grouting up and swallowed them, still only inches from his moving snout.

Beyond them a small herd of fallow deer hinds and lovely fawns emerged from the bushes and began grazing in the dappled shade of a cork oak. I heard '*chukar*' sounds behind me, and took photos of a pair of red-legged partridges feeding by a pond, their black, red and white flank bars gleaming like medals in the sun. Later I saw there were eight wild boar, some with young, grubbing among the fallow deer (*gamos*), and neither species showed any alarm at the other. I noticed the boar, blackish-brown all over, had fluffy ears, and were prettier than their domestic cousins. Red kites kept flying around and I saw one swoop into a tree to the right of the hide, where it had a nest with a mate already in residence. One of them picked up a twig and rearranged it, preparing the nest as early as February 18. Before long I saw another kite go into a tree behind the first, where there was another nest.

I forgot about time and it was gone 2 o'clock before I left the hide. I hurried to the lynx enclosure, to find Rafael no longer there. Nor was the lynx. It had doubtless taken its daily rabbit into the bushes and was now having a nap. Damn, I had missed the feeding! I gave a few of the '*Brroo*' trills wildcats make when attracting each other – without result. I had to hike in the hot sun all the way back to the Palacio, where I apologised to Rafael in his laboratory. He took me to the cookhouse where neat-suited biologists were served fillet steak and chips. I was handed a bowl of gruel made from chicken skin, tripe, pigs feet and chick peas. I spooned down some of the vegetables I could stomach, then repaired to my van to eat the cheese, hard boiled eggs and red sausage I had brought with me.

Rafael later showed me some of his lynx traps, agreeing that the hollow tree ones were the best, though he thought that if they had not been entered within two weeks of setting, they never would be. They were then extremely heavy to move somewhere else! I drew for him the Canadian cougar trap, a smaller version of which I had used in Scotland for wildcats, foxes and, once, an injured badger. This was a box-cage device in which an animal taking the bait would activate a nylon line attached to a mouse or rat trap spring, yanking out a nail that held up a heavy sliding door behind the animal. Rafael liked the idea and said he would try it. His method, in both the hollow tree and portable metal traps, was similar. When the lynx entered, it trod on a tipped up plywood platform which was tied by a strong wire through a smooth copper pipe to a metal bolt propping up the rear door. As the platform went down, so the bolt was pulled out. His metal cage traps, however, had two doors, one at the back and one at the front, through which the entering lynx could see two exits and therefore felt safer. When the platform went down both doors were activated, and both had complicated spring devices on them to prevent the animal from pushing its way out again. He had caught four lynxes in the hollow tree traps but only one adult in the metal ones; the other nine lynxes caught in metal traps had been youngsters. Rafael also had leg-hold traps, the cruel teeth of which had been bound round with thick plastic so as not to break a limb or tear the animal's skin. Between these traps and the securing stake was a long spring which further prevented injury if the lynx leaped about trying to get free. He said a lynx never went to carrion, only staying around dead meat if it had made the kill itself. I could not reconcile this with the way I had seen the captive lynx whip a dead rabbit off like lightning, but then I suppose it had no other choice. He baited his traps with live rabbits or mallards, contained in a special cage.

Later, Juan and Rafael took me on their lynx radio-tracking rounds.

It was a crazy, exhilarating drive for the Land Rover blundered in and out of thick sand between the marshes, swerving, waltzing in the drifts, and almost aquaplaning over deep water. Approaching a 50-metre slough of water, they revved up and plunged the vehicle straight into it, great gouts of beery-coloured liquid washing over the bonnet and windscreen. None of the traps we checked had been set for it was not quite the end of the breeding season.

The radio tracking equipment had two channels which could work separately with 24 collars, and that day we tracked three females and a young male lynx that was wandering and had not yet found a territory. Each female had a territory of about four square kilometres, Juan explained, and only once had they found two females within two kilometres of each other. To gain the best signals as we toured the scrubland among bushes of gorse, broom, rosemary, lavender, tree-heath and brambles, between the juniper, arbutus and cork oaks, Juan climbed on to the Land Rover roof, holding the heavy antennae high. He read out the details to Rafael who made notes for their study. The tom wildcat had moved overnight and was now close to some houses skirting the Reserve, still apparently looking for domestic females with which to mate.

Rafael told me that rabbits accounted for 90% of lynx prey, and that sometimes the lynx killed young deer, mainly fallow. In 1980, when 1,537 lynx droppings were analysed from a 68 km square in the Reserve, Dr Delibes had found that the diet consisted of 79.2% rabbits, 8.9% ducks, 5.2% other birds, 2.6% ungulates (young deer) and 4.1% other small mammals. Rabbits were most important from July to October, when there were more young about, and they were preferred to deer calves. From October, when rabbit numbers were fewer, and those left were adult and healthy, the most important prey was young deer. There was a probable increase in the vulnerability of fawns during and after the mating season in September and October, when the maternal-filial bond is weakened and the protection provided by the mother diminished. Severe autumn droughts also made deer more susceptible, for some even died from starvation. From March to June the most important prey were ducks, mainly mallards, which left the marshes to mate and nest in the small fresh water pools of the scrubland. They walked about on dry ground and were noisy both night and day, making them more vulnerable.

It was estimated that 10 lynxes occupied the study area, and that each lynx consumed about 74 grams of food for each kilo (2.2lbs) of body weight daily. In a year one lynx killed and consumed 261 rabbits, 9 deer (at most), 14 other mammals (including one hare), 31 ducks and 19 other birds (including 7 partridges).

Another study, published in 1975 by Miguel Delibes, Jesus Garzon, Javier Castroviejo and F. Palacios, investigated 16 digestive tracts and 37 scats of the Spanish lynx found in Sierra Morena, Montes de Toledo, Sierra de Lagunilla and Sierra de Gata. All were mountain areas under 1,400 metres high which supported a typical Mediterranean vegetation. From 85 prey identified, 56.5% were rabbits, 26.9% were rodents, 11.7% were birds (including partridge and thrush), and one hare was found. The biologists made it abundantly clear that epidemics of myxomatosis had damaged the last populations of this endangered cat.

Lynx kill deer by biting their throats, causing suffocation, then drag them into the bush. They usually eat the muscle tissue from shoulders and thighs, and will eat from the same carcass three or four times in two days. Predation by lynx accounts for about 50% of fallow deer fawn mortality in Doñana. Now that the wolf is extinct in the Doñana region, the lynx is the only coursing predator left capable of killing half-grown deer.

On the way back to the Palacio I saw a new tower and hide that was far closer to the trees of nesting herons and rare spoonbills than my morning one had been. I asked if I could go into it. Juan said firmly no − it was being used for the three days of my stay by a biologist and his two helpers, who were doing a census on nest densities and populations. I retorted equally briskly that the hide was *there*, I had a permit, and I wanted to go into it. He did not reply.

Just then we saw an imperial eagle soar in and swoop up to land on a dense but fairly low cork oak between the two hides, and there was the dark blob of a nest below it. I asked if I could site one of my invisible hides in the bushes near by when the chicks were about a month old? Juan said that no photography of imperial eagles at the nest had been allowed for several years.

20 · The Elusive Lynx

It was obvious next morning that allowing me to use the new tower and hide was the last thing Juan wanted to do. He drove me further than ever before, to a wooden tower and hide out in the open scrubland but near a fenced compartment of young pines. There was no nest tree of any bird in photographable distance. He insisted that this tower would give me my best chance of seeing a lynx in the wild. The bushes were shorter here and a lynx often went along a sandy track 40 metres behind the hide.

I had a hard task climbing up to the hide with my big heavy pack, for the wooden rungs were rotting, and I made sure I stepped only on their edges. When Juan also climbed up to hand me the cushion I had borrowed from his lab, there was a loud crack and a gasp. He had broken one rung completely.

'Be careful when you come down,' he said.

He did not seem able to get any higher and I almost overbalanced as I reached low to grab the cushion and saw there was now a 5-foot gap in the wooden ladder. Perhaps I would not be able to get down.

It was bitterly cold in that hide. Many of the side slats were missing, and the freezing north-east wind came blasting through the gaps. I never saw any lynx. Within ten minutes a horseman went singing happily down the sandy track and I felt the noise and his scent would keep any lynx away for hours. I took a photo of two migratory spotted redshanks on a marshy area, and even saw an osprey on a westward hunting flight. Twice it dived, talons first, into the shallow waters of the *marisma* but it caught nothing and was too far off for good photos.

Within half an hour another horseman came down the sandy track and, to my surprise, turned into the forestry compartment and began to harass a red deer hind. He did not chase her, or put his horse into a trot, but just ambled at walking pace round and across, round and across the path of the hind, which became frenzied with fear and dashed around trying to escape, bloodying her nose and lips against the fencing. She came near to the hide and I took close-ups, showing the fear in her eyes. I thought the rider was trying to hunt her, wear her down to exhaustion, so I took a picture of him too! After forty minutes I saw her burst through a gap in the fence to the south east and race off through the bushy scrub to freedom. The horseman, who later I learned was a warden, cut some bushes, stuffed them into the fence hole, and casually wended his way home down the track to the west. I realised then that he had been trying to get the hind out of the young trees.

It was Rafael who came to collect me, and I was glad when he did so for my feet were frozen. Although I was wearing gloves, my hands had gone white. To save weight while I negotiated myself across the gap, I tried to lower my hefty pack down on garden cord, which broke and sent the pack crashing to the ground. Fortunately only a lens dust cap and a container of anti-wasp and snake bite hystamine pills were broken. Somehow, clinging hard to the side logs rather than putting my full weight on the rungs, I eventually got down safely.

He then drove me to a small sandy *camino* which he said was the best place for me to see lynx droppings and good examples of their four-toed tracks. As with cougars and wildcats, the tracks did not show the animals' claws. Rafael told me that two pairs of lynxes were there, each holding a territory on either side of the *camino*. They always marked their territorial boundaries by depositing scats on the slim band of grass in the centre of the *camino*. If a tom lynx crossed into another tom's territory, and they met, they would fight like hell, claw each other badly and tear lumps out of the rival. I told him how cougars urinated on special scratch piles of earth made with their paws, to advertise their presence to rivals and to attract females. He said lynxes did much the same, and we found one example.

Lynxes usually breed between mid-December and early February

This 35lb wild male lynx, kept in the Doñana reserve, stood his ground when we went to feed him.

Undaunted by our presence, the lynx dashed for the fallow deer haunch, and seized it, unhindered by the radio collar.

From the best hide in Doñana, reserved for biologists, I watched spoonbills nesting with the herons.

I was astonished when mongooses waddled towards me, and a large male emerged from his burrow below the hide.

A unique sight in Spain – only near Malpartida de Cáceres do white storks nest on huge rocks.

After a long wait by a deserted sandy track I succeeded in photographing a rare Spanish lynx in the wild.

To have white storks nesting on your roof, as they are on this church, is a symbol of good luck in Spain.

White storks mating.

The black-winged kite comes from Africa.

and, after a gestation of 65 to 73 days, give birth usually to two kits but any number from one to four in March or April. Dens can be found in dry sandy hollows or small caves amid thick bushes, but lynxes have also been known to use low white stork nests in trees. The young usually stay in the area where they are born until their second winter, and the males leave first, travelling further to find a territory of their own.

I noticed that 40 metres south sou-west of the *camino* there was a deep sand slake gouged out by recent heavy rains. With the north-east wind blowing and the sun behind me, it would have been an ideal place to wait for a lynx, but I knew it would not be allowed. Just then a female Montagu's harrier, showing her white rump, flapped over some banks of reedmace.

In the afternoon I was driven again to the lynx enclosure, and this time the tom was even hungrier for his late meal. I recorded him on tape hissing and growling. While Rafael planted more young oaks on the far side of the enclosure, Juan threw, not a rabbit, but a chunk of deer haunch to the lynx. This time the sequence button worked well and I clicked off six pictures of it dashing in from the left, grabbing the meat and rushing away with it. The haunch was heavy (about 9lbs) and the lynx kept tripping up like an over-eager but inexperienced football player getting too far ahead of the ball. It was a comical sight, with its short stumpy tail bobbing, its white bum flashing, as it tried to get its meal away from us as fast as it could.

As we drove out I asked Juan again if I could go into the best hide – at least when the biologists went for lunch. He said they did not go for lunch. I told him they had done so yesterday for I had seen them in the cookhouse! He gave me a long look and said he would try.

To my dismay, early next morning, he drove me back to the first tower. I certainly did not want to photograph those rather distant herons again. Luck, however, was on my side for Juan let slip the fact that the census biologist and his helpers were not there today. Looking downcast, I pointed to the best hide half a mile away and begged to use it. Eventually he sighed and said –

'All right. But you have to walk in from here.'

I thanked him and scuffed off through the grass and bushes before he had time to change his mind. As I approached the tower great clouds of gawky grey herons, night herons and spoonbills left the close nesting trees, darkening the sky momentarily, like huge flies scared off a cowpat. The snow-white spoonbills were hefty birds, some 2ft 10ins long, and as they held their weird spatular-shaped beaks before them, they looked as if they were taking part in an odd egg and spoon race. These are rare birds – with about 200 pairs in Holland, 250 pairs in Austria, 240 pairs in Greece – and by far the largest nesting colony in western Europe is that of 500 pairs in Spain.

After climbing the tower safely with my pack, I found the door of the wooden hide locked. With no time to waste I wrenched the padlock and staples out with my hands. Luckily I had a small screwdriver with me and could reset it all when I left. The birds, which had gone almost out of sight, must have thought I had walked past for they soon returned to the trees.

The spoonbills now began an odd courting routine. Their long grotesque-looking black bills, which end in a flattened spoon, and which they use to sift out small fish, molluscs and crustaceans when wading in shallow water, did not look likely instruments for nest building. Yet the nests were large, neat, and the reeds, twigs and leaves were well woven. One spoonbill took a twig from the nest on which it was standing and almost overbalanced as it reached down to pass it to another on a nest far below. Either they were trying to find their old mates, or courting new ones for they sometimes flew to each other's nests, raised and lowered their yellowish crests of head plumes, and clopped their mandibles.

Suddenly I saw some greyish creatures waddling along under the nest trees, in and out of the bushes. At first I thought they were badgers but I could see no white head stripes. As they wended their way through the herbage I could get only the odd glimpse of fur here and there. Luckily a pair of magpies pursued them, perching above them and chattering, so that I could follow their progress. At last the animals came out briefly into the open and I could see there were three ichneumons, or Egyptian mongooses. They were larger than otters but smaller than badgers with grey-yellowish sleek fur. As they came nearer I realised they were going to some sand burrows directly below the tower. I clicked off many photos – one of the biggest, a male, on his own; another of the male and a female, then of the two together coming out of a hole and staring intently to my left. I had to change to a 200mm lens for they were too close to get in frame. What an unexpected bonus!

After radio tracking a male mongoose for a month between July and August, M. Delibes and J. F. Beltran estimated it ranged an average daily distance of 2.9 km, varying between 0.6 km to 6.4 km, and did not occupy a permanent den. Like the lynx, it feeds chiefly on rabbits in Spain, though it also eats birds and eggs, amphibians, fish, insects, carrion, berries and mushrooms. It is the daily activity and the frequent hunting of reptiles which make the mongoose different from other carnivores in its range.

I would have been lucky to see just one mongoose clearly in the wild, but to have three come so close was almost a miracle. And it would not have happened if I had not talked my way into this hide. If only I could see and photograph a lynx in the wild. I glanced at my watch. I had well over three and a half hours before I had to rendezvous again with Juan, when my permit would run out. I thought again of the *camino* Rafael had shown me, where lynx came to deposit scats to mark their territorial boundaries. It was more than a kilometre away. Dammit, I would take a chance and go there right now. If this was one of those lucky days I would press that good luck as far as it would go. I moved out of the hide, reset the padlock staples by making tight holes with my little screwdriver, and climbed down the tower. It was good to get into the warmth of the sun again.

Moving quietly but fast, I trekked where the bushes were thickest and in a wide arc to the south west, in the hope that no lynx would pick up my scent in the cold north-east wind. For the same reason I wanted to approach from the south and it was hard to locate the deep sand slake on the main track below the *camino*. I paused behind a tall bush, straining eyes and ears to make sure the coast was clear. Leaving pack behind and keeping my head low, I crawled on hands and knees to the gouge in the sandy track. I lay still for about a minute, then carefully edged the long lens over its brittle top edge. The position was a little too low for a clear view of the *camino* some 30 metres away. I lifted the rear of the camera and made a fulcrum of sand for it. Now I could see clearly and settled down to wait.

The sun was still shining but it was surprising how fast my body heat from the exercise of the trek was sucked out of me by the cold wind. My hands soon went white and I had to pull the sleeves of two sweaters and camouflage jacket over them to keep my fingers warm enough to work the camera. Because of the noise it would make, I would not use motor drive. I would probably get only one shot. The depth of the sand gouge was such that my chest and feet were higher than my belly, causing my spine to be strained backwards unnaturally, and the pain was excruciating. I could only relieve it for a minute or two by lying in the foetal position on one side or the other. After nearly two hours I felt I was wasting my time.

Suddenly there was a movement in the bushes to the right of the *camino* some 80 metres ahead, different from those being caused by the wind. Out came a blunt nose and muzzle with a little white beard below. My heart began to pound. The feline face turned towards me, the beard became two snowy mutton chops, and I was aware through the lens of a pair of lustrous greeny-grey eyes and sharp ears adorned by long tufts of dark hair. I did not press the button for I wanted the whole lynx to emerge. Soon it did, and took a few trotting steps towards the *camino* as my camera clicked. It did not appear to hear that noise. Frantically I wound on to the next frame as it reached the grassy centre of the *camino* and bent down to sniff something, perhaps another lynx's scat.

I was just too slow, for as my camera clicked, it whirled away from me and bounded up the track, showing the bright white alarm patch under its stumpy black-tipped tail before vanishing into the bushes. It was clearly scared, had perhaps heard the winding of the film or the second click of the shutter, and I knew it would not show itself again.

The long hike back to meet Juan seemed interminable, and after the excitement of the last two days I felt tired. But no fatigue could affect the sense of elation and victory that now buoyed me up. At last I had seen and photographed the rare elusive lynx in the wild, and if one of the two pictures came out well, it seemed I had won yet again.

I said goodbye at the locked gate and promised to send Juan and Rafael copies of my books. I longed to tell them of my success with the lynx but dared not do so. What I had done was strictly against the rules.

21 · The Wary Wolf

After spending Sunday in a pine wood glade, typing out notes on my observations, I called on Dr Migual Delibes in Seville. He photocopied what he wanted from my books and told me that a group of biologists was trying to start a centre for breeding imperial eagles near Madrid. I had almost no chance of obtaining a permit to photograph them at Doñana, though I was welcome to return for anything else. Apart from one Japanese film unit five years ago, which had obtained permission at government level, he reckoned no foreign photographer had received a permit for imperials for ten years or more.

I drove back to Extremadura to look for Belarmino Martín, whom Suso had co-opted to help find me a new remote home. I took a circuitous route without seeing any wildlife of great interest until I reached Aliseda on the N521, where white storks were nesting on a large building. I also spotted a red kite dive to the ground below a tree and pass the morsel of food it found there from claw to beak while it flew off. I had never seen that before.

Driving on towards Malpartida de Cáceres, I remembered being told that white storks nested on rocks in this area, and that they were easy to photograph without a hide. I worked my way south through the town, feeling pretty sceptical, until suddenly there they were — the stork rocks, to the side of a small road. For a moment I let my attention to driving lapse. Without warning, the front wheel

213

went over the edge of a steep drop to the fields below. I struggled to bring it back on to the road again, but it had gone too far. There was a grinding crunch and the van came to a stop, teetering on the very edge. Instead of rolling over and crashing down the steep slope, it leaned at a dangerous angle while gingerly I climbed out with something to eat for lunch.

For two hours no-one came down that road, and I envisaged myself sleeping in the field below in sub-zero temperatures. At last a black car appeared and turned down a *camino* past the stork rocks. I waved frantically. The driver came over and saw my plight.

'*Espere!*' Wait, was all he said.

He drove back the way he had come, and I waited. Presently he returned with two other men who tied a rope to their car bumper and hauled me out of trouble. They said they were working on a boat platform on a lake near the stork rocks, and I asked if I could go in there and take some pictures. They looked doubtful and mentioned a permit. Nowhere else in Spain, they assured me, did white storks nest on rocks as they did here at Los Barruecos. Then they waved me over – if I hurried, they said, no-one would stop me.

As I stalked close I realised that some of these rounded rocks were as large as two storey houses and I felt dwarfed by them. I crept cautiously, trying to stay hidden behind small trees, but it was all unnecessary. The birds must have been used to people, for they flew in and out casually, greeting their mates at the nest with clopping beaks, while I exposed a roll of film.

Later I photographed seven white stork nests together on the roof of Malpartida's church and found one nesting pair under the church bell. Storks were clearly being encouraged, for two nests were on artificial platforms. I reached my imperial eagle camping site above Salto de Torrejón by nightfall. It was colder here than in Doñana, and I had to use a sleeping bag inside my blanket bed.

When I saw him next day, José Antonio told me that he had received a telegram from the Provinces' ICONA chief saying that no photography of imperial eagles at the nest was to be allowed in Monfragüe this year. He also said that he had been unable to find any isolated cottages for sale, which did not surprise me, for nowhere in all my travels in Extremadura had I seen a '*Se Vende*' notice on any property. Estate agents did not exist here. Everything was sold by word of mouth.

I saw more white stork nests on the high roof of the cathedral of

Malpartida de Plasencia when I drove there for supplies. But the streets were so narrow that I could not get far enough away for a good slanting view of the birds. One street led downhill from the cathedral, which I thought would only make matters worse, but in the end I found I could see more of the roof from down there. I photographed the storks on the lowest nest beautifully lit by the sun. To my surprise, they then started mating, the male mounting the female with lazy flaps of his white and black wings. Both clapped their bills, and the female thrust her head, neck and beak right up into his thick breast feathers until I could no longer see them. Then she twisted her head from side to side in a loving way. Take a little trouble and you can see something new every day.

No sooner had I returned to the camp site than I saw the imperial eagles in courtship display. The male was chasing his larger mate up and down, first below and then above the trees. He swooped up from beneath her and rolled over to touch her talons. Then he flapped high beyond her and dived down as she turned over to greet his.

When the sun went down, it became bitterly cold again, and at times I was shivering in my bed in the van. It was slowly registering with me that this Extremadura region could be as cold as Scotland in winter − and that reminded me forcefully once more of my homeless state. Truth was, I had no clue about what I was going to do. In finding my previous three wilderness homes, in Canada and in Scotland, luck had intervened before so long. Maybe, as one's energy force field diminishes with age, one runs out of 'luck'. I forced myself to visit Belarmino Martín, but he was not at home. I left a note for him with his wife.

As I drifted along a country road next day I saw a bluey-white bird fly from a marsh on the left up into an *encina* tree. I thought it a cock hen harrier. I stopped and saw through the camera lens that, despite similar colouring, it was smaller than a harrier and had black ridges on its shoulders. It also had a much broader, rounder, altogether prettier face and head. It was a rare black-winged kite, the first I had ever seen. As it flew to another tree I stalked closer, and then saw another perched in the tree the first bird had just left, clearly its mate. Presently the first bird flew off, dived into some grass, pouncing twice, and then shot up again to take a mouse to its mate. Having handed over the mouse, the kite then snatched it back again and flew off round the trees. It did not seem much of a courtship technique.

I reached Candelada by early evening and decided to give Beltran a call. When we met at the garage bar, the first thing he said was –

'You are as slippery as a toad!'

I reminded him that, while frogs are slippery, toads are not. But what on earth did he mean? Then I remembered that while driving from Madrid to meet Suso, I had stopped to phone Beltran. There had been a long pause before his wife had returned to the phone to say that he was down at the *finca*. Maybe I was becoming a nuisance, I had thought, and just carried on with my journey. Now he told me he had gone to the *finca* to MEET me, not dodge me, and I had failed to show up.

While waiting for me to arrive, he had let the two wild boars out for a run, whereupon they started a boisterous fight near his daughter, and Beltran had stepped in front to protect her. In the mêlée, the bigger boar gored Beltran's left leg with a tusk, making a deep gash. The wound had to be cleaned and sewn up with 27 stitches, leaving Beltran in hospital for four days. He was still on antibiotics.

Later, while I was eating a late lunch in my van near Toledo, I saw a large brown, orange and white bird land on the grass at the edge of the road and begin probing about for grubs and insects. It was a great spotted cuckoo, another first sighting for me. I took a few photos of it through the window, and ended a film. Surely it would not stay while I threaded in a new one – but it did, and I opened the window carefully, poking the barrel lens through for more pictures. This 16-inch bird is found only in Spain, Portugal and the very south of France in all western Europe, and I felt almost as pleased as I was with the black-winged kite. Again it was clear that I need to *move*, to be *active*; day after day at a lonely desk was death to my spirit.

I nursed the old *caballo* back to the Red Villa with a heavy heart. A shock awaited me in the sack of mail that had accumulated at the post office during my absence. My Surrey friend, who was housing all my surplus gear, wanted it out of her house by the end of April, for her aged mother now needed a resident nurse, who would have to use my room. Panic! I wrote to Suso and to Belarmino Martín but neither replied by the time I left for Santander. There was no escaping a return to England to find new lodging for my things.

I decided to deviate slightly from the direct route north and have another look at the tree nest of the imperial eagles. I camped on a blind turn-off just past Consuegra on the C400 road to Toledo.

I was ready to drive away next morning when I saw a huge dark harrier-type bird flying about the marshes on the far side of the road. With twigs in its talons, it turned abruptly and landed in grass near a reedbank and a green bush. Presently it flew up again with empty talons, so I deduced it was making a nest there. The bird, which I thought was a female marsh harrier, quartered the ground for a further 200 metres, then dropped down again. Through the binoculars I saw her pulling rushes and reeds about with her beak and one foot. Then up she went again, her talons filled with rushes. As she flew back to the nest site I saw her switch the rushes so that they pointed fore and aft, like an osprey turns a fish to reduce wind resistance during flight. She stayed at the nest for half a minute before flying away again to repeat the procedure. On her return, she always flew past the nest and made an abrupt banking turn to the left to go down to it. This ensured that she did not get the rushes and reeds she was carrying caught up in the growing vegetation around the nest. She could dive down on to the nest from directly above. The cock bird, with grey patches on wing and tail, was loitering around too, but not with any great intent. I did not see him help the female to build the nest.

I had lunch at the kites' rubbish tip near Oropesa, then went to the imperial eagles' nest in the eucalyptus. There was something white and red in the nest when I reached it. As the bird shifted some nearby branches I saw the head and great beak of a white stork! She was clearly on eggs. When her mate swept in from the left, she stood up to greet him, clattering her bill. He had some food for her. I would never have expected an imperial eagle nest to be taken over by white storks, but the earlier nesters had obviously found this ready-made home cosily near to the ample food at the dump, and had moved in. Good for them! Bad for me, and the eagles. Though I could not in any case stay to watch developments in the present circumstances. And furthermore some bird or other, I was reminded, was about to take over my temporary quarters in Britain. I hurried on northwards, full of anxiety about what I would find and do . . .

With more than a day in hand before the Santander ferry sailed I decided to cut across to the mountains of León and Zamora provinces which, I had been told, held Spain's largest populations of wolves. There are believed to be over 1,200 wild wolves still in the country, and some estimates go as high as 2,000. They are found mainly in the west and north western mountains of both Spain and Portugal, with smaller packs (or 'clans') in the Sierra de la Demanda region of Burgos Province, the border hills west of Cáceres. A few are occasionally seen in the Montes de Toledo. The Spanish *lobo* is difficult to see, and to study, for packs can travel over 100 km in a single night, and during the day they hide up in the most dense thickets in the deepest woods. I knew I had very little chance of seeing a wolf – but every new route holds the possibility of suspense and mystery.

I took the road through Medina del Campo and Tordesillas, where the Rio Duero looked black and polluted, then turned along the N122 towards Zamora. Long before I reached Morales de Toro the sky seemed suddenly to be filled with red kites, flop-flying all over the place. I counted nine, and most of them seemed to be paired up, flying over plantations of large umbrella pines where clearly they were about to nest. After Zamora I kept on the same road almost to Alcañices, where the terrain became very Scottish, with granite outcrops, folds of rock and many little cliffs and valleys amid the green grass and heather. There were black cattle here, and many dry stone walls of unique construction, the stones laid diagonally with gaps between them, and every so often containing a large boulder or fang-shaped rock that reared up between the stones.

After Alcañices I turned up the rough road through San Vitero for it seemed the only one to cross the heart of the Sierra de la Culebra. The walled fields soon petered out. Apart from the odd scrap of land clawed back from the wilderness and ploughed up, the first rolling hills were covered in sessile oaks and saplings, with tamarisks and other deciduous trees, and between them spread a dense *matorral* of cistus, heathers, lentiscus and other bushes which seemed to gang up on any animal or human that sought to penetrate their depths. It was certainly the sort of country to hide wolves.

I passed through one poor village after another, where women dressed in black carried bundles of vegetation on their backs and mules were still being driven. The villages became fewer nearer the top of the pass. I saw a railway line passing below the southern side of the peaks, and beyond it a small stony track off to the right. I turned up it and drove for about 3 km into rougher terrain. There were large forestry compartments up to my left, with bare jagged granite peaks cutting weird angles in the sky above them, while bushy tree-lined hills below the track ran into folding grassland valleys, which in turn gave way to swampy areas surrounded with thickets.

At length I saw that the forestry section was giving way to rough open 'slash' country which had been logged off. It reminded me of cougar terrain in Canada in which rabbits and deer left the forest shelter to feed on the grasses and bushes that grew up where once the trees had been. Before reaching the edge of the forest I thought I would stop and scan the steep open area ahead. I put on camouflaged trekking jacket and bush hat, took out my binoculars, and walked along the track, staying close to the trees. Keeping my eyes to the left, I picked my way between the slabs of rock. Beyond them I saw a large animal legging it up the hill in the sinking sun. Then another got up and went after it, changing its gait from a gallop to a trot after about 20 metres. I could hardly believe what I was watching as my heart quickened. The first animal turned left and vanished into the forest, but the second paused, and I saw that its muzzle was more pointed than that of an Alsatian. It was not as big as a full-grown German shepherd dog and was greyer in colour, with blackish hairs in its coat. As it turned its head to look back at me, there was no doubt about the distinct width of the skull, the yellowish chops and the fawny throat patch. I was gazing at a wolf.

Perhaps they were a young pair which had left their packs and were setting up in a territory of their own. They had been warming themselves in the last of the sun.

I shrank back behind a rock slab and hurried to get the camera from the van. There was no sign of them when I returned. Clearly the second wolf had gone to join the first in the shelter of the forest. It would have been a hopeless task to attempt penetrating that dense wood, never mind attempting to track down so wary an animal in it. I waited until dusk, but was not surprised to see no further sign of them. I drove on another 5 km to a hunting reserve before turning back. I camped amid pine trees overlooking the open slash area.

When I woke, the sun was already fingering the high peaks with gold as it rose above the eastern hills, though inside the van's windows were still covered in thick frost. I scraped away a portion of ice and kept watch, but there was no sign of life. After breakfast I walked by the side of the forest, keeping in the shade, working upwards until the trees came to an end. As I expected, I saw nothing, not even a feral dog. I was no longer certain that the animals had been wolves at all, and I was angry with myself for not having the camera ready in my hands. Months later I told Suso about the incident and he thought it more than likely that they had been wolves. These mountains – the

Sierra de la Culebra, and the Sierra de la Cabrera above them — were one of the last strongholds of the Spanish wolf.

I was surprised to learn that the species is not totally protected, and that there is a strong lobby against protection mounted by the small farming communities in wolf terrain. Most of the peasants living here keep only a few animals — sheep, goats or cows — and the loss of just one beast can be a disaster to them. Most of the wolves wander in small packs and cover great distances. A farmer finding a sheep ripped apart has very little hope of catching any of the culprits that will be miles away by dawn. The tendency therefore is to shoot a wolf on sight.

Dr Rodriguez de la Fuente campaigned energetically on behalf of the wolf for many years. In a paper in 1975 he wrote:

In Spain, although the wolf population has suffered a notable decrease in recent years, these beautiful animals are still present in almost all our sierras and steep moorlands . . . Imagine what would have happened in the famous Serengeti or in the crater of the Ngorongoro if, on the plea of preserving the goats and antelopes, people had killed all the lions and leopards, as we have been doing here with the wolves and lynxes of Asturias, the mountains of Toledo and the mountain ranges of the south. What would have happened, of course, would quite simply have been that there would now have been fewer zebras, fewer antelopes and, moreover, that they would be diseased and degenerate. Naturally, not a single tourist would now be going to photograph these herds, so goodbye to a valuable source of foreign exchange.

The truth is that the wolf is a carnivorous animal which can balance the degenerating selective pressure that hunters exercise in the big game preserves. It has been proved time and time again that wolves, slower-paced than any deer or antelope, always pick out injured or maimed individuals, the sick or old, which are the first to become exhausted in the chase. It is through this selective hunting, that the most vigorous breeding animals capable of maintaining the purity of genetic lines, are the ones that survive. Contrariwise, human hunters always pick out the finest specimens as trophies, thus eliminating the best males and unleashing a negative selection which, on many estates, has already given rise to generations of deer with small and misshapen horns. A total lack of wolves to compensate for this situation could be catastrophic. We should also remember the vast numbers of rats, mice and other rodents, which wolves devour in spring and summer, and the control they exercise over foxes, weasels and other small predatory animals. It is logical that in zones where it is proved that wolves cause damage to flocks, they should be persecuted and killed. But on estates and in the game preserves, their extermination would constitute and create a real imbalance in the biological communities.

The wolf was first afforded some protection in 1970, when it was made a big game animal. That rendered it illegal to shoot the animal in the close season, in other words during the breeding period of spring and summer, though it often is even today. Poisoning was also made illegal. In recent years conservationists have campaigned for full protection, as is enjoyed by bears, and for farmers to be compensated by the government for their losses due to wolves. In fact the Spanish wolf was included in a 1989 Directive drawn up by the Common Market Commission to cover some 1,300 wildlife species, including plants (see the Appendix) — so maybe the wolf can expect full protection before much longer.

When I returned to the van, I was surprised to find the milometer had gone through 90,000 miles. My poor old *caballo*! The front brakes were making ominous noises but the engine was still slogging gamely on despite an oil leak.

Now short of time, I headed for Palencia and the direct route to the ferry. I was beginning to worry about the nightmare facing me in Britain, which lessened my appetite for wildlife on the way — though I did spot a hen harrier before Amusco and three cock harriers in flight. A few griffons were soaring from the cliffs of Puerto de Pozazal, and I saw three black kites flying on the outskirts of Reinosa, where belching smoke from a huge factory spoiled an otherwise idyllic backdrop of snowy mountain peaks. I did not take it as an omen, though the vision matched the mood of the dislocated and unsettling months that were to follow.

Arriving homeless in Britain, I moved all my gear out of the Surrey house and scattered it around in five locations, including a timber warehouse owned by Bill Baldwin, a birdwatcher who had

221

read my books and came to the rescue at the last moment. Another reader rented me a room in her less than quiet flat, from which I launched an obsessive search for a new home in the wilds. Estate agents were uncomprehending, house prices were rocketing, and I trekked hundreds of miles through fields and woods in surprisingly remote areas of southern England on the unrewarding quest.

Eventually, with my van overhauled, I returned to Scotland to finish, in pouring rain, the wildlife movie that no-one wanted. At the same time I gave a few media interviews for the publication of *Moobli*, which was largely ignored by book reviewers — though it brought me more enthusiastic mail from readers than anything I had written since *A Last Wild Place*. In October I gave up the frantic chase and returned to Spain more insecure and dispossessed than ever. I felt like a tramp, a wandering vagabond in an old van, as I pulled into the San Clemente pine wood to camp, tired, dispirited, and convinced I would find the Red Villa once more plundered in my absence and the last of my gear gone. I had visions of typing the new book my publisher had urged me to finish this winter with frozen fingers at the red kites' rubbish tip.

But things are rarely as bad as they seem, and the villa stood untouched when I reached it. I felt a flood of relief, almost love for the place. There was also a letter in my mail from Belarmino Martín, written three days after my departure all those months ago. He looked forward to a visit from me, for he was eager to help me to find a home in Extremadura.

Belarmino turned out to be an energetic, dark-haired man in his early thirties when eventually I met him in his office. He had an untrimmed Nietszche-style moustache, and he bustled round on my behalf finding, among others, a place 4 km from the village that was approachable only by mule over a massive trackless escarpment. There was also a gloomy and damp old farmhouse in a muddy pic- nic area used for grazing sheep and goats, and a boarded-up window- less cottage with a concrete tank 50 metres away that collected spring water. The owner might rent it if the key could be found. Should I be so choosy as to turn down such a place just because it was close to a polluted river a few kilometres downstream from a nuclear power station? Belarmino, who was very warm-hearted and took a great deal of trouble, said he would keep on looking.

I found the most promising place myself, by chance. I was making my way along the tree-lined overgrown banks of the Tiétar river when I came to a little house, with a stout chimney, by the water's edge at the end of a steeply sloping bank between a cattle fence and the river. To get to the door I had to break through a 15-foot high thicket of brambles – only to find that the door had been stolen. I stepped on to the red-tiled floor of a large rectangular room which admitted light through two large glassless windows that looked across a 200-metre reach of the river. A square metal-rimmed hole in the floor revealed another room, five metres deep, beneath my feet. Another door led on to a patio, with secure iron fence, that overlooked a group of islets in the river. A snipe flew up in front of me. Stone steps went down to the lower dungeon, which had two small window holes facing north and south. Water flowed from a semi-tiled tunnel (probably from a spring) into the deep river beside the house. The roof was of thick concrete, and girdered. Could this be it . . . ?

I hastened to tell Belarmino who, on seeing it, told me it was an old disused pumping station, the lower room once housing engine and pipe for getting water up to the *finca*. I could probably have it for a symbolic rent if I could make it habitable. The only trouble was that, in winter rains, the Tiétar river could rise by four to five metres and flood the lower room. Well, I had always wanted an indoor swimming pool! Belarmino made encouraging sounds about getting the electricity brought down here and a builder to fit windows, shutters and doors to make it reasonably watertight. He talked of getting some hardcore put down on the muddy track so that I could get my vehicle close, but I went off the idea when suddenly I heard screams and shouts coming from a favourite picnic area a few metres away that I had not noticed behind a screen of trees. Even so, I wrote to His Excellency, the President of the Diputación Provincial de Cáceres, for permission to renovate, but received no reply.

While Belarmino promised to look for a small piece of land in a vast pinewood north west of Majadas, on which I could build something simple for myself, I returned to the lonely slog at my desk in the draughty Red Villa. I had intended to head north to the mountains of Asturias, to look for wild bears, but I was told that the snows had arrived and the bears would be in hibernation early this year. I contented myself with quick sorties to watch the colony of bustards and cranes near Talavan between long spells at the typewriter, speaking to hardly a soul for weeks on end. I heard no more from Belarmino before setting off, too early in March, on what seemed in more rational moments to be an absurd quest for bears.

22 · *Frozen on Bear Mountain*

I was in real trouble this time. For a day and two bitterly cold nights my van had been bogged down in deep snow halfway up a stupendous canyon in the spectacular mountains of the Asturias. I was running short of both food and petrol. After the first miserable day, occasionally running the engine so that the heater kept the van tolerably warm, I dared not use it any more. I had a little bottled-gas heater but it was less than half full, as was the canister which supplied my twin-burner cooker. I did not know how much longer the snow would last and was forced to ration both carefully.

It was a mid-March day, and the last thing I had expected when setting off from Murcia in searing heat was to become trapped in a snow blizzard. The entire 1,450 km drive from the Red Villa to the Somiedo area, which both Beltran and Suso had told me probably held the best nucleus of wild brown bears in the country, had been made in bright sunny weather. Only the mornings had been cold, with hoar frost lining the inside of the van's windows when I got up.

Having passed through rolling hills and valleys dotted with clumps of trees, where the villages were built along the banks of the river Sil, a sense of excitement mounted as the first rugged bare granite peaks came into view before Palacios del Sil, and after it when I reached the first of the great gorges which scored these mountains.

The slopes of this first ravine were clothed with trees, mostly leaf-less oaks and saplings, but there were also thick-trunked tamarisks

224

Spanish squirrels often use insulated electricity cables to travel through the woods.

Thousands of cranes migrate to winter in Spain from their far northern nesting grounds, and are hard to approach.

The magnificent mountains of Asturias are the main stronghold of the last wild brown bears in Spain.

After being trapped in blizzards for three days I found a family of bears in the ravine, romping in the snow.

The cubs loved sliding down the snowy slopes, and once went down backwards, almost cannoning into their mother.

The mother sometimes lay on her back or side, inviting a cub to jump on her so that they could roll down the snowslide together.

Snow games over for the day, the mother led the cubs away
down the valley.

with gnarled bark and clumps of sallow and poplar along the river banks, as well as other trees I could not identify. Here and there were a few pines. A broad snowy peak emerged high to my right as I rounded a bend towards Piedrafita. As I made the ascent to the 1,486-metres-high Puerto de Somiedo I was disappointed when the forest ran out. Here were just a few birches among the deep heathers and rocky outcrops, the landscape and icy roads reminding me of Scotland. Somiedo village itself seemed deserted, with just the odd car outside a shuttered house, and snow lying in sunless gullies beside the road. It did not look like bear country to me any more. I told myself there must be more woods on the other side of the pass. I drove downhill for a long time, through Caunedo and Pola de Somiedo, and suddenly — there it all was again.

Vast deep forested canyons rose on either side, with etiolated crags towering up into the sky as if they were trying to block out the light, like scenes from a wonderful dream, or nightmare. The Somiedo river flowed through the valley below, and the colossal slopes were clothed with more trees than before — bare oaks interspersed with evergreen holm oaks and what looked like holly oak bushes which had somehow rooted on the cliffs. As well as poplar, sallow and willow lower down I could recognise ash trees, aspen, a few eucalyptus, fewer pines, and others I could not name. Old man's beard festooned many bushes. There was plenty of shelter for bears in this rugged, vegetation-strewn country, I thought. As I drove on, the valley opened out to reveal nearly all the riverside land to be intensely cultivated. While there might not be bears in this particular valley, it was clear that far more pristine wooded gorges stretched for miles in every direction. In them bears would find what they most needed — undisturbed space, food and plenty of cover.

There are still a few trigger-happy hunters about, men who would break the law and shoot a bear if they think they can get away with it, so I will not reveal precisely where I ended up. Enough to say that, for three days, I explored the whole Somiedo region, the rough square bounded by Piedrafita, La Plaza, Belmonte, Cangas de Narcea, and Muniellos to the south west. I drove and trekked, drove and trekked, making short sorties on foot into woods and up gorges. After tracking grizzlies in Canada I knew what to look for, but not once did I find any trace of bears.

What surprised me about all this woodland was that so little of it seemed to be commercially planted — hence there were few *caminos* or side roads into the gorges. Just before dusk on the third day, I was driving through a truly savage-looking area at about 1,000 metres when one of the rare *caminos* appeared at the side of a bend in the road. It seemed to lead along the south side of a huge wooded canyon which broadened out near its top some 10 km away. Without thinking, I swung into the *camino* and drove up a rough stony track, bouncing along for about 3 km until I was far beyond sight and sound of the road.

Suddenly I saw a small clearing in the trees up ahead, to the right, the entrance to which was partly blocked by some abandoned rotting firewood logs. The little clearing sloped down from the track slightly, and as I like to sleep with my head a few inches higher than my feet (this helps to stop acidic stomach pains after drinking wine), it seemed an ideal place to camp for the night. I drove past, got out to remove some of the logs, then backed the van down the slope amid the trees until the bonnet was a metre from the track.

It had been bitterly cold all day, so I lit the little bottled-gas heater, turning it up full while I tape recorded the daily diary. That done, I switched on the radio. Even though I had tied it up to the roof for the best reception, I could not get Radio 4 or any British programme. The canyon walls were blocking everything but a Spanish chat show and a French pop music programme. I settled for the music while I drank some wine and prepared supper. After eating, for once I did the washing up the same night and put all the utensils away before climbing into bed.

Two hours later I awoke so chilled under four thick blankets that my uppermost hip and thigh were cold to the touch. I got the sleeping bag from a side cupboard, lay on it stomach-down for a minute or so to warm it up, then clambered in. With that *under* the blankets I was tolerably warm again. All the time I was doing this, I fancied I could hear a soft whispering sound. Just a breeze soughing through the leafless trees, I told myself.

It was so bright when I roused next morning that I felt sure I must have overslept until 10 o'clock. I looked at the little travel clock – it was only 8 a.m. Puzzled, I pulled one of the curtains aside.

I was astonished to find myself surrounded by a sea of white. An overnight blizzard had engulfed the van in over a foot of snow, and even as I stared out more huge soft flakes were falling. Instantly, I realised my plight, but I tried to keep calm. I dressed, shovelled snow away from front and rear wheels, and then went through the motions of extricating the van. As soon as the thrusting rear wheels hit the next lot of snow they slipped, revolving uselessly, and would have dug the van into even more trouble in the mud had I not given up. There was no way my old *caballo* could force itself up that slight slope. And even if I did succeed here, it would certainly get stuck in a drift somewhere along the 3 km of slippery track. With such a snowfall, even the main road would be impassable on the steep slopes along the gorges.

As I sipped tea and ate some toast I realised that the chance of another human being coming this way in a 4-wheel drive vehicle was remote. I had to face it — until the snow melted I was stuck, marooned. And if the snow did not melt before my supplies ran out, I would have to hike a long way for help. I kept the engine running for a while to try and warm up the van with the heater, but the air-cooled engine needed the draught of movement to fan in the hot air. I switched off again. I rationed the little bottled-gas heater to a two minute burst, to take the chill off the air, then checked my food. There was a quarter pound of minced beef, two eggs, a pack of margarine and half a tin of condensed milk in the tiny gas fridge. No need to keep the valuable gas alight just for them. Out went the flame, and I stuffed hard-packed snow into the fridge instead. I also had half a loaf, one tin of Spanish meatballs, four potatoes, two onions, one tomato and a packet of dried soup. Worst of all, I had only one bottle of wine left!

To hell with this, I thought, as the van chilled again. The snow had stopped falling. I would keep warm by exercise. I donned the camera backpack and started zig-zagging up the steep slopes of the gorge directly above the van. The silence was eerie. As I climbed I saw and heard no signs of other life; no birds of prey in the sky, not a single small bird flitting among the trees or bushes. My steps crunched loudly as they pressed down the snow, and occasionally I trod in small drifts deep enough to send it over the tops of my rubber boots. After half an hour I was fairly warm again, but it was clear I was wasting my time as far as wildlife was concerned, especially anything as big as a bear, so I returned to the van. I sat huddled in the bedclothes and took out the few cuttings and research notes by Spanish naturalists that I had assembled about this rare and magnificient animal.

The Spanish brown bear, usually classified as *Ursus arctos pyrenaicus* (though it might be better called *U. a. Hispanicus* since the Pyrenean population is almost extinct) is a sub-species of the European brown bear. It ranged many of Spain's highest and most densely wooded mountain ranges up until some three hundred years ago, and in 1582 it was recorded as far south as the valley of the Lozoya river, just north of Madrid. Since it was both worshipped (as recorded in wall paintings) and hunted by Palaeolithic cave-dwellers 50,000 years ago, the bear has in one way or another been persecuted by man. The Romans began the tradition of hunting them with hounds and spears, and countless numbers were trapped alive to be sent back to Rome for bear baiting at the Colosseum, or to help fill the demand for animal circuses by an increasingly corrupt populace. In the Middle Ages the bear was hunted also for its prized meat, the flesh of its paws being a great delicacy. The rendered-down fat, or grease, was considered an important balm for rheumatism.

In more recent years civilisation's encroachments, the pressures of human population, the changing of the bear's habitats by logging and clearing the woods to make way for arable cultivation, as well as the planting of artificial eucalyptus and conifer forests, have all helped to reduce its numbers. Added to these influences have been the effect of agricultural poisons, pesticides and herbicides, and a great deal of over-hunting. As a game animal it was eagerly sought for the head trophies, the paws and valuable hide. It was also often shot for any (real or imagined) predations on farm or domestic livestock.

The Spanish bear is smaller than the great grizzly of north America and Canada, the adults weighing sometimes as little as 200lbs. It was first protected by law in 1967, when sport hunting was stopped. Stiffer legislation was passed in October 1973 and December 1980, and today all forms of hunting are banned, as is the capture and possessing of live or dead bears, or any hide, skull or any part of one. Despite this, there is known to be a small international gang that guides wealthy hunters on clandestine missions to the wildest mountains to poach bears. In November 1988 a hunter from Palencia shot and killed a 400lb bear which was known locally as '*El Rubio*' (The Blond). In answer to the official legal charge, when some 70,000 people also signed a denouncing petition, the accused claimed he had acted in self defence; that the bear had attacked him. At the time of writing, all the evidence was being closely scrutinised before bringing the hunter to trial.

ICONA, and protection organisations like FAPAS, have spear-headed campaigns to stress the rarity of '*el gran señor*' of the mountains and its importance as a magnificient species of Spain's wildlife heritage, and to make local people and farmers more friendly towards the animal and its survival. The fine for killing a bear today can be as high as 3,000,000 pesetas (£15,000).

Studies in the Pyrenees have shown that brown bears are largely herbivorous, especially in the autumn, when they feed on many kinds of nut, seeds and berries. Three French scientists analysed 482 faeces collected between 1977 and 1979 and found that their diet consisted of 80% vegetable, 7% to 9% insects, beetles and grubs, and 5% to 10% flesh from wild or domestic mammals, most of which had come from carrion. If a bear does kill a sheep, goat or sick cow, or wreck bee hives when after the honey, the farmer is not permitted to shoot it in a 'revenge killing' nor to employ a hunter to do so. He fills in a compensation form and (I am told) almost invariably it is swiftly approved and recompense is paid by the government. This sum is further increased by conservation bodies anxious to placate farmers.

In spite of these late efforts, *'el gran señor'* is the most seriously endangered large mammal in the country. While in the past few years its numbers have been put between 120 and 160 individuals, more recent expert estimates have set the last populations at only some 85 individuals left. Most of these (about 60 animals) live in the most western stronghold, the natural parks and biological reserves of Asturias. Further east is the next largest enclave, with little more than a score of bears to be found in the remotest hills of the provinces of León, north Palencia and Cantabria. Some 4 or 5 bears (individuals being rarely seen) are thought to exist in a rough oblong of mountains between Roncesvalles and the Puerto de Somport in the Spanish–French Pyrenees, and one or two are occasionally sighted in the Vall d'Aran region, also border country, further east. Some of the bears sighted on the Spanish side may have wandered over the border from the French Pyrenees, where the species has been totally protected since 1958, yet only number an estimated 20 to 30 animals.

I looked out of the window. More snow was falling. I knew then, as I shivered in the tent of blankets in my old *caballo* in that lonely place, that I was crazy! There was as much chance of seeing a wild bear out in this lot as of seeing giant panda.

I played some music tapes on my little casette recorder and sipped a glass of wine. Then I mixed half a chopped onion into half the mince, poured on a beaten egg with lots of flour and cooked it up with one potato and a smidgen of cabbage. Giving the heater a two minute burst, I forked down the food and was abed by 4.30 p.m. To my surprise, I slept soundly through the long night.

The snow lay thick when I woke in the morning. A gentle breeze was blowing from the south west, and outside the air seemed slightly warmer. I decided to go for a trek, partly to keep warm. This time I would go up the *camino* towards the end of the gorge, taking it slowly. I put my last film into the camera, slung the pack on my back and set off.

After half an hour the *camino* petered out. Great high cliffs thrust out from the steep tree-lined slopes which led up to a series of crooked white peaks on each side of the canyon. Nearer the end, the precipitous slopes along which I was now stumbling flattened out. The walking became easier as I wended my way through a patch of small oaks and came into the open. I stared at the ground in amazement.

There were huge tracks coming down the mountain from the right, crossing my path and continuing to my left over a large fairly flat area. The prints in the snow were like those of the naked human foot, though bigger and much broader. From my years in Canada I knew bear tracks when I saw them, and my first reaction was one of fear. There must have been two animals, maybe three, for the prints were all mixed up, as if the creatures had been walking in erratic single file. One set of tracks were larger than the others. When I scanned the terrain with binoculars, I could see the bears' trail disappearing round the righthand side of a broad rise in the ground. My compass told me that the tracks were heading north west. With the breeze still in the south west, I had a cross wind, so that if the bears were still in the area they probably would not get my scent. With a brief prayer, I set off alongside the bear tracks, keeping a sharp lookout ahead. After a kilometre or so they turned round a cluster of trees, and I decided to cut straight through. On the far side something made me stop abruptly. I could hear noises ahead, odd slithering sounds accompanied now and then by a muffled thump.

My heart began to pound. I could see nothing, yet large animals of some kind sounded as if they were fighting! Were they coming this way? I felt scared and wanted to turn back. I paused, listening with hands cupped at the back of my ears. The sounds were coming from a fair distance and were not approaching. A few metres ahead to my right stood a stunted tree with a thick trunk, and about 20 metres beyond that I saw what looked like a rocky ridge overhanging a deep drop. I put the camera and lens, all ready, back in the pack and crept stealthily over to the tree. Its first branch was less than two metres from the ground and, after scraping away the covering of snow, I managed to scramble on to it. I made a grab at the next branch so that I could steady myself enough to stand up. Moving slowly, keeping the trunk between myself and the rocky ridge, so that anything beyond it would have less movement to see, I climbed a little higher, then peered round, my face pressed close to the bark. I almost fell out of the tree with surprise.

In front of me were three big bears having a fine old romp in the snow. The rocky ridge was in fact the top of a 13-metre cliff, and the bears were on the far side of it, a good 250 metres away. The largest bear was clearly the mother, and I judged her weight to be around 400lbs. The cubs, which must have been two years old, were roughly two thirds her size. They were giving her a playfully hard time. One grabbed the thick fur on the side of her throat with its teeth and she responded with a sporty biff round the head with a huge paw. Then she rolled downhill with the cub spreadeagled across her stomach, pinning it down with her body on completion of the roll. She gave it a nip on the neck and sprang clear — only to be mock-attacked by the other cub.

I managed to extricate the camera from the pack but it was almost impossible to cling to a branch with my left elbow and steady the long heavy lens enough to focus it properly. After the first few pictures, the arm and leg strain beginning to tell, I knew that I could not keep this up for long. Surely the bears were far enough away for it to be safe to watch from gaps between the boulders on the ridge? The mother might attack, to protect the cubs, though I thought it more likely that they would bolt if disturbed. At that distance, in any case, I would have time to get back up the tree.

Like a sloth I slithered down until I was out of their sight. Then, as quickly as possible, I crossed to a gap in the ridge, carefully poked my lens through and lay down behind it in the snow. The bears obviously saw and heard nothing for they were still playing snow games.

Behaving rather like an otter, one cub gallumphed up the steep slope for about 20 metres, hunching itself forward like a great hairy caterpillar, then rolled on to its back and slid all the way down again. Its bottom caught up on some hidden rock halfway down, turning its body right round and sending it on down at the different angle. Then — thump — its thick furry head struck the trunk of a small pine. The bear appeared not to feel it. The collision turned the cub round again, so that it carried on down, tail first, on its back until it was set upon by its brother, or sister. They produced mock snarls — I could see their white teeth flashing — and cuffed and clubbed each other round the head with their fat paws, all the time enjoying roly-poly in the snow, their great rubbery brown soles sticking up in the air. They did everything you could imagine that monkeys might do.

After a few minutes, as if by some silent agreement, they got to their feet and launched a play attack on their mother, one going for her throat, the other leaping right on to her back. I heard her give a loud growling groan, but she soon re-entered the spirit of the game, cuffing and mock-biting them back. They tugged hard and pulled a few guard hairs and fur from each other. After another rolling skirmish sent all three bears another ten metres down the hill, the mother broke away and tried to gallop uphill. Being older and a good deal heavier she could not go as fast as her cubs. They gallumphed past her and waited at the top of the slope until she arrived. She seemed to realise they were planning to jump on her, for she turned round at once to go downhill again. The cubs then had another punch-up, rearing up on their hind feet and clouting each other, both falling down backwards and landing heavily on their bums, whereupon they slid backwards down the slope, still exchanging mock bites, and cannoned into their mother! One cub carried on down, running normally, while the mother rolled on to her back and scratched snow off her belly. The remaining cub, still above her, looked on for a few moments until the soft invitation of the open belly, where it had suckled in babyhood, was too much of a temptation to resist. It jumped on to its mother, who received it with open arms in a real bear hug, and away they went, roly-poly, over and over, down the snowy hill. Again they slid for a while on their backs, heads first, and this time the mother's cranium cannoned into a tree trunk. *Boomf!* Apart from a brief shake of her head as she slid on down, she too appeared to be unhurt.

The cubs just would not leave that slope alone, and kept bounding up it so that they could slide down again, sometimes on their stomachs. One found it could stop by digging its front paws into the snow, sending the white powder shooting ahead in small cascading sprays. I watched them for about twenty minutes, realising how fortunate I was to see these great creatures, three of the rarest mammals in the world, frolicking and completely at ease in their wild environment.

I began to feel bitterly cold, and an icy feeling on the tops of my thighs told me that my body heat had melted the snow, which had then soaked through my trousers. I kept shivering, and my hands were greeny-white when I pulled the gloves back to examine them. I was sure the cold had made me mistime some of the pictures. My feet felt as if they would never thaw out again. A feeling of faintness swept over me momentarily. I put my head down on my right forearm, my face numb and wanting to sleep. Hypothermia was setting in. I *had* to move!

When I looked up again, the mother bear was higher up the slope, the cubs behind her, sniffing the air in all directions. I could see she wanted to be on the move, and I prayed they would not come in my direction for I was too cold to run. Having gained no alarming scents, she turned downhill, gave a coughing grunt and scuffed through the snow in a rhythmic hip-swinging saunter as she led the cubs down the valley.

I watched them go, and felt an intense gratitude. What a marvellous experience! But when I tried to stand up, I found I could not move. It was as if ice had locked all my joints. Wonder was replaced by fear, and then panic at the thought that I might be paralysed by the cold. I pushed hard with my left hand on the ground and rolled on to my side. With an effort I lifted my left thigh and bent my leg at the knee. The panic passed. I *could* move. By pushing with both hands on the ground and rolling on to my left foot I managed to stand up, feeling faint again. I waited until my head cleared. Each movement after that seemed to make the next one easier, but everything seemed to be in slow motion, as if my mind was distanced from my body and could not communicate commands normally. It seemed to take an age to take camera and lens apart, put on the caps, set them in the pack, do up the tie cords, and get it all on to my back. I stared around me again. I had just seen some of the rarest mammals in Europe yet I felt that part of me was not there any more.

'Put one foot in front of the other, *nada más*,' I told myself.

I stumbled back through the snow alongside my own tracks, moving like an automaton. I was sure my days of hard trekking were coming to an end. The wilderness life was teaching me how old I was, for to survive one has to be both efficient and fit. By my own standards, it seemed I was no longer either. My once proud boast, that I lived as close to the animal state as possible, had found me out. If I kept it up, I would die like an animal, alone.

As I scuffed along, twisting my pelvis to relieve what seemed to be arthritic pains in my hips, I told myself that this was finally IT, the last trek. I did not climb mountains just to reach the summits; I climbed them to find out their intimate wildlife secrets, and I had done enough of it, more than enough. It was a long way back to the *camino,* and a lot further than that to the van. For a moment the thought occurred to me that I might not make it. The constant movement, however, eased the pain in my hips until it disappeared altogether.

Then suddenly the light improved, and I felt a welcome warmth on my back. I looked behind; a small gap had appeared in the clouds and the sun, now high, was beaming through. Before long I saw drops falling from the trees, the snow on their branches melting and making bullet holes in the white carpet beneath. By the time I reached the van the gap in the clouds had widened and steam was rising from the warmed windscreen and metal surfaces. I crashed open the sliding door, made a hot cup of honeyed tea, cooked the rest of the food in the pressure cooker and ate hungrily. I felt better then, but was sure nonetheless that it was time for me to retire from the really hard stuff. I slid into bed for a nap.

It was late afternoon when I awoke, and the sun shone from an almost cloudless sky. Most of the snow around the van had melted, and inside it was now so hot that I had to open both side windows to cool the air again.

As I drove back to the road I saw the peaks of yet another *cordillera* glittering and twinkling far ahead in the blue haze. There are wild wolves up there, I thought. Maybe if I go there in spring, when they are breeding – maybe if I use my brains and really work out where they could be, keep to lower ground, go slower. . .

I knew then that while there were still secrets to be learned, I would plod on into an eternal landscape, and probably never know what retirement means.

Appendix

Why and how does Spain's splendid variety of wildlife survive when its rarest creatures have all but disappeared from the rest of Europe? It is too easy to say that the country is an isolated peninsula separated by the Pyrenees, or has lagged behind in industrial development, or is under populated for its size, and leave it there. So let us first take a look at its turbulent human history.

When the Romans withdrew, they left Spain a prosperous country. Then came the Visigoth occupations, the Moorish conquest which lasted 700 years, and the re-conquest in the years of E1 Cid. There followed the rise of the Catholic Monarchs in the 15th century, when Columbus discovered America and her great armies strode through Central and South America, sending home the gold. She then held the greatest empire since the Romans. Through all this the wild and remote fastnesses of Spain's 505,020 square kilometres remained inviolate.

They also remained largely untouched through all the strife that followed, when the inevitable atrophy that besets all great military empires set in, and the war of the Spanish Succession stripped her European empire. She fought the Napoleonic Wars, the Peninsula War when she ousted the French occupation, and the colonial wars that ended her domination of South America. Next followed the internal strife of the two Carlist wars over the succession to the throne. Initially, the Industrial Revolution ignited only in the north of Spain – in the Basque country, in the Asturias and in Catalonia. Several coups d'etat weakened her internally during the hundred and ten years up to 1923. Then came the bloodbath of the Spanish Civil War which led to

General Franco's autocracy of the Right (which, for all its faults, maintained peace in the country for more than forty years).

Through all this mayhem, wild bear, wolf and lynx still found space in which to pursue their lives − though in dwindling numbers. So did the eagles and vultures and similar rare creatures, many of which have not survived at all in other areas of western Europe. Now, with King Juan Carlos on the throne, as Franco decreed, and the country rapidly feeling her way into liberal democracy, there are encouraging signs that the wild-life legislation begun under the Generalísimo is not only being upheld but slowly advanced.

The trouble is that implementation of the laws is extremely weak. The very existence of many wild places has been and still is endangered by speculation and short-sighted forestry policies. Between 1947 and 1975 Spain lost some 900,000 hectares of woodland. Since then a further 2.1 million hectares have been de-forested, and on 1.2 million hectares fast-growing eucalyptus and conifers have been planted for the paper industry. In some years, between spring and autumn, more than half a million acres of woodland have been burned down. Early in the century fires were started in order to drive out wolves and wild boar. More recently forests have been set ablaze deliberately by the owners of former cattle and sheep pastures protesting against the new paper plantations. Before planting eucalyptus and pine, everything was first cleared away − trees, shrubs and grass − and this led to horrific erosion problems. Some estimates say that 30% of Spain is today either desert or seriously threatened by desertification.

Until 1971 nature and wildlife came under the aegis of the General Directorate for Hunting, Inland Fisheries and National Parks, and conservation lagged far behind the demands for production and even hunting. Then ICONA (National Institute for the Conservation of Nature) was formed and built *into* the Ministry of Agriculture, which is also responsible for forestry and fisheries. To begin with the demands for production took precedence and government bounties were still paid for killing and trapping raptors and other 'vermin' because of alleged predation on farm stock, and on birds like the red-legged partridge, a favourite game species. But by 1973 the ICONA conservationists had made some headway − the first laws protecting all birds of prey were passed, and the bounties stopped. However, other rare birds (some 300 species) were not protected by law until early 1981. Even so, the illicit killing and stuffing of some protected birds still goes on, and the stealing of eggs and chicks from nests continues to be a small but flourishing illegal business in Spain.

At the same time as the birds of prey were protected by Spanish government decree, so were seven mammals − the bear, stoat, otter, mongoose, wildcat, lynx and the Spanish ibex − plus the chameleon and two tortoise species.

In 1985, as part of the process of Spain becoming a democracy, the powers of the central government ICONA organisation were passed to the 17 autonomous regions, and there are now 17 separate ICONAs. Many conservationists claim this has led to bureaucratic confusion, that laws are not enforced strongly enough, and that the protection of habitat is now more difficult than before. With over a third of Spain's population of 3.8 million living in the seven biggest cities, wildlife owes its survival to the great deal of empty space where people could not make a living. Until now there has been room in which it was not greatly disturbed. There are signs that this could change. In recent years the car has liberated the modern city Spaniard and families take every chance to get out into their *campo* at weekends and on fiesta days. Tourism is Spain's biggest source of foreign currency, bringing record earnings into the coffers recently, and there is great pressure to build new roads, hotels, cable cars, ski lifts, golf courses and so forth, in more of the wild places. Recent years have also seen an economic boom in Spain, with foreign investment rising rapidly, the export industry showing record profits, and inflation coming down yearly – to some 3.8% in 1988. With her entry into the Common Market there has also been pressure to increase agricultural output, to make the industry more efficient, and to reduce the list of nearly three million unemployed.

The slow establishment of the great wildlife National Parks by ICONA was a huge step forward but the future largely depends on how effective the new breed of conservationists can be. It is true that more and more nature biologists have been absorbed into the ICONA bureaus, replacing the old guard of agricultural and forestry chiefs, who were more interested in productivity, so the situation seems to be slowly improving. New growth in the number of conservation bodies and 'green' groups will also help to move environmental issues to the forefront of political thinking.

One major victory for conservation began in 1983 when the Spanish Air Force announced it would purchase Cabaneros, a 25,000 hectare private estate in the mountains between Toledo and Ciudad Real, and turn it into a bombing and aircraft training range. Hitherto only a quarter of the land had been used for cereal production, the rest being left to nature. The area had become a stronghold for 60 breeding pairs of black vultures, three pairs of imperial eagles, plus booted and short-toed eagles, great bustards and black storks. It also possessed a unique flora. The World Wildlife Fund, the International Council for Bird Preservation, the Spanish Ornithological Society and other bodies protested vigorously. One persuasive argument was that not only would planes harm the birds but a collision with something the size of a vulture would wreck a jet engine, and so the birds were a hazard to the aircraft. After experiencing low-flying planes which rattled their windows and scared their stock, local residents added their protests. Conservationists gave interviews to the media and in 1988, fearing a loss of votes, the Defence

Ministry finally backed off. At the time of writing the Air Force was looking for a more tolerable site. It was a victory for nature, for common sense, and for Spain in the long term.

In the mountainous Asturias region a newly formed animal protection society, FAPAS, conducted a campaign to get the farmers and local populace on the side of the birds and established a feeding station for endangered griffon vultures. Dead sheep, goats and other animals are driven to it by keen naturalists. In 1988 the Ministry of Agriculture announced a 20,000 million pesetas scheme for preventing and dealing with destructive forest fires, with ICONA providing half the funds and with the National Institute for Employment giving 500 million pesetas to finance the labour force required. Environmental issues occupy more space in the media than ever before and the government has promised to slow down the desertification process, and to provide more money for cleaning up the Mediterranean. Professional people are even campaigning for the abolition of bullfighting. The will is there but Spain's wildlife laws certainly need stronger enforcement.

Here is a west European country which still contains nearly 100 wild bears, over 1,200 wild wolves (some estimates are as high as 2,000), some 400 rare Iberian lynxes, uncounted thousands of wild boar, six species of eagle, four species of vulture (of which two are extremely rare). While the peregrine is known as the '*halcón común*' (common falcon) and numbers some 2,000 breeding pairs over most of Spain, it is surprisingly eclipsed by the dashing little hobby falcons (8,000 pairs) so rare in Britain, and even the conifer forest-loving goshawk (3,000 pairs). Sparrowhawks are common (9,000 pairs) and while one may think one is seeing kestrels almost everywhere, one is more likely to be watching the lesser kestrel (50,000 pairs) which is paler beneath than the common kestrel (30,000 pairs). Rarest is the little Eleanora's falcon (only 300 pairs) which nests in the Balearics and other Mediterranean islands. The honey buzzard survives in Spain but is local, confined to small pockets of broad leaf forests in the north and south west, though it numbers some 1,000 pairs. Red and black kites are plentiful, but they have an extremely rare cousin, the black-winged kite, with only 100 pairs. It is extremely local, mainly in the south west, but believed to be increasing slightly.

The harriers fare quite well in Spain, with Montagu's harrier (6,000 pairs) the most numerous. The spectacular aerial courtship display, where the ghostly blue-white male passes food to the browner female, can be seen in many heathland and wetland margins throughout the country, but they are threatened through agricultural changes in biotopes and illegal destruction of nests. The marsh harrier (1,000 pairs) can also be seen quartering over wetland areas with large reedbeds, though it is thought to be declining through habitat change and illegal hunting. The hen harrier is confined mainly as a breeder to the north west, haunting young tree plantations, moorland and wetland margins, but is the least common (500 pairs) and is possibly also in regression.

Spain has all the European owls and it is almost impossible to travel in country regions towards dusk without seeing one. The commonest is the little owl (120,000 pairs) gazing goggle-eyed at you from telephone poles, cables, tree branches or rocks, for it also hunts by day and locates prey from such perches. Second is the Scops owl (80,000 pairs), third is the tawny owl (50,000 pairs) and fourth is the barn owl (40,000 pairs) but it, like the little owl, is often hit by vehicles and hundreds of each are killed annually. Both these birds succumb to pesticides too. Next comes the great 30 inch-long eagle owl (2,000 pairs), with its stronghold in Extremadura. Rarest is the short-eared owl, with only about 50 pairs.

The last natural west European population of that impressive land bird, the great bustard, lives in Spain. In open undulating country in the centre, south and west, its elaborate courtship display can still be seen. The big males stand, bristly moustaches quivering, heads back, neck and breast feathers puffed out, their orange-brown barred tails held high to show the snowy white rump feathers, and making guttural *'ump ump'* sounds. When these birds take to flight — and wings 25 inches long are lifting weights up to 25lbs — the sound is unforgettable.

In all western Europe, apart from a few scattered pairs in West Germany, Greece and Austria, the black stork survives only in Spain, and of the 140 pairs, 90 are found in Extremadura. White storks are far more common and can be seen all over south and central Spain, clopping their huge bills from their nests on church and cathedral roofs, chimney pots of ordinary houses, and even on electric pylons. Their main population is in the province of Cáceres.

Taken aback by the speed of recent development in the Asturias and the whole Cordillera Cantábrica, conservationists seem to be fighting a losing battle to preserve the dwindling wild bear population. Bad though poaching still is (in 1986 six animals were known to have been killed by illegal shooting), the biggest threat to Spanish bears today comes from development, some of it for tourism. A huge dam has been built at Riaño in the heart of the Picos de Europa region, with the idea of flooding some 1,500 hectares of a fertile valley to provide low cost electricity and enough water to irrigate the dry plains of Zamora province many miles to the south. Some 3,000 people were evicted and a new concrete town, Riaño Nuevo, was built higher up in the mountains to house them. Incredibly, it was built on a former forest which had been the main feeding habitat of a small sub-population of bears. The flooded valley itself has cut these animals off from another relict population in north Palencia, so that healthy breeding and maintenance of a viable genetic pool may no longer be possible. The building of electrical pylon lines as well as new roads and ski-lifts and cable cars for an increasing tourist trade, are also cutting across vital bear areas. Unless conservationists can succeed in enforcing far stricter planning controls, and increase effective wardening against the bear poachers, the last wild bears in western Europe face a bleak future.

In my view it was a serious mistake on the part of the Spanish government to omit the Iberian wolf from the list of totally protected animals in 1973 (although it was classified as a *game* animal in 1970). However, it may soon be fully protected for in 1988, the EEC, in an attempt to get its conservation policy in order, issued a directive to member countries listing 1,300 endangered species, brown bear and wolf among them. The directive required countries to produce wildlife legislation to protect all these species, to *enforce* that legislation, and also set aside protected areas. Failure to do so would result in an offending country being taken to the European Court.

It is true that more reserves of one kind or another are being declared yearly. These are: National Parks, Natural Parks, Sea-Land Natural Parks, Hunting Reserves, Biological Reserves, Natural-Archeological Parks, and just Declared areas which can be designated at any time by local authorities. The Asturias region (taking in the Picos de Europa), for instance, has 34 such reserves, covering over 40% of the land. Extremadura has 54 such reserves, covering about 38% of the land. Even Valencia province has 35, though they cover only some 15% of the terrain. It is my view that, contrary to popular opinion, when it comes to designating and guarding such reserves, Spain is well ahead of most other EEC countries. I have met several EEC biologists from nations like Belgium, the Netherlands, Germany and Italy who were visiting Spain not only to make a census of species but to learn how the country had achieved what it has so far.

In her excellent book, *Spain,* Jan Morris wrote: 'It is thought that Spain can support double her present population, if the land is worked properly, but even then half her country will be uncultivated. Even in the arable areas, there is plenty of room for wildness; and beyond the fields there always rise the vast, spare, rock-ribbed mountains, which can never be spoilt or tamed.'